A

Historical Studies IX

HISTORICAL STUDIES

Papers read before the Irish
Conference of Historians

IX

CORK

29–31 May 1971

and two papers read at a symposium
before the Department of Medieval
History, University College, Cork,
entitled

'Approaches to History'
6–9 March 1969

W. L. WARREN   K. F. ROCHE
N. MANSERGH   D. HAY
R. B. McDOWELL   K. B. NOWLAN
D. FENLON   F. J. BYRNE

Edited by J. G. BARRY

BELFAST
BLACKSTAFF PRESS
1974

First published in 1974 by
Blackstaff Press Belfast

©

W. L. Warren,   K. F. Roche,
N. Mansergh,   D. Hay,
R. B. McDowell,   K. B. Nowlan,
D. Fenlon,   F. J. Byrne,
                1974.

SBN 85640 035 1

Contents

Introduction   vii

The Historian as 'Private Eye'   1
by W. L. Warren

The Government of Ireland Act, 1920: its Origins and
Purposes. The Working of the 'Official' Mind   19
by N. Mansergh

Ireland in the Eighteenth Century British Empire   49
by R. B. McDowell

Encore une Question. Lucien Febvre, the Reformation
and the School of 'Annales'   65
by Dermot Fenlon

Some Stoic Inspiration in the Thought of
J.-J. Rousseau   83
by K. F. Roche

The Church in Italy in the Fifteenth Century   99
by Denys Hay

The Catholic Clergy and Irish Politics in the Eighteen
Thirties and Forties   119
by K. B. Nowlan

'Senchas': the Nature of Gaelic Historical Tradition   137
by F. J. Byrne

List of Articles in Historical Studies, volumes I–IX
inclusive   161

Introduction

The Irish Committee of Historical Sciences, founded in March 1938 to provide for the representation of Irish historical interests on the Comité International des Sciences Historiques, has held a conference of historians annually since 1939, to transact routine business and to hear papers on historical subjects. In July 1953 a conference, which was no longer confined to Irish history, was held and it was decided that a conference of this kind should be held every second year.

The second biennial conference was held at Dublin in 1955, and the papers read at the conference were published under the title 'Historical Studies: papers read before the second Irish Conference of Historians'. This was the first of a continuing series, and since then the conference has been circulating amongst all the university colleges of Ireland. The following is a complete list of the volumes already published and of the conferences at which they were read:

Historical Studies: papers read before the
Irish Conference of Historians

Vol.	Conference	Editor	Date of publication
I	Trinity College and University College, Dublin, 11–13 July 1955.	T. D. Williams	1958
II	The Queen's University of Belfast, 22–23 May 1957.	Michael Roberts	1959
III	University College, Cork, 27–29 May 1959.	James Hogan	1961
IV	University College, Galway, 25–27 May 1961.	G. A. Hayes-McCoy	1963

V   Magee University   J. L. McCracken   1965
College, Londonderry,
30 May–1 June 1963

VI   Trinity College,   T. W. Moody   1968
Dublin, 2–5 June
1965.

VII   The Queen's University J. C. Beckett   1969
of Belfast, 24–27 May
1967.

VIII   University College,   T. D. Williams   1971
Dublin, 27–30 May
1969

IX   University College,   J. G. Barry   1974
Cork, 29–31 May
1971.

The present volume comprises six of the eight papers read at the Ninth Conference of Irish Historians held at University College, Cork, between May 29 and May 31, 1971. It further includes two papers, those by Professor W. L. Warren and Professor F. J. Byrne read at a symposium held by the Department of Medieval History, University College, Cork, entitled 'Approaches to History' between March 6 and March 8, 1969.

The Committee takes this opportunity to express its gratitude to University College, Cork, for its hospitality and for the grant which made this publication possible. The editor would like to express his appreciation of the help and co-operation which he received from Professor R. Dudley Edwards and Dr. Ronan Fanning, Department of History, University College, Dublin.

J. G. Barry

The Historian as 'Private Eye'

W. L. Warren

Those of us who practice the art (or should I say, the craft?) of history know that the historian is *sui generis*. He is not quite like other scholars, although he must at times give plausible impersonations of them. Since the bounds of his subject are as wide as human experience, the historian may find himself by turns psychologist, economist, jurist, theologian, social philosopher, or political scientist, for his way leads him wherever men have trod, and into recesses of their thoughts and assumptions, their teachings and dogmas, their anxieties and ambitions, as well as into their decisions and actions. The individual historian may choose to be a specialist, but history itself is not a specialism. It is an exploiter of specialisms. In the reconstruction of the past the historian rubs shoulders with, sometimes shakes hand with, and frequently picks the pockets of the archaeologist, the genealogist, the numismatist, the geographer, the anthropologist, and the philologist. He ought, more often than he does, to rub shoulders and share minds with the technologist, for technology, in its widest sense, is, much more often than ideology, the shaper of society.

It is no doubt this many-sidedness of *homo historicus* which makes it so difficult to determine his location on the academic spectrum. In its classification of disciplines the American Philosophical Society places modern history among the social sciences and medieval history among the humanities, which presumably proves something—either the propensity of modern historians in the United States to succumb to sociological theorising, or the bewilderment of American philosophers.[1] Philosophers have frequently tried to tell the historian who he is and what it is that he does; but I am probably not alone in thinking that the kind of history philosophers of history talk about is rarely the kind of history you and I write. Even those who have, of late,

[1] Cf. *American Philosophical Society: Year Book*. Medieval history is placed in 'Class IV: Humanities', together with ancient and cultural history.

1

tried to analyse the language which historians use have not penetrated to the way historians go about their business, for it is a characteristic of historians to cover their tracks. In the processes of historical reconstruction, interpretation, and presentation, we tend to disguise rather than reveal the processes by which we in fact reach our conclusions. In the space of a page or even of a paragraph we conceal the ruminations of a month, and reduce a mountain of research to the molehill of a footnote. Perhaps I exaggerate; but it can hardly be denied, I think, that it is rarely possible to deduce from the examination of a piece of historical writing the whole of the mental processes of he who wrote it, any more than it is possible to divine from simply looking at a building the inner secrets of the way it came to be constructed. To know history it is only necessary to read good historians, but to know how history is written it is necessary to *be* an historian. We belong to a guild or mystery, admission to which is by the long apprenticeship of Ph.D. research. I state this as a fact without regarding it as altogether desirable, for I fear that in hiding our processes from the public we too often hide them even from ourselves, and rely on instinctive judgements and innate wisdom while at the same time believing that we are methodical. Too much historical writing contains shallow assumptions about the nature of society or makes unreasoned generalisations about the behaviour of men. Some of us, it is true, take refuge from such hazards in the dug-outs of textual criticism. But invaluable, indeed essential, as is the scholarly work of processing the materials to make them usable, it is not in itself history, for the distinctive work of the historian consists in converting the detritus of the past into a comprehensible legacy.

A hundred years ago historians tried to convince themselves that the past could speak for itself, and history be turned into a legitimate scientific discipline, if historians confined themselves to uncovering the buried treasures of documentary sources, to validating data, and to laying the unvarnished facts before the public. It was with this conviction that men such as Ranke, Mommsen, and Fustel de Coulanges rescued history from the myth-makers and propagandists, from the romantics and belles-lettrists. The methodology they devised, a methodology for sifting, testing, and evaluating source material, made of history an academic discipline. But although their influence was beneficial, their goal of an ultimate, objective, record of the past was a chimera. The goal was unattainable, the attempt undesirable. If the historian pursues objectivity by forswearing interpretation, and declines to bridge the gaps in the record by intelligent

2

reconstruction, he is abdicating a part of his responsibility. The facts of the past, even when knowable, are as mute as cemeteries.[2]

One of the basic fallacies of the objective school of historians is the supposition that the past is actually there, somewhere, waiting to be discovered and expounded, just as the truth about the physical world is always there, waiting to be discovered and expounded by the natural scientist. But the past cannot, except perhaps in some metaphysical sense, be said to exist at all. The past is dead. The historian cannot study the past, but only the traces of the past. He has to read the past from its footprints, like the skilled hunter reading his spoor. But since the past is dead its remains have a different sort of existence from that which they had in life. Something has gone out of them. The historian has not merely to clarify and arrange his material—he has also to transform it by giving it the kiss of life. History does not exist until the historian makes it. To suppose anything else is to be the victim of an illusion. It is a recognition of reality that in English, French and German we use one word, be it *history*, *histoire*, or *Geschichte*, to refer both to what happened in the past and to what the historian writes about it.

The historian like the anatomist conducts his studies *post mortem*, but his interests should be more akin to those of the physiologist, who is concerned with the workings of the living organism. I say 'should be' because too many historians, I fear, remain in practice anatomists—corpse historians—transmitting the icy touch of death even to those who read them. Yet the *rigor mortis*, with which so much historical writing may be rebuked, is not entirely the fault of unimaginative historians: it is at least partly attributable to the defective training we give our apprentices. Although we have, by and large, abandoned the premises and assumptions of the objective school of historians, we have advanced little beyond the methodology they gave us. It is, of course, a splendid tool, but is a tool for research not for inter- pretation—necessarily so, for they eschewed interpretation. It is a method for anatomy not a method for resuscitation. We train our graduate students in the techniques of deciphering evidence and understanding its provenance, we inculcate rigorous standards of criticism and evaluation, we coerce them into distinguishing the niceties of an *undoubtedly* from a *maybe*, a *perhaps* from a *probably* —then we leave them alone to grope in the dark after a framework of explanation for causes and motives. If they are prudent they stick to compilation and analysis; but how often, as a result, is

---

[2] For a review of the arguments for and against objective history, see H. Meyerhoff, *The Philosophy of History in Our Time* (New York, 1959).

the Ph.D. thesis merely a contribution towards history rather than a piece of history itself.

The historian, I have said, concerned as he should be with the whole of human experience, will find himself involved with psychology, economics, law, social philosophy, political theory, and theology, not to mention historical and environmental geography and social anthropology. But how good are we at it? Are we the polymaths our attempts at explanation assume us to be? How often do we sneer at psychologists and sociologists for being seduced by fashionable but ill-founded systems of explanation, while at the same time resting ourselves upon systems of explanation which are not only unfashionable but also unconscious? How often do we revile the Marxist for his dogmas of interpretation, while at the same time offering nothing in their place save for trite assumptions drawn from the conventional wisdom of explanations in everyday life? Do we really believe that the class war is contradicted by commonsense? How often do we criticise other peoples' systems of explanation with a confidence which is unimpaired by any critical analysis of our own? How often do we claim to be relying on our data when in fact we are generalising from assumptions drawn, as Robert Morton has said, from 'a private world inhabited exclusively by penetrating but unfathomable insights and ineffable understandings'?[3]

Here, it seems to me, is the central dilemma of historians today. If we stop short of fitting our researches into a framework of interpretation and explanation we may preserve a reputation for sound scholarship, but we are not historians. But if we venture into interpretation and explanation, how well-equipped are we in the techniques and insights of other disciplines to do it properly? This is why I believe that we should acknowledge frankly that history is not the solitary pursuit we so often seem to try to make it, but the product of many minds. This is why I believe that the quality of historical writing (though not necessarily of historical

[3] R. K. Merton, *Social Theory and Social Structure* (London, 1957), p. 16. On the unconscious assumptions of historians cf. D. M. Potter, 'Explicit data and unconscious assumptions in historical study', *Generalisation in the Writing of History*, ed. L. Gottschalk (Chicago, 1963). The problem has been well reviewed by S. W. F. Holloway, 'History and sociology: what history is and what it ought to be', in *Studies in the Nature and Teaching of History*, ed. W. H. Burston and D. Thompson (London, 1967). I am not at all sure, however, that I can accept his contention that the historian will discover his interpretive schemes from sociologists. I am inclined to agree with Elton that the historian is well occupied in confounding the rashness of sociologists with particular instances: but no doubt there is much to be gained by a closer liaison between the two. Cf. G. R. Elton, *The Practice of History* (London, 1967), pp. 23–39.

scholarship) has improved with the expansion of history depart-
ments and the increased opportunities to recruit our interpretative
schemes from the experience of others. Above all, it seems to me,
we should give more thought to improving and rationalising our
techniques of explanation, at least by discussing them.

It is one small area of the process of explanation which I
propose to explore now; but have no fear that I am embarking on
philosophical analysis or sociological theorising, for it is my
contention that the topic is more conveniently approached by
way of detective fiction.

The historian going about his business is, more particularly
than any other seeker after knowledge, the detective, for like the
detective he is concerned not simply with the discovery and
correlation of data, but with men's motives and intentions. The
detective, like the historian, has to reconstruct events from
traces—traces which are often scored and rubbed, overlaid,
and partly effaced. They differ in that the detective may examine
participants *viva voca*, while the historian usually has to make do
with the witness of chronicles, diaries, and letters—but this is a
difference of method not of essence.

We are all familiar, of course, with exercises in historical
detection. There are many elements of the mystery novel in
W. H. Stevenson's demonstration that Asser's *Life of Alfred* was
at least written by a near contemporary and not, as had been
supposed, by a twelfth century forger. Among many subtle
arguments he advances these. The author refers in passing to the
eclipse of 878 and mentions the time of day at which it occurred.
Now although the eclipse is mentioned in other sources, none of
them gives the time of day; and no later forger could have supplied
the missing information since on his medieval assumptions about
the movements of the sun he would have reached an erroneous
conclusion.[4] This is not conclusive: it is conceivable that a later
forger had access to sources of information which are lost to us.
Consider, however, the reference to *King* Edmund of East Anglia—
murdered in 870 by the Danes, in the lifetime of King Alfred of
Wessex. His cult as a saint was developed by the time of Alfred's
death, and was soon to become immensely popular.[5] Are we to
suppose a forger so astute that he would feign ignorance of
Edmund's sanctity—and to what purpose? In arguments such as
these Stevenson displays, for all his scholarly rectitude, what
Sherlock Holmes identified as the three qualities necessary in the

[4] *Asser's Life of Alfred*, ed. W. H. Stevenson (Oxford, 1904), pp. cxxviii, 280ff.
[5] *Ibid.*, pp. 231–2.

ideal detective: the powers of observation, knowledge and deduction.[6]

I do not, however, wish to dwell on this aspect of the topic.[7] The similarities between the detective and the historian are here obvious enough. Historical investigation may indeed proceed by the discovery of fresh evidence, or by noticing fresh features of readily available evidence—observing instead of merely seeing, as Holmes frequently reminded Watson[8]—but it does not happen as often as we might wish. Indeed I suspect that our training gives us an obsessive concern with hunting down clues in archives, when we might be more profitably employed reflecting about the evidence we already have. The popular impression of Sherlock Holmes applying his lens to the scene of the crime is not, as a matter of fact, one that is well sustained in the stories. Holmes was a man, Watson tells us, 'who, when he had an unsolved problem upon his mind would go for days, and even for a week, without rest, turning it over, rearranging the facts, looking at it from every point of view, until he had either fathomed it, or convinced himself that his data were insufficient.[9]' He would during these sessions fill the room with clouds of smoke from his pipe—the clay, not the cherrywood which he reserved for relaxation. He solved *A Case of Identity* without once leaving his rooms in Baker Street.[10] It was a simple problem, as he explained to Watson: he had several parallel cases on his file which suggested the solution; it happened to be the personalities involved which made the case interesting.[11] It is a method of analogy with which the historian is very familiar.

But more instructive perhaps, is the very mysterious case of *The Man with the Twisted Lip*. Holmes's inquiries led him, at first, by all the normal rules of deduction, to reach a perfectly clear, logical conclusion. There was just one scrap of doubtful evidence

[6] 'The Sign of Four', *Sherlock Holmes: Selected Stories by Sir Arthur Conan Doyle* (World's Classics, 1951), p. 71.

[7] For another particularly good example see R. H. C. Davis' revision of our understanding of Anglo-Saxon Society in East Anglia, arguing from an apparent discrepancy in the geld returns of Babergh hundred, *The Kalendar of Abbot Samson of Bury St Edmunds* (Selden Society, 1954), and 'East Anglia and the Danelaw', *Transactions of the Royal Historical Society*, 5th series, v (1955), 23–9.

[8] 'Not invisible but unnoticed, Watson. You did not know where to look, and so you missed all that was important': 'A Case of Identity', *The Adventures of Sherlock Holmes*, by Sir Arthur Conan Doyle (Folio Society, 1958), p. 61.

[9] 'The Man with the Twisted Lip', *The Adventures of Sherlock Holmes*, p. 137.

[10] 'The Five Orange Pips': 'The ideal reasoner would, when he has once been shown a single fact in all its bearings, deduce from it not only all the chain of events which led up to it, but also all the results which would follow from it', *The Adventures of Sherlock Holmes*, p. 111.

[11] 'A Case of Identity', *The Adventures of Sherlock Holmes*, p. 61.

which suggested that the conclusion might be false. Once aware, however, that there could conceivably be another explanation he solved the problem comfortably ensconced on five pillows while he smoked precisely one ounce of shag.[12] He then put his theory to the test by taking a bath sponge and wiping the twisted lip from the face of the man who had disguised himself by assuming it. Holmes had recognised in this case that the pursuit of evidence could go no further, so he resorted, quite properly, to speculation, looking for an explanation which would resolve the mystery while at the same time embracing all the known facts. The historian, of course, can rarely test his conclusions as readily as Sherlock Holmes did: he must often be content (at least provisionally) with explanations which the available evidence does not contradict.

I am prompted to reflect on this approach to explanation by the conviction among some historians (mistaken, it seems to me) that speculation is improper, or at best a sort of professional solecism. Go no further than the evidence allows, says this dogma, the implication being that if the evidence is insufficient for deduction the problem should be set aside. I suspect that this attitude is partly a hangover from the methodology of the objective school; but it is probably also influenced by the fact that for many modern historians the available data is copious enough for the method of correlation and deduction to suffice. I derive some ironical amusement from the lamentations of modern historians at the invention of the telephone and the aeroplane, which, by allowing statesmen to discuss and decide by personal contact, have eliminated the written evidence upon which such historians have been accustomed to rely. The situation is only too familiar for medieval historians: for us the decisive evidence is almost always missing; but we do not allow this to confound us.

'There are periods in history', says G. M. Young at the start of his brilliant lecture on 'The Origins of the West Saxon Kingdom', 'where it is impossible to say this or that happened, because the evidence is lost; but where, nevertheless, we are bound to say: something like this must have happened, because we can see the result.'[13]

At this point we should perhaps distinguish two kinds of historian corresponding to two kinds of detective. The historian who will not venture beyond deduction from clear evidence is like the police detective, who is obliged to prepare a case which will stand up in court. He may in fact be tolerably sure of who did it and how it was done, but unless he can prove it by unimpeachable

---

[12] 'The Man with the Twisted Lip', *The Adventures of Sherlock Holmes*, p. 137.
[13] G. M. Young, *Last Essays* (London, 1950), p. 112.

B

testimony he must shelve the case. But there is another kind of detective and another kind of historian who are both happily embraced by that graphic American term, the 'private eye'. The police detective has respectability but constricting rules; the private eye may more readily resort to unorthodox methods to illumine dark places, not necessarily to prove a case, but at least to provide an explanation which will satisfy his client.

The thrillers of Raymond Chandler follow, by and large, the same basic pattern. The private investigator, Philip Marlowe, is presented with a problem. He begins by following up the obvious leads, but these not only stop short of a solution, they intensify the problem or change its nature. Faced with an *impasse*, Marlowe, like Holmes, broods. He then, unlike Holmes, intrudes himself into a series of situations which appear to the reader to have little direct connection with the original problem, but which, in the event, serve to illuminate it. Indeed as the story moves to a conclusion it becomes apparent that what Marlowe has done has been to apply his mind to thinking up a context within which the problem will achieve an explanation. He is not so much attempting to prove a theory (for the nature of the problem may make proof positive impossible) as offering a challenge to the context, forcing it to admit its connection with the original problem and by absorbing the problem confirming the explanation.[14]

Chandler, who, like Conan Doyle, had reflected about the methods he attributed to his detective, offers in *Farewell My Lovely* a more than usually explicit statement of his approach. Marlowe is here working, intermittently, in conjunction with a woman whose father had once been chief of police. She represents the orthodox methodology and reproaches Marlowe for what she regards as his lack of professional standards. She expects him to be out looking for clues when he knows that it is time to think. Towards the end, after Marlowe had provoked a *dénouement* she acts as the foil for his explanation of how he had read the problem, and she teasingly refers to the traditions of more commonplace detective fiction.

'You ought to have given a dinner party', Anne Riordan said . . . 'Gleaming silver and crystal, bright crisp linen, . . . candlelight, the women in their best jewels and the men in white ties, the servants hovering discreetly with wrapped bottles of wine, the cops looking uncomfortable in their hired evening clothes, . . . the suspects with their brittle smiles and restless hands, and you at the head of the table telling all about it, little by little, with your charming light smile and a phoney English accent like Philo Vance.' . . .

[14] Raymond Chandler, *The High Window, The Big Sleep, The Lady in the Lake, Farewell, My Lovely, The Long Goodbye.*

'And suddenly the butler fainted', I said, 'only it wasn't the butler who did the murder. He just fainted to be cute.' I inhaled some of my drink. 'It's not that kind of story,' I said. 'It's not lithe and clever. It's just dark and full of blood.'

As he reconstructs what had happened, she interrupts him to protest that some of it he could not possibly *know:* 'That's just guessing', she said. But to him it was more than *just* guessing; it was rational guessing. Some elements of guessing had to be added to the facts to make them explicable. The guessing was checked by a confrontation with the facts. It was not *just* guessing. As he says to her: 'It had to be that way'.[15]

Now it seems to me that there are pointers here to the way many historians actually work—whether or not they recognise or admit it. A great part of historical explanation consists in the construction of contexts. It is rare in practice to find historians proving theories. What they actually do is to find and elaborate contexts within which facts achieve meaning, problems disappear, and questions answer themselves. If we inquire into the aims of Henry II in the controversy with Archbishop Becket, it is not sufficient to tell the story (although many have supposed that it is), for although the story, as we know it, is amply documented, it tells of Becket's aims not Henry's. Nor can we find the answer to the problem by analysing the Constitutions of Clarendon—this is an exercise which has to be performed, but it demonstrates that the Constitutions can be understood only when we know what the king's aims were. Henry II's conception of his 'rights' over the Church can be appreciated only in the context of the way he pressed his other rights, political, economic, and jurisdictional. His intentions become apparent only in the context of his grandfather's attempt at a concordat with the Church, and the necessity of adjusting its formulation to the changing circumstances of ecclesiastical government. His conduct becomes explicable only in the context of his relations with Becket's predecessor as archbishop. And the controversy achieves perspective not (as many historians have falsely assumed) in the context of the church in England, but in that of Henry II's relations with the churches throughout his extensive dominions.

It is in the identification and elaboration of contexts that the historian deploys his knowledge and experience. His explanatory structures improve with his ever expanding knowledge and his opportunities to borrow from other historians and from workers in related fields. It is the progressive improvement of explanatory

[15] Raymond Chandler, *Farewell, My Lovely* (Penguin Books, 1949), pp. 246–7.

structures, more often than the revelation of newly discovered sources which enables us to advance beyond the work of our predecessors. This is one good reason why graduate students are well advised to stick to compilation and analysis: their capacity for context-building is limited by their relative lack of experience. This is why amateur history is so often unsatisfactory: the facts presented may all be irreproachable, but the amateur is an amateur because he lacks the professional's expertise over the whole field, which is the prerequisite for constructing contexts within which the facts achieve their true significance.

So much for exposition: now let me try to give a concrete example—by, for once, recalling the mental processes by which I reached a particular conclusion.

In the Red Book of the Exchequer (a rather curious place to find it) there is a copy of letters patent from the barons of Ireland, headed by William Marshal, earl of Pembroke and lord of Leinster. It may be dated to 1212. In it they profess their support of King John's stand on the liberties and dignities of the Crown of England against the threats of the pope to absolve his subjects from their allegiance. They conclude by declaring 'We are ready to go with him whether in death or in life, . . . and, both in this cause and all others, we will to the last faithfully and inseparably adhere to him'.[16]

When I first read this I supposed that the initiative came from William Marshal, attempting to restore himself to the favour of the king, from which he had been excluded since 1206.[17] This was what I said in my book *King John;* but it was not a happy guess, for although it might explain William Marshal's action it could not explain why twenty-six other barons agreed to add their seals too. Admittedly some of them were Marshal's vassals, but not all were. An alternative explanation, proffered by Richardson and Sayles, fits the bill rather better: pointing to cognate royal letters on the Close Roll, which may be dated to the end of 1212, they show that it is more than likely that the suggestion that such letters would be welcomed came from the king and was part of his propaganda war on the Church.[18]

There, it may be thought, the matter may be laid to rest, but

[16] Red Book of the Exchequer, fo. s 180–180v. This letter was omitted from Hubert Hall's edition in the Rolls Series, but is printed in H. G. Richardson and G. O. Sayles, *The Irish Parliament in the Middle Ages* (Philadelphia, 1952), pp. 286–7.

[17] W. L. Warren, *King John* (London, 1961), p. 201; cf. Kate Norgate *John Lackland* (London, 1902), pp. 172–4, G. H. Orpen, *Ireland Under tne Normans* (Oxford, 1911), ii. 309–11.

[18] Richardson and Sayles, *op. cit.*, pp. 285–6, citing royal letters addressed to William Marshall and to the justiciar, John de Grey, in October 1212, *Rotuli Litterarum Clausarum*, vol. i (Record Commission, 1833), 132b.

can it? What is really significant is that the barons of Ireland not merely responded to the suggestion, they kept their word: they did stick to John through thick and thin, right through the Magna Carta crisis and the civil war which followed, right to the end. William Marshal was not merely John's main prop in the war, he was the executor of his will, rescued the kingdom for his infant son, and was *rector regis et regni* until his death in 1219.[19] Now in view of John's crushing treatment of the Irish baronies on his expedition of 1210, this is, to say the least, surprising.[20]

Moreover, consider Walter de Lacy, lord of Meath. He was not among the signatories of the letters patent—he was at the time dispossessed, for John had refused the appeal of his vassals dissociating him from the perfidy of his brother Hugh, earl of Ulster, and asking for his reinstatement.[21] It might have been expected that Walter would have been, like his distant cousin John de Lacy, constable of Chester, among the front rank of the rebels of 1215.[22] But on the eve of the Magna Carta crisis Walter de Lacy recovered his lands from the king, and joined his loyalty to that of William Marshal. He provided troops from his Welsh estates which largely sustained the king at the height of the civil war, and was one of the executors of his will.[23] If we wonder at this, we should recall also that Walter de Lacy's wife was the daughter of William de Briouze, and that it was her mother and brother who starved to death in Windsor castle.[24]

'Curiouser and curiouser', as Alice said.[25] And it gets curiouser the more one looks. Note how the change of front by the barons is accompanied (to put it no stronger) by a change in the justiciarship of Ireland. When King John had begun seriously to assert his authority in Ireland he had appointed one of his ablest

[19] Cf., Orpen *op.. cit*, ii, 31 1ff S. Painter, *William Marshal* (Baltimore, 1933).
[20] For the expedition of 1210 see Orpen, *op. cit.*, ii, chapter xxi Warren, *op. cit.*, pp. 194–7.
[21] The appeal of Walter de Lacy's vassals follows the letter of the Irish barons in the Red Book of the Exchequer, calendared in *Calendar of Documents relating to Ireland*, i, no. 402.
[22] It seems likely that the two of them had been conspiring against John in 1209, cf., S. Painter, *The Reign of King John* (Baltimore, 1949), pp. 253ff. Walter's estate of La Pin in Normandy had been taken into the king's hand in 1202, but his father-in-law, William de Briouze, obtained permission to administer it, W. E. Wightman, *The Lacy Family in England and Normandy* (Oxford, 1966), p. 223.
[23] *Rotuli Litterarum Patentium* (Record Commission, 1835), i. 181; *Rotuli Litterarum Clausarum*, i. 147; Painter, *The Reign of King John*, p. 278; *Foedera* (Record Commission, 1816–19), i, part 1, p. 144.
[24] Cf. Painter, *The Reign of King John*, pp. 242–50. Shortly before his death John granted to Margaret de Lacy permission to clear a site in the royal forest of Aconbury to found a religious house for the souls of her father, William de Briouze, her mother, and her brother, *Rotuli Litterarum Patentium*, i. 199.
[25] Lewis Carroll, *Alice in Wonderland*, chapter 2.

11

administrators, John de Grey, as justiciar. In 1213, on the morrow of the Irish barons' profession of loyalty, John de Grey was recalled and replaced by Henry archbishop of Dublin, a man notorious for his identification with the narrower interests of the settlers.[26] The suspicion that some sort of bargain had been struck grows stronger. One would have expected the barons of Ireland to be in the forefront of rebellion against John. Something has happened to change the attitude of the barons of Ireland; but what? Consideration of such scanty evidence as there is only serves to deepen the mystery—but we need not despair for this is the classic thriller story situation.

'Well Watson', said Holmes [in the story of the *Red-Headed League*][27], 'What do you make of it all?'
'I make nothing of it,' I answered frankly. 'It is a most mysterious business.'
'As a rule', said Holmes, 'the more bizarre a thing is the less mysterious it proves to be. It is your commonplace, featureless crimes which are really puzzling, just as a commonplace face is the most difficult to identify.' . . .
'What are you going to do then?' I asked
'To smoke', he answered. 'It is quite a three-pipe problem'

I must confess that it took me more than three pipes even to decide where to start looking for a solution. There is no obvious explanation in the chronicles or documents, so it becomes a matter of trying to find a context in which the problem may achieve an explanation.

The first consequence of my tobacco ruminations was an expansion of the problem. Granted that there was a *rapprochement* between King John and the barons of Ireland late in 1212 or early in 1213, why were they at odds in the first place? Put more concretely: why did John mount an expensive expedition to Ireland in 1210? The obvious, indeed the advertised explanation, was the pursuit of William de Briouze for defaulting on the instalments of his proffer for the lordship of Limerick. But this is patently unsatisfactory: Briouze had crossed over to his Welsh estates before John landed in Ireland, and the expedition was obviously hunting even bigger game. It was directed as much against Marshal and the Lacys as against Briouze, and Leinster escaped

---

[26] John de Grey replaced Meiler FitzHenry as justiciar in 1208, and was himself replaced early in 1213, H. G. Richardson and G. O. Sayles, *The Administration of Ireland*, p. 75. On Henry of London, archbishop of Dublin and justiciar 1213–15 and 1221–4, see A. Gwynn, *Studies*, xxxviii (1949), 295–306, 389–402.
[27] 'The Red-Headed League', *Sherlock Holmes: Selected Stories by Sir Arthur Conan Doyle* (World's Classics), p. 344; *The Adventures of Sherlock Holmes* (Folio Society), p. 38.

the confiscation of Meath and Ulster only because William Marshal prudently submitted and surrendered his charter. Their harbouring of Briouze was only a convenient excuse for a deeper purpose which could not so easily be explained or justified.

Now Marshal and Briouze (and, we might add, Hugh de Lacy) had until recently been among the king's most trusted advisers.[28] Why the breakdown in their relations? Sidney Painter's explanation is that they had become too powerful, and John distrusted people when they became too powerful.[29] This is plausible, but it is the sort of explanation from general observations which should be resorted to only in default of a more specific explanation, and after all the possibilities have been exhausted. There is a common tendency to accept the first plausible explanation which comes our way—against which detective stories should warn us. We should hesitate to accept Painter's explanation for at least three reasons. In the first place it was John himself who had made them powerful. If he came to distrust them as too powerful, this must have been because they were no longer his friends and allies. In other words it must be a breakdown of relations which causes the distrust, not the distrust which causes the breakdown. Secondly, there were easier and cheaper ways of trimming their power than an expedition to Ireland: they held important lordships in Wales and had English estates too. Thirdly, they were considerably less powerful than they had been: they had lost their Norman estates when King John lost Normandy to Philip of France in 1204.

It was at this point in my ruminations that it occurred to me that John's loss of Normandy is conceivably the element which has been omitted from the context in which we have hitherto tried to explain this Irish mystery. The fact that it enters into no book on Irish history which I have ever read is a reminder of the danger of artificial limitations—such as national boundaries—on context-building.

When King Philip overran Normandy in 1204 he posed a cruel dilemma for the barons. They now had two masters in a war to the death. Some elected to sacrifice their English estates and remain in Normandy. But others had too much to lose in England, Wales, and Ireland and retreated across the English Channel. Neither John nor they regarded the loss of Normandy as final; but although they cast their lot with John they fell out with him

---

[28] It was John who made Hugh de Lacy earl of Ulster on 29 May 1205, *Rotuli Chartarum* (Record Commission, 1837), p. 151. Cf. Orpen, *Ireland under the Normans*, ii. 141, *n.* 1.
[29] Painter, *The Reign of King John*, pp. 228, 240.

over what to do next. John's policy, strategically a sound one, was to mount a flank attack from the lands which remained to him in southern France for the recovery first of Anjou; but the barons were all for a seaborne assault on Normandy. The dispute prevented any action being taken at all in 1205.[30] Yet the situation was urgent for the barons: King Philip had already granted away the greater part of the Lacy estates in Normandy.[31] William Marshal attempted to do a deal with Philip, recognising his *de facto* lordship in return for the protection of his Norman estates: but John refused to sanction any such arrangement and denounced him as a traitor.[32] Marshal then retired to his lordship of Leinster. He had not been in Ireland before, so far as we know, but he was to spend most of his time there until the middle of 1213. Now there was one obvious reason for going to Ireland: to get out of John's way. But this, I suspect, was not the only reason: Marshal's diligent concern with his Irish lordship suggests that he was trying to make his Irish estates render compensation for the loss of his estates in Normandy.

It is noticeable that it was only after Marshal went to Ireland that John started to worry about the Irish situation.[33] We can see signs of his worry in the curious instructions to the justiciar, Meiler FitzHenry, in 1206 to harass the barons. There was open but undeclared warfare between the justiciar's men and the barons' men. And when Meiler got rather the worse of it the king replaced him by John de Grey.[34]

But what was King John worried about? I suggest that Marshal's example in seeking to make Ireland render compensation was infectious; and that the more intensive exploitation of Irish lordships ran counter to royal policy for Ireland. This involves me in explaining what that policy was—a dark subject which I have time to illuminate only dimly.[35] The royal policy for Ireland has been obscured by changes in tactics and by misunderstandings about why Henry II involved himself with Ireland in the first

[30] Cf. Warren, *King John*, pp. 103ff.
[31] L. Delisle, *Catalogue des Actes de Philippe-Auguste* (Paris, 1856), p. 185; Wightman, *The Lacy Family*, p. 220.
[32] *Histoire de Guillaume le Mareschal*, ed. P. Meyer (Paris, 1891–1901), iii. 176–8, 180–2; Delisle, *Catalogue des Actes de Philippe-Auguste*, no. 818, p. 186; cf. Warren, *King John*, pp. 104, 113–14.
[33] Shortly after William Marshal left for Ireland, John deprived him of the sheriffdom of Gloucester, and custody of Cardigan and the forest of Dean, Painter, *William Marshal*, p. 147.
[34] For the details see Orpen, *Ireland under the Normans*, ii. 209ff., and Painter, *The Reign of King John*, pp. 240–2.
[35] It is investigated more thoroughly in W. L. Warren, 'The interpretation of twelfth century Irish Society', *Historical Studies*, vii (1969) and W. L. Warren, *Henry II*, (1973) chapter 4.

place. I cannot see that his policy here was any different from his policy towards the rest of those western peoples who had not yet been thoroughly assimilated into post-Carolingian forms of government, the Basques, the Bretons, the Cornish, the Welsh, the Scots—and the Irish. Henry's policy was simply to stabilise his western frontier, for his real problem was always on his eastern frontier with the Capetians. He never set foot in Scotland, for although it lay within his claim to lordship, it had developed an effective monarchy; he pulled out of Brittany, and he virtually withdrew from Wales, once he had succeeded in stabilising them. I am pretty sure that he intended to pull out of Ireland too, and was only prevented from doing so by the frustration of all his attempts to stabilise it. His approval for Dermot McMurrough to recruit freelances gave prospect that Ireland would develop as Scotland had done after the sons of Malcolm Canmore appealed for Norman aid. But this was frustrated by Strongbow's attempt to make himself Dermot's heir, for the prospect then was not of another Scotland but of another Sicily developing on his doorstep. Henry was forced to intervene and to try to stabilise the Irish situation as he stabilised the Welsh situation by doing a deal with the native rulers; the Treaty of Windsor has a close parallel in the Treaty of Geddington. But this was frustrated by the inability of the High King of Ireland to control the Irish. So he then proposed to solve the problem of Ireland as he had solved the problem of Brittany, by separating it off and putting in one of his sons to unify it under a strong government. This, of course was frustrated, first by John's youthful foolishness, and then by that astonishing accident that the youngest of his four sons succeeded to the whole of his dominions. It is tolerably clear, however, that John adopted his father's policy and continued to think of Ireland as a separate entity, indeed as a separate monarchy: note how in his submission to Pope Innocent III John speaks of 'My whole kingdom of England and my whole kingdom of Ireland.'[36]

Now since, for practical reasons if nothing else, a thorough conquest was ruled out, all these solutions to the problem of Ireland, and particularly the last, depended on winning a large measure of co-operation from the Irish themselves. It was not impossible: Normans in large numbers had settled peaceably into Scotland.[37] The prominence given to battles in the chronicles has tended to obscure the considerable amount of co-operation that

[36] W. Stubbs, *Select Charters* (9th edition, Oxford, 1913), p. 280; '. . . totum regnum Angliae et totum regnum Hiberniae . . .'.
[37] For the Scottish story see R. L. G. Ritchie, *The Normans in Scotland* (Edinburgh, 1954).

went on in the first generation of Norman settlement. It was, of course, a complex situation; but let us not ignore, for example, the fact that the Treaty of Windsor made provision for the peaceful return of the Irish to lands invaded by the Normans. Let us call to mind the elder Hugh Lacy's reputation for winning the confidence of the Irish by resettling displaced peasants, and by his strict regard for treaties.[38] Hugh de Lacy indeed very nearly went too far in arranging a marriage with O'Connor's daughter.[39] For John's continuation of his father's policy of trying to make the Irish feel that they were to be partners not victims, consider his close relations with their leaders on his expedition of 1210: indeed a prominent element in the army which marched against the Lacys was the contingent of Cathal Crovderg of Connaught.[40] There was no question here of the Norman settlement in Ireland reproducing the Norman Conquest of England. Nor, of course, did the Crown intend that it should reproduce the Norman settlement of Wales: there were to be no private baronial empires. But the Crown's insistence that the barons in Ireland should observe the conditions of English feudal tenure has tended to make us think that the lordships in Ireland were just like English fiefs. They were not: the great lordships of Leinster and Meath were province kingships, and royal policy rested, somewhat precariously, on them remaining more like province kingships than palatinates. Whatever the nature of their lordships over Norman settlers, the barons' lordship over their Irish subjects was assumed to reproduce the lordship of their Irish predecessors.

But how do we square this royal policy with the royal writ of 1217 which directed the justiciar in Ireland not for the future to allow any Irishman to be promoted to an ecclesiastical dignity?[41] We cannot square it, but we can explain it: the man responsible for that writ was the man in charge of the English government in 1217 after John's death—William Marshal, *rector regis et regni*.

This was the man and this was the sort of policy which I suggest made John start worrying about Ireland when Marshal went there in 1206. Marshal's determination to make Ireland render him compensation could be satisfied in one of two ways, either of which was inimical to royal policy. It might be satisfied by fresh conquests, or by a more intensive exploitation of the economic resources of the lordship. The justiciar might hinder the former,

[38] Cf. Gerald of Wales, *Opera* (Rolls Series), v. 353.
[39] *Gesta Regis Henrici Secundi Benedicti Abbatis* (Rolls Series), i. 270.
[40] Cf. Orpen, *Ireland under the Normans*, ii. 248–50, 262–4, and R. Dudley Edwards, 'Anglo-Norman relations with Connacht, 1169–1224', *Irish Historical Studies*, i (1938–9), 135ff.
[41] *Patent Roll Henry III, 1216–25*, pp. 22, 23.

16

but what about the latter? Now Ireland was, economically speaking, the most under-developed country of western Europe. The Irish economy rested chiefly upon cattle-grazing in a land ideally suited to the most advanced techniques of the European agricultural revolution: spring as well as winter sowing, three-field crop rotation, and peasants organised in manors to raise wheat, oats, beans, peas, and pigs.[42] The dues payable by Irish subjects were no doubt substantial, but far less than could be got by the economic exploitation of manorial peasants. It is partly for this reason, I would guess, that warfare played so large a part in the Irish polity: plunder was for the Irish lord an economic necessity, and in recognising his right to a share in the spoils of raids, the law was simply recognising his right to exploit other people's peasants rather than his own. But a Norman lord of the late twelfth century did not want plunder, he wanted rents, and if the Irish would not adapt themselves then he would sweep away the existing social and economic organisation and import English peasants to work his manorial fields.[43] This I suggest was the new policy of the barons in Ireland, following the lead of William Marshal, in the early years of the thirteenth century. And John's expedition of 1210 had the two-fold objective of putting the barons in their place and recovering the confidence of the Irish.

He was crushingly successful. The marks of his policy are the revision of baronial charters, and the sequestration of Lacy's fief of Meath. But two years later John was in dire difficulties with the barons of England: 1212 sees the first serious threat of rebellion which John was only just able to master. It was then that Robert FitzWalter and Eustace de Vesci fled abroad. Conspiracy and the threat of conspiracy were everywhere. It was at this time that John was taking loyalty oaths from members of his household. This was the time when anyone wanting favours from John could bargain for their support. William Marshal seized the opportunity: he and the barons of Ireland publicly pledged their loyalty. And the price of their loyalty?—I have little doubt that it was a free hand in Ireland. A free hand to exploit their Irish lordships with the utmost efficiency, and if necessary ruthlessness—with no interference from the justiciar in Dublin, and no political nonsense about concern for the welfare of the Irish.

[42] For the agricultural revolution see Lynn White, *Medieval Technology and Social Change* (Oxford, 1962), chapter 2. There is on the one surviving pipe roll of the Irish exchequer for John's reign, a striking contrast between the renders of corn from the Norman lordships and of cattle from Irish lands, cf. for example, the account for Meath, 'The Irish Pipe Roll of 14 John, 1211–1212', *Ulster Journal of Archaeology*, iv (1941), Supplement, pp. 32, 36.
[43] Cf. Jocelyn Otway-Ruthven, 'The organisation of Anglo-Irish agriculture in the middle ages', *Journal of the Royal Society of Antiquaries of Ireland*, lxxxi (1951), 1–13.

That a bargain was struck is suggested by the replacement of John de Grey by Henry of Dublin as justiciar of Ireland, and confirmed by the consistent support which the barons of Ireland gave to John and his son throughout the Magna Carta crisis and the civil war in England. Whatever they thought of John personally (and several of them must have detested him heartily), they had too much at stake to renege on their bargain. It paid off handsomely: after John's unexpected death the barons of Ireland found themselves governing England.

It seems highly probable that this bargain—hitherto unsuspected —played an important, perhaps even a crucial part, in the histories of both England and Ireland. It is arguable that the support of the barons of Ireland tipped the scales in the civil war of 1215-17. It is arguable too that John's *volte face* over the royal policy towards Ireland and the settlers there marked the demise of any hope of the creation of a kingdom of Ireland in which Irish and Normans were equal partners. This had been the basic objective of royal policy earlier—following the example of Scotland. It is interesting that Henry III seems to have tried to revert to it: in 1227, as soon as he was effectively king, he revoked that instruction to the justiciar of Ireland which William Marshal had issued in his name. It was too late: a generation had passed in which the interests of Irish and Normans had been in fundamental and open conflict.

Let me be perfectly frank about the status of this argument. This theory of mine rests on slender foundations. The facts which it embraces are not open to dispute; but the arrangement of the facts into a pattern and the links between them are entirely guesswork. It is a theory which I cannot prove, and which by its very nature is probably incapable of proof.

I am adding to a familiar story just two elements of context— equally familiar but previously omitted from this particular context: the loss of Normandy in 1204 (which, I suggest, made the barons with estates in Ireland look to those estates for compensation); and secondly, the demands of the English situation in 1212, which impelled John to allow the pursuit of those baronial interests at the expense of long-term royal policy. It is only in this context, it seems to me, that the facts are explicable and the puzzles to which the facts give rise can be resolved. I cannot prove any of this—but 'It had to be that way'.

The Government of Ireland Act, 1920: Its Origins and Purposes

The Working of the 'Official' Mind

N. Mansergh

Professor Lyons, in his recently published history of *Ireland since the Famine*, describes the offer implicit in Lloyd George's Government of Ireland Bill, 1919, as being 'totally divorced . . . from the realities of political life in Ireland'.[1] It is not the purpose of this paper to weigh that verdict but to pose a question peripheral to it. The question is this: if it be accepted that the Bill was 'totally divorced' from the realities of political life in Ireland, was it then in whole, or in part, an essay in political fantasy? Or was it related to other realities, namely the realities of political life in war and post-war England? This paper seeks to isolate and elucidate the second and inherently more probable of these alternatives by reviewing some of the important discussions in Parliament and more especially in Cabinet, which preceded Cabinet agreement in 1919 to sponsor what was in effect the fourth and last Home Rule Bill.

The Bill was first formulated by a Committee of the Cabinet appointed for this purpose in 1919 and then, in draft, its principal provisions and purposes were discussed and debated first in Cabinet and then in Parliament. The thinking of the Cabinet was largely derivative, as was inevitable on a matter already so much deliberated upon, and it is the purpose of this paper to trace its development over what seems to be a natural and meaningful period of time. It may, of course, be objected at the outset that to speak of the 'thinking' of a Cabinet, and still more of a number of Cabinets, even though with overlapping personnel, is otiose,— that there were *per contra* only the thoughts of individual members.

[1] F. S. L. Lyons, *Ireland since the Famine* (London, 1971), p. 412.

Clearly there is force in this contention, but it may be urged on the other side that any such committee, or succession of committees engaged upon a common undertaking or enterprise is apt either to develop an outlook that is more than the sum of the outlook of its members or else to disintegrate, at any rate, psychologically. Disintegration, actual over and above psychological, appeared indeed to be the likely destiny of Asquith's coalition in the summer of 1916 on Irish policy, but the succeeding Lloyd George coalitions achieved sufficient sense of common purpose to embark upon common action. In the light of their composition and of the controversies of the recent past this was in itself sufficiently remarkable to deserve enquiry as to how it came about. The essential source material for such an enquiry is to be found in the records of Cabinet or Cabinet Committee discussions and conclusions.[2]

It is, of course, the case that opinions, as expressed in Cabinet, or for that matter in Parliament, were rarely spontaneous and that more often than not they reflected a conclusion or consensus or compromise reached after individual or party exchanges of view. That is certainly important, especially to biographers and students of English politics, but from the broader perspective of Anglo-Irish relations—something apt to be lost sight of in dramatic reconstruction of personal and party in-fighting in the coalition era—what mattered was the extent to which there was a convergence of English political opinion at the highest level upon a particular, and *per se* improbable and, as it proved, inadequate panacea for the problem of Anglo-Irish relations.

The interest of such an analysis of the evolution of opinion on Irish policy that preceded the enactment of the 1920 Act is enhanced by reason of the fact that it took place in three successive Coalition Cabinets of a steadily increasing Unionist and steadily diminishing Liberal proportionate content—that of Asquith, formed in May 1915, that of Lloyd George's War Cabinet formed in December 1916 and finally of Lloyd George's post-war administration formed in January 1919. This meant, given party attitudes to the Third Home Rule Bill, a presumption in each case, not of agreement, but of difference on Irish policy within each succeeding Cabinet. Yet by 1920 there had emerged, if not agreement upon, at least acquiescence in a particular settlement. One necessary condition of its emergence was Unionist preparedness to abandon Union and to accept the view that Home Rule, not merely with partition, but with two parliaments in Ireland, was the best

---

[2] *The Records of the Cabinet Office till 1922* (H.M.S.O. 1966), pp. 3–17 provide a helpful guide to the material available.

practicable solution of the Irish question in terms of British interests; and another was that Coalition Liberals, who after 1916, and more especially after 1919, were not necessarily the most reputable of Liberals, should be persuaded that there was recognition, at least in principle, of the concept of the unity of Ireland to which earlier they had been committed by their support for the Third Home Rule Bill. By what processes of argument, pressure of events or personal power of persuasion were these ends achieved? A. J. P. Taylor would have us believe that credit, if that is the right word, is to be attributed to the last, as exercised by Lloyd George who 'devised an arrangement of fantastic complexity, the Government of Ireland Act (1920): the United Kingdom, United Ireland, a separate Ulster, all mixed together'.[3] But while Lloyd George certainly placed his *imprimatur* upon the Act, not least by his Parliamentary exposition of its purposes,[4] the level at which it may be said to have been of his devising is another matter. An explanation of so complex an outcome to so controversial an issue in personal terms may appear at first sight somewhat over-simple to be satisfying.

The remoter landmarks on the road that led to the formulation of the 1920 Act need only brief recall. There was no provision for the partitioning of Ireland in any of the Home Rule Bills, though the possibility of special treatment for Ulster had been considered and rejected by the Cabinet before the introduction of the Third. On the first day, however, of the Committee stage, 11 June 1912,[5] two young Liberal members, Agar-Robartes and Neil Primrose moved an amendment making acceptance of a Home Rule Parliament conditional upon the exclusion of the four North-Eastern Counties, Antrim, Armagh, Down and Derry from its provisions, Agar-Robartes explaining that the amendment was intended to remove the chief stumbling block to Home Rule, which was, in his judgement, the attempt to achieve the impossible, the fusing together of two incongruous elements in one polity and the corresponding failure to recognize that Ireland was not one but two nations. This argument commended itself neither to the Liberal Government nor to the Unionists, Bonar Law, however, saying on behalf of the Unionist party that he would vote in favour of the amendment, not because he was the less opposed to Home Rule for the rest of Ireland, but because it would make a bad Bill less bad.[6] 'We do not,' said Carson, 'accept this Amendment'—which he described as the most vital

---

[3] *English History 1914–1945*, Oxford 1965 p. 156.
[4] H. of C. Deb., 22 December, 1919, Vol. 123, coll. 1168–75.
[5] H. of C. Deb. Fifth Series Vol. xxxix, col. 771.
[6] *Ibid.*, col. 779.

which probably could be moved—'as a compromise of the question. There is no compromise possible.'[7] And because that was so there ought to be no Home Rule. But he noted also that he would never leave out Fermanagh and Tyrone. From another standpoint the amendment was dismissed by the Prime Minister as the most self-stultifying he had known. No wonder it had not been moved by any of the representatives of Ulster itself. 'Are these chivalrous champions of the rights of the Protestant minority', he asked 'going to take shelter . . . in this oasis, or Alsatia . . . in which they are a majority, in which they are exposed to no kind of hardship or injustice . . .?'[8] Lloyd George also opposed the amendment on the significantly different ground that if four Counties were to be excluded, 'there ought to be an overwhelming demand for it,' and clear agreement about which Counties were to be excluded. He saw no evidence of either; on the contrary the Ulster Unionist demand was not exclusion for a given area but 'the right to veto autonomy to the rest of Ireland',[9] and as such to be discounted and dismissed. If, however, there were such a demand from Ulster, the government, of course, should give it serious consideration.

The Buckingham Palace conference, 21–23 July, 1914, conveniently reflected the next stage—that reached at the outbreak of the War. There were two essential points at issue at the Conference—the nature of the exclusion, i.e. open or veiled, temporary or permanent, and the extent of the area to be excluded —and neither was settled. Indeed the first was never discussed because there was no agreement on the second. What happened was that Asquith, presuming that there was no possibility of profitable discussion of a settlement other than on the lines of exclusion of some sort, identified the two serious outstanding points as area and time limit, and urged that the former should be discussed first. Carson, Bonar Law, Lansdowne and Craig argued strongly for the reverse.[10] Redmond, however, protested saying it was impossible to consider the question of time limit until that area had been disposed of. His view prevailed and the question of area was thereupon discussed. Carson, according to Redmond's typescript notes of discussions which had no official rapporteur, urged the exclusion of all Ulster, commending it to Redmond and Dillon with the argument that if a smaller, more homogeneous area were to be excluded, reunion of the whole of Ireland would be delayed. The contention had force but acceptance

[7] *Ibid.*, cols. 1065 and 1068.
[8] *Ibid.*, col. 786.
[9] *Ibid.*, col. 1126.
[10] *Redmond Papers* (National Library, Dublin), 21 July, 1914.

of the conclusion was 'quite impossible' for Redmond. Carson then demanded as a minimum, 'a clean cut' excluding a *block* consisting of the six counties of Antrim, Down, Armagh, Derry, Tyrone and Fermanagh, including Derry City and Belfast,[11] all to vote as one unit and to remain under the Imperial Parliament, but with administrative responsibility for their own affairs[12]. The debate, however, was for the most part focussed on detailed delimitation by district and the submissions made by Redmond were in direct line with those examined by the Boundary Commission ten years later. More generally a study of Redmond's records indicates the shift of emphasis from the 1912 amendment. The premise of debate was now the exclusion of six *not* four counties, with the nature of the exclusion yet to be explored—a fact which had its bearing on the 1916 negotiations.

At the outbreak of War, or to be more precise, in October 1914, a Home Rule Act[13] was placed on the Statute Book, coupled with an Act[14] suspending its operation till a date to be determined 'not being later than the end of the present War' and with an understanding that Parliament would then have an opportunity of passing an amending bill making special provision for Ulster or some part of it. But in effect these were paper transactions placing on record the political equipoise in August 1914. Essentially their intention was to put the Irish question 'on ice' for the duration. The first coalition imperilled the balance of political forces on which such a possibility depended and the Easter Rebellion destroyed it, not merely in rather obvious political terms, but also at a deeper psychological level. It was not so much that the Dublin Castle system had been exposed as inadequate on a particular and momentous occasion as that it was felt in Cabinet, and most of all by the Prime Minister, that in itself and in what it represented, it no longer provided a possible basis for the administration and government of Ireland.

It is in this context that the Memorandum which Asquith submitted to the Cabinet in two parts on 19 and 21 May, 1916[15] on his return from Ireland, may be taken to mark the unfreezing at that level of the Irish question. Asquith, on his visit, had formed two distinct impressions. The first was that despite the

[11] The counties listed were referred to as the six 'plantation' counties. But historically this is not warranted. Six Ulster counties were planted under the 1609 'articles of plantation' but Cavan and Donegal were included in that number and Antrim and Down were not.
[12] *Redmond Papers* July 23, 1914.
[13] Government of Ireland Act, 1914, 4 & 5 Geo. 5, Ch. 90.
[14] Suspensory Act, 1914, 4 & 5 Geo. 5, Ch. 88.
[15] Cab. 37/148/18.

c

prudence and discretion of the military command, there had been incidents which had aroused 'a good deal of uneasiness and sympathy in many people in Dublin and elsewhere in Ireland who lent no countenance to the outbreak' with the rebels and the second that there did not seem to be 'any general or widespread feeling of bitterness between the civil population and the soldiers.' He himself 'went one day on foot partly through a considerable crowd and was received, not only without disrespect, but with remarkable warmth.' These impressions would seem to have reinforced his natural predisposition to think yet again in terms of the classical Liberal solution of self-government as a step not to estrangement but to closer and more harmonious relations.

But classical Liberal solvents of imperial-national relations were apt to subsume that if there were majority-minority tensions, they too, were susceptible to similar panaceas. In Belfast, Asquith was reminded that there existed quite different possibilities. The Lord Mayor of Belfast, 'a level headed and public spirited man', told him that during the early autumn of 1915 'a sort of atmospheric wave' overspread Protestant Ulster. 'We had sent' (such was or became the prevailing opinion) 'the best of our manhood to the front; the Catholic[s] of the South and West have contributed substantially less; if we were now to allow what remains of our available men to recruit, we shall be left defenceless against a possible, even probable, Nationalist invasion of our province; and our wives, our children, our homes, our industry, our religion will be at the mercy of our hereditary foes. From that day to this recruiting in Ulster has practically ceased; and so long as this belief, and the temper which it engenders, persists, not only will there be no effective recruiting for the Army, but there will be a determined resistance to any attempt on the part of the State to disarm those who remain at home.'

Ulster leaders confirmed to the Prime Minister that what he had been told was a correct interpretation of the state of mind of the vast majority of the Protestant population of Belfast and industrial Ulster and that nothing could dislodge such feelings from their minds. Those feelings rendered domestic disarmament, however desirable, impracticable. What then remained? One or two repeated to Asquith the old forumla of resolute government but the large majority 'were clearly of [the] opinion that the only way to escape was by prompt settlement of the whole problem. . . .' It was, said Campbell, the Attorney-General, 'a case of now or never.' But what did such a settlement require? The answer came clear—Home Rule with an amendment of the Home Rule Act, 1914 such as would adequately safeguard the future of the Ulster

Protestants, and that was deemed to mean the permanent exclusion of Ulster or some part of it.

The Prime Minister acquiesced reluctantly in this conclusion. It appeared to him to be 'the duty of the Government to do everything in their power to force a general settlement.' By that means alone could arms be controlled and it was all important that this should be so, lest otherwise the two armies of North and South should be held in leash 'for a final spring at one another's throats when peace was declared.' In 1914 the possibility of a settlement on such lines had broken down on the problem of the area to be excluded but, now, Asquith was by no means sure that the Nationalists (apart from the O'Brienites in Cork from whom he had received a deputation) would not 'be disposed to prefer the total exclusion (for the time being at any rate) of Ulster', to the continued withholding of Home Rule from the rest of Ireland. If, however, the ultimate solution was to be thought of on Home Rule cum partition lines, there had to be wartime transition arrangements and there Asquith contemplated the disappearance 'of the fiction' of a Chief Secretary, the appointment of no successor to the Lord Lieutenant—the Vice-royalty having become 'a costly and futile anachronism' — and single British ministerial control of Irish administration operating with the help of an Irish advisory council.

The Asquith memorandum of 19–21 May led on naturally to the Lloyd George negotiations, undertaken at the Prime Minister's invitation at the end of the month. Asquith spoke in the House of Commons of a bold effort on fresh lines that might lead to an agreed settlement[16] between those representing different interests and parties in Ireland and told members that the Minister of Munitions, Lloyd George, at the unanimous request of his colleagues had undertaken to devote his energies to the task. But while there may have been occasion for boldness, there was little opportunity for freshness and, as might confidently have been predicted, Lloyd George sought to manipulate familiar formulae with the one overriding purpose of obtaining a settlement if not by agreement, at least with a semblance of agreement. This was easy in respect of negotiating method, for Lloyd George, unlike Cripps in India in 1942, was bound by no Cabinet declaration, for the good reason that the Coalition Cabinet in 1916 would not have been able to reach agreement upon its terms. His task, accordingly, realistically viewed, was not merely to secure the assent, however reluctant, of the Nationalist and Ulster Unionist

[16] H. of C. Deb. Vol. lxxxii, Coll. 2309–11.

leadership to a 'prompt' settlement, but having done that to persuade the Cabinet collectively to accept it.[17]

It was later an allegation of Lloyd George's Unionist critics that there was on the Cabinet side a 'blue print for negotiations,' namely Asquith's Memorandum. The point was put by Lansdowne in a paper[18] circulated to the Cabinet on 21 June, in which he wrote that 'while it would have been unwise to fetter Lloyd George with meticulous restrictions' it was understood in Cabinet that Lloyd George in negotiations would not go beyond the lines of the Memorandum.[19] In view of the transitional arrangements there outlined he [Lansdowne] had no idea that anything so far reaching as the terms of Lloyd George's reported discussions with Irish leaders was in mind. In particular, Asquith had concluded that the Home Rule Act could not take effect till after the War and by implication, so Lansdowne considered, this conclusion had received public affirmation in the Prime Minister's speech at Ladybank on 14 June, when Asquith had said that at the end of the War 'the fabric of the Empire will have been refashioned, and the relations not only between Great Britain and Ireland but also between the United Kingdom and our Dominions will of necessity be brought under close and connected review.' In reply Lloyd George, in fact, conceded that he had not been authorized to bind the Cabinet, but he deemed nonetheless that he had been authorized to deal with the Irish leaders on the assumption that Home Rule might be brought into immediate operation. He had thus clearly conveyed to the Irish leaders the impression that he was not merely, in Lansdowne's phrase, 'gathering up' their opinions, but was in a position to and had in fact made them a firm offer.

On 23 June Long echoed Lansdowne's complaints about the scope of the discussions. The Irish business was, he wrote, 'unhappily involved in mystery and the consequence is that a great deal of deplorable misapprehension has arisen.' Both Carson and Redmond appeared to have misinterpreted the Prime Minister's reference to the breakdown of the existing machinery of Irish government, as meaning that the whole form of government under the Union had failed and that Home Rule was the only alternative. But in his Memorandum the Prime Minister had written that the Home Rule Act could not come into force until the end of the War. Moreover, alleged Long, Lloyd George

[17] For an account of the negotiations that followed as recalled by Lloyd George see *War Memoirs*, 2 vols. (London, 1938), Vol. 1 pp. 418–25, and as interpreted by Asquith's biographer see Roy Jenkins' *Asquith* (London, 1964), pp. 397–402.
[18] Cab. 37/150/11.
[19] Cab. 37/150/15.

had been commissioned to undertake *confidential* negotiations
and to report results to the Cabinet before any public announcement was made. The first was obviously unrealistic, since Irish
leaders had to consult and persuade their respective supporters,
but there may have been more substance in the second, in view of
Lansdowne's further complaint in the House of Lords on 29 June
that the Cabinet were still insufficiently seized of all the points
involved in the negotiations.[20]

To the Unionists' sense of grievance about the conduct of
negotiations was to be added their protests in Cabinet at their
content and direction. The two, inevitably, were not readily to be
disentangled and on one point Lloyd George seemingly attached
more significance to the Asquithian adjective 'prompt' than
Asquith himself, for he moved with remarkable speed towards
a settlement formulated by the end of May, the basis of which
was the application of the Home Rule Act as soon as possible,
with acceptance of a Nationalist modification to the effect that
the number of Irish members at Westminster should remain
unaltered at 103 instead of being reduced, as contemplated in the
1914 Act, to 42, and of a Unionist demand that the six 'plantation'
counties of the North East should be excluded from the jurisdiction of the Home Rule Parliament and directly administered
by a secretary of State responsible to the Imperial Parliament
for the period of the War, with the longer term resolution of the
Irish question to be referred to a post-war Imperial Conference.
But such an overall settlement could win Irish acceptance only
by ambivalence in personal presentation and from that Lloyd
George was not one to shrink. He assured Redmond, and this
is very familiar ground, that the arrangements, including exclusion
should in fact be temporary, i.e. for the period of the War and
in his own words he had 'placed his life upon the table, and would
stand or fall by the agreement come to', while to Carson he wrote,
'We must make it quite clear that at the end of the provisional
period, Ulster does not, whether she wills it or not, merge in the
rest of Ireland.' The contradiction, which allegedly alone enabled
Carson to persuade the Ulster Unionists to renounce three of the
Ulster counties on plea of permanence, and actually enabled
Redmond to persuade a majority of his party to acquiesce in
what he deemed to be a temporary—though clearly open to
perpetuation on any reckoning—partition, has been regarded as
of critical significance.[21] But four points are to be noted, the

[20] H. of L. Deb. Vol. xxii, col. 506.
[21] The story is told in Denis Gwynn, *History of Partition* (1912–25) (Dublin, 1950),
Chap. v. Lloyd George's letter to Carson was dated 29 May, 1916.

first three in passing and the fourth for fuller consideration. The first is that without Lloyd George's negotiating dexterity the historian is well advised to refrain from semblance of moral judgement there was no prospect whatever of a 'prompt' settlement. The second is that in essence Lloyd George was employing a procrastinating device, since the issue of transient or lasting exclusion would in legislative terms be deferred till the end of the War, and the third that in fact the difference, as Devlin surmised, between temporary and permanent exclusion was, politically as distinct from psychologically, minimal or even non-existent, since what the Ulster Unionists had obtained and enjoyed they would assuredly not have abandoned after a period of years. The fourth—and this is a tangled skein that needs to be more deliberately unravelled—is that the Cabinet would have been divided, to the point of partial disruption, had the attempt been made to give effect to the proposed heads of settlement, not only because of the Ulster question but also, and immediately more so, because of Home Rule and the nature of it, for the rest of Ireland.

Lansdowne's objections on this second point certainly lacked nothing in directness of statement. 'Is this', he asked, in his Memorandum of 21 June, 'the moment for imposing upon the country, in the guise of an interim arrangement, a bold and startling scheme which at once concedes in principle all that the most extreme Nationalists have been demanding, viz the disappearance of Castle Government and the establishment of an Irish Parliament with an Irish Executive responsible to it? The triumph of lawlessness and disloyalty would be complete. We may delude ourselves by saying that this arrangement is purely provisional, but the capitulation will be palpable and its significance will not be diminished by the exclusion of Ulster or part of the province.' Sinn Féin would not be conciliated and, he proceeded in a passage that foreshadowed the evolution of Southern Unionist sentiment that received public expression at the Convention a year later: 'I have always thought that any measure of Home Rule which presented to the World as a new Irish nation, an Ireland from which Ulster or any part of it was excluded, would be a deplorable and humiliating confession of failure; and if Home Rule is to come I should prefer a measure embracing the whole of Ireland, with safeguards for the minority wherever found.'

In a less cogent paper of 23 June, Long supported Lansdowne specifically on the point that Home Rule during the War was not, as alleged by Lloyd George, an imperial necessity but would prove an imperial disaster. The following day, however, a Unionist of quite different intellectual calibre, A. J. Balfour, countered with a Memorandum[22] circulated to the Unionist members of the Cabinet. Balfour took as his starting point an assertion by Lord Selborne, a vehement critic of the proposed settlement, to the effect that there was no guarantee he [Selborne] was not prepared to give that a Home Rule Parliament be established immediately after the War, but that he would rather resign than see it set up a moment earlier. Balfour's feeling was rather the other way. If Home Rule there had to be 'let us at least exclude from its operation as much of Unionist Ulster as possible'. Were Lloyd George's scheme to be carried through 'the six Ulster counties would have permanently secured to them—by consent and without bloodshed—their place in the United Kingdom. Will anybody assert that, if the settlement of their fate be deferred till peace is declared, terms equally good could be obtained without a dangerous struggle?' He had always held that rather than submit to Home Rule, Ulster should fight and Ulster would be right, but equally he had no illusions about the price in terms of civilized society and damage to property this would entail. 'Very strong therefore,' he argued, 'must be the arguments which would induce me to run the hazard of civil war, when we have offered to us voluntarily all that successful civil war could give.' He did not think the arguments were strong. An Irish government was unlikely to countenance a suicidal policy of assisting Germany and were they to prove as incapable of government as Mexicans, why then Home Rule would perish never to be revived. But he did not himself entertain such ideas, nor did he believe that Redmond and his friends would tolerate Sinn Féin notions of an Irish Republic dependent on Germany any more than 'we can tolerate it ourselves.' Therefore, concluded Balfour, 'the war supplies no sufficient justification for neglecting the unique opportunity now offered for settling peacefully and permanently the problem of Ulster.'

Ironically enough Balfour's Memorandum was written the same day as a report[23] from General Maxwell, also circulated to the Cabinet, which might have been thought to knock from under it the principal prop on which it rested. People in Ireland, noted Maxwell, 'think Sinn Féinism and patriotism are synonymous terms.' Home Rule was again being discussed and that in itself was evidence that rebellion paid. Redmond and his party were discredited, the North was quiet only because the Unionists had the arms and they knew they could defend themselves and the

[22] Cab. 37/150/17.
[23] Cab. 37/150/18.

only conclusion was that the Irish question would never be settled in Ireland.

Lord Robert Cecil followed with a paper on 26 June[24], to express disagreement with Balfour partly on these same grounds, but further alleging that, of the triumvirate by whom a Home Rule administration would be principally directed, Redmond had no administrative experience and had given no evidence of administrative ability, that Dillon had always been a convinced enemy of this country, that Devlin had announced that his first act would be to free all 'rebel' prisoners and that none—and this was clearly the telling point—would have the authority of popular choice. Sinn Féin, on the other hand would, and its two principal tenets were: (i) 'vehement rejection' of any proposal for the division of Ireland, (ii) profound mistrust of the Irish Parliamentary Party. Sinn Féin would not be conciliated by the proposals in debate. To withdraw the offer of Home Rule would be equally dangerous, Carson having warned that to withdraw the proposals now 'would throw Ulster into a ferment and convert the rest of Ireland into "hell".' So what did Lord Robert suggest? Something perhaps a little devious for so high minded a man—for the duration of the War, martial law with symbolic Home Rule, i.e. if the necessary Amending Bill excluding the six counties were passed, a Home Rule Parliament could meet, elect a Speaker and then adjourn till the end of the War!

The Cabinet met on 27 June and Asquith reported[25] to the King that despite the hardly won concurrence of Carson and Redmond to the settlement, Lansdowne on grounds of concession to rebellion and risk of encouraging further rebellion, especially in view of the terms of Maxwell's report, and Long on grounds of lack of a genuine acceptance of the basis of it by the Nationalists, could accept no responsibility for it; Cecil advanced in the English interest his symbolic Home Rule *cum* suspension of executive power till the end of the war stratagem; Curzon feared defeat in the Lords, with the consequent risk of an election and newly elected fresh members 'of a revolutionary tinge being returned'; but Crewe and Grey on the Liberal side strongly supported the settlement and Bonar Law on the Unionist side, who wondered what was the alternative to the proposal, said he would recommend his party to ratify it at their meeting the next day. But, according to Asquith, it was Balfour who 'delivered the most effective pronouncement in the long conclave.' He dissociated himself entirely from Lansdowne and Long and far from believing the

[24] Cab. 37/150/21.
[25] Cab. 37/150/23. See also Jenkins, *op. cit.* pp. 399–401.

proposed settlement 'a concession to rebellion,' he thought 'it might be far more fairly represented as a Unionist triumph,' the exclusion of the six Ulster counties having been the maximum demand of the Unionist leaders at the Buckingham Palace Conference. 'With unanswerable logic', he [Balfour] proceeded to point out the absurdity of the contention that the establishment of a Home Rule Parliament at a distance of 6 or 8, and more probably 12 or 18 months could seriously embarrass action in the War, stressed the importance of not alienating United States opinion and declared himself a whole-hearted supporter of the policy of Carson and Bonar Law. Clearly the moment of truth was approaching. But before it came Lloyd George intervened. He suggested the appointment of a small committee of the Cabinet to consider further safeguards, which might avert the resignation of Unionist members of the Cabinet. Curzon and Chamberlain agreed, Lansdowne acquiesced, Long held out to the last. The proposal was adopted and the Committee (the Prime Minister, Lloyd George, Cecil and the Attorney General, F. E. Smith) appointed to consider and formulate such additions as seemed to be necessary. By this means, Asquith observed, a series of resignations, with the consequent possible dissolution of the government, which 'would not only be a national calamity but a national crime', had been averted. What he did not tell the King—perhaps he did not wholly understand—was that some resignations were the price of settlement. Even a week later, on 5 July, (when the Cabinet met to receive the report of the committee it had set up) and when Lansdowne spoke of his dilemma 'either horn of which seemed to promise danger if not disaster' as between a settlement he disliked and distrusted and the risk of political chaos 'which might necessitate the worst of evils—a general election'—and Long of his position as a 'cruel' one, Asquith found cause for much satisfaction in the fact that both decided to remain and that Selborne's was accordingly the only resignation. He contended that this had amply justified the delay which had obviated 'premature and precipitate decisions'.[26] But on 11 July in a speech in the House of Lords which, as Asquith wrote to Crewe, gave the 'greatest offence to the Irish',[27] Lansdowne made it brutally clear that his continued membership of the Cabinet was on the basis of 'permanent and enduring' exclusion of the six counties together with continuing British wartime control over defence dispositions in the twenty-six

[26] Cab. 37/151/8. See also Roy Jenkins, *Asquith* (London, 1964), p. 401.
[27] Quoted *Ibid.*, p. 402.

regardless of the existence of a Home Rule administration of which his mistrust was ostentatiously displayed.[28]

The headings of the settlement as outlined by the committee and preliminary to the drafting of legislation, were laid before the Cabinet on 17 July. They provided principally:

(1) that the Government of Ireland Act 1914 should be brought into force as soon as possible subject to certain modifications,

(2) that the Act was not to apply to an excluded six counties area, which was to be administered by a Secretary of State,

(3) that the Irish representation in the House of Commons was to remain unaltered at 103.

To reassure critics, special safeguards were included to protect British military and naval interests. The Act was to remain in force for twelve months but the period could be extended and a permanent settlement considered after the War at an Imperial Conference concerned with closer cooperation of the Dominions with Imperial Government.

The submission of the outline of legislation which did not foreclose the Ulster options provoked renewed Unionist opposition. Cecil, Lansdowne and Long all returned to the charge. It was essential, argued Cecil,[29] that exclusion should be definite until the excluded areas wished to return. Equally it was impossible for the Unionist party to support a settlement unless Irish representation at Westminster were diminished—the one boon of Home Rule—since otherwise Ulster would be at the mercy of eighty Irish Nationalist members. It was impossible, therefore, to proceed with the experiment, though he allowed that something had been gained in that Unionist leaders were now definitely pledged to Home Rule for the South and West of Ireland and the Liberal party had conceded that six Ulster counties could not be included in a Home Rule Ireland without their consent. Lansdowne argued that the Ulster Unionists had 'notoriously' accepted the settlement only on the assumption of permanent exclusion,[30] while Long, supporting Lansdowne's demand for a structural change in the Home Rule Act to exclude the six counties, enquired further whether it was right to divert attention from the War.[31]

On 19 July Asquith reported[32] to the King that he could not assent to further postponement, but that the Cabinet after much discussion of the draft Bill agreed (i) that Carson's claim for the

[28] H. of L. Deb. Fifth Series, Vol. xxii, Coll. 645–9.
[29] Cab. 37/151/37.
[30] Cab. 37/151/38.
[31] Cab. 37/151/42.
[32] Cab. 37/152/1.

definitive exclusion of Ulster could not be resisted, (ii) that the Nationalists should be told that after the Home Rule Parliament had been set up, Irish representation in the Imperial House of Commons must be reduced, with the proviso that it should be restored when an Amending Irish Bill was introduced. This was to make an already dangerously disadvantageous compromise impossible for the Irish Nationalist leaders and thus destroy, as intended, the basis of the settlement. When a Bill with such provision was introduced on 25 July Redmond declined to support it and on 27 July, by which date Redmond, for whom the negotiations had disastrous consequences, was extricating himself finally from them, Asquith reported to the King; 'It was agreed that for the immediate future in Ireland the simplest and least objectionable plan would be to revert for a time to the old system of Lord Lieutenant and Chief Secretary.'[33] What it must have cost him to pen those words!

What conclusions may be drawn from the complex and abortive negotiations of the summer of 1916? The first and most important in general terms was that the options before any composite coalition Cabinet were extremely limited. Hard-core English Unionist opinion, reinforced by the most highly placed spokesman of the Southern Unionists, would not acquiesce in Home Rule, even with six county exclusion, in wartime, short of safeguards which would render Home Rule meaningless, despite the readiness of the new leadership in the persons of Bonar Law and F. E. Smith, and the old in the person of Balfour, to contemplate imminent Home Rule, given permanent exclusion for the six counties; the Liberal leadership, including presumably Lloyd George, though he remained a negotiator without personal commitment, desired Home Rule forthwith, acquiescing in the exclusion of the 'six' counties as a necessary condition of it, but with such exclusion decently veiled in deference to the concept of unity, to which their allegiance was already bespoken; the Irish nationalist leadership, in a position of nominal strength with a Home Rule Act on the Statute book and the special treatment for the North Eastern counties still to be decided, but politically altogether insecure at home, were neither willing nor able to negotiate on the basis of a lasting partition, but had however, shown themselves prepared to acquiesce in the temporary exclusion of six counties—the possibility of four now being discounted and disregarded—as the price of immediate Home Rule, the Ulster Unionists, having in effect twice diminished their pretensions, first by abandoning, for the period of the Lloyd

[33] Cab. 37/152/22.

George negotiations, their objection to Home Rule in principle and second their claim to the whole province of Ulster, had little more to concede short of conceding all. Within this complex clearly something had to give or to be sacrificed and in 1916 what gave in general terms was liberal, more particularly, Asquithian resolution in the face of aristocratic Unionist opposition to Home Rule in war time on the basis of a divided Ireland.

But such a general conclusion in isolation is insufficient. Why precisely did the 1916 negotiations fail? To argue that this was to be attributed to Lloyd George's dexterity, or duplicity, does no more than push the question back two stages further. Why in the first instance did he feel compelled to resort to a negotiating gamble with the odds on premature and damaging revelation so obviously against him? The answer is that in no other way could he hope to take even a first step towards a settlement. And then secondly, was it because of Lloyd George's conflicting assurances that the settlement collapsed? To this long-standing assumption A. J. P. Taylor gives a categoric negative.[34] The objection, he writes of Lansdowne, Long and other hard-core Unionists, was over Southern Ireland, not over Ulster. The first was certainly so. But it was not their only objection, as emerged very clearly in July with reiterated demands for permanent exclusion of the six counties. Would Asquith indeed have made the concession to a 'little aristocratic clique'[35] which finally wrecked the proposals, had it not been for the additional demands for a reduction in the number of Irish members and for a structural alteration in the 1914 Act, voiced publicly by Lansdowne in his speech of 11 July in the Lords, and both assured of broadly based Unionist support precisely because they were designed to safeguard the 'plantation' counties? The truth would seem to be that, in the initial stages of the controversy, the opposition was to war-time Home Rule in the rest of Ireland, but as it progressed, demands for a reduction of Irish members and structural amendment of the Home Rule Act indicated that it was the future of Ulster that was fundamental. Moreover, unless the view is taken that Asquith was deliberately misleading Redmond, that was the purport of a letter to him dated 28 July 1916 and marked 'for you *alone*'. 'I say nothing,' wrote the Prime Minister, 'as to the responsibility of this person or that' [for the breakdown of the negotiations] but 'I am sure you agree that the actual breaking point was not the figure at which the Irish members should be retained in the

[34] Taylor, *op. cit*. pp. 71–2, Note B.
[35] Quoted in Trevor Wilson, *The Downfall of the Liberal Party 1914–1935* (London, 1968, Fontana Edition), p. 74 from *Manchester Guardian*, 26 July 1916.

Imperial Parliament. This could easily be arranged by some form of compromise. . . . The real point is the future of the Excluded area. Carson (naturally) wants safeguards against "automatic inclusion". You (with equal reason) desire to keep open, and effectively open, the possibility of revision and review—at an early date.'[36]

Asquith told Redmond in that same letter of 28 July, that the important thing was to keep the negotiating spirit alive. It was superfluous advice—neither could stop negotiating and in the end it helped to bring disaster to both. Lloyd George, who displaced Asquith in December, was also a negotiator, but he negotiated for appearance as well as for ends. The Irish Convention, of which Professor McDowell has written the detailed story,[37] was his grand essay in the art. It is to be noted, however, that Lloyd George's own first choice, as set out in his letter to Redmond of 16 May, 1917,[38] was not for a Convention at all, but for a Home Rule settlement with the exclusion of the six counties, subject to reconsideration by Parliament after five years and with a Council of Ireland composed in equal numbers of delegations from the two parts of Ireland with powers to extend or to initiate the ending of the area of exclusion. It was only in view of its rejection, that Lloyd George reverted to the South African Convention precedent which loomed so large in the minds of most Liberal and some Unionist leaders. The Convention indeed took place, but it was the proposal that was discarded that foreshadowed the future, including not only partition, but the notion of a Council and the idea of parity as between majority and minority in the membership of that Council. The changes that took place in 1919–20 marked in fact a further retreat from the concept of unity in as much as the five year initial period of exclusion adumbrated in 1917 was to disappear and the Council to be restricted in respect of the initiatives open to it.

Lloyd George's letter to Redmond reinforces other evidence to the effect that within a few months of his accession to the highest office Lloyd George was probing for a solution along the lines of exclusion for the six counties, increasingly thought of in quasi-permanent terms and Home Rule for the twenty six. 'I saw Lloyd George two or three times in Paris,' wrote T. P. O'Connor, 'on 10 May, 1917; so far as I could gather he was still on his absurd "clean cut" proposition.'[39] There is a certain

[36] *Redmond Papers.*
[37] R. B. McDowell, *The Irish Convention 1917–18* (London, 1970).
[38] Cd 8573 and also reprinted in *Report of the Proceedings of the Irish Convention* Cd 9019, pp. 50–1.
[39] *Redmond Papers.*

ring of conviction in Lloyd George's repeated comments, as on 7 March, 1917, on the differences between North and South—the inhabitants of the former being 'as alien in blood, in religious faith, in traditions, in outlook—as alien from the rest of Ireland in this respect as the inhabitants of Fife or Aberdeen.'[40] This was the view made explicit in the Agar-Robartes amendment in 1912 and while the majority of Liberals may be thought to have stood firm by the principle of unity, there was evidently a minority of them who felt that self-determination, preferably on the basis of county option for the North-Eastern counties, at the least was not inconsistent with their principles. It is true that at the Convention the Ulster representatives had reverted to their all-Ulster exclusion demand as the price of Home Rule but, vulnerable though he was to Unionist pressures in Parliament and Cabinet, Lloyd George was well placed to discount claims, which no longer commended themselves to much influential English Unionist opinion.

In early 1918 two questions compelled attention—the first the follow-up to the Convention and the second, in its Irish context, the manpower shortage. The Coalition Cabinet, aware that they were separate issues, decided to treat them as though they were not and as a result produced a package deal—Home Rule and conscription to be extended to Ireland as near simultaneously as was practicable, on the argument that, since there was no prospect of agreement on either separately, objections to each might cancel out if they were taken in conjunction. The one positive result was that the Cabinet *appeared* to have a policy in respect of Ireland, which was important in its English political context, but which, in its Irish, may well have been worse than having none. Inevitably, in such circumstances, the composite policy was pursued with an almost total lack of conviction.

On 28 March, 1918, the Cabinet, without waiting for the final Report of the Convention, decided to extend conscription to Ireland as soon as that Report was received.[41] It was an abrupt decision on a matter long debated in a desultory way and the decision taken was against the weight of official opinion over a period of time, Duke, on his appointment as Chief Secretary, having assured Maxwell (September 1916) that 'from my knowledge of English politics and all I could learn of the Irish situation an extension of the Military Service Act to Ireland must be regarded as impracticable', and Maxwell in a Memorandum circulated to the Cabinet a month later having questioned whether,

[40] H. of C. Deb. Vol. xci col. 459.
[41] Cab. 23/14. 28:3:18.

in 1916, such a policy were not already too late, adding that it would, however, 'please militant Sinn Féiners and Unionists, the former because it would play into their hands . . . the latter because they consider what is good enough for England is good for Ireland, but the motive imputed to them would be their desire to kill Home Rule'.[42] Duke reiterated his strong objections to conscription in Ireland on 20 and again on 29 March, 1918,[43] i.e. immediately after the Cabinet decision. Why then was it taken? The answer is first and fundamentally because of a near-desperate shortage of men on the Western Front, with gloomy forebodings even in the highest circles about the stopping of the German offensive short of Calais—there had been for the same fundamental reason earlier conscription crises in Australia and Canada;— second, the pressure of opinion in Parliament and country upon the Cabinet demanding equality of sacrifice, the more insistently with the age of conscription about to be raised from forty-five to fifty. Embedded in the demand was doubtless the feeling, expressed very characteristically by Lansdowne in 1916, who had then forecast that the Government would be eventually driven to conscription,[44] that 'nothing in the end would be more beneficial socially to Ireland than to pass the bulk of her young men through the army' since it would mean that they 'would return to ordinary life with ideas of duty and discipline', not otherwise to be acquired. But it was the added inducement of a package deal that persuaded the majority of the Cabinet, including Curzon, Smuts and Lloyd George, whose attitude on Ireland was evidently hardening, as Hankey noted[45] in April, 1918, to line up with Milner and Balfour on this issue. Smuts' reasoning is of some interest. In the event of the Convention agreeing on a Report, and indeed in any event, he thought the passage of a Home Rule Bill and conscription, while in effect simultaneous, should be so timed that Home Rule would come 'first on the ground that this would remove the Irish sense of historic wrong and satisfy United States and Dominion opinion on Home Rule.' Evidently he attached importance to these, in one respect surely altogether misconceived, views for the record of what he said is amended and extended.

There was a full scale discussion on Ireland at a Cabinet conference on 3 April,[46] at which the Viceroy, Lord Wimborne

[42] Cab. 37/155/8 and 37/155/40.
[43] Cab. 24/5.
[44] Cab. 37/157/8.
[45] Thomas Jones, *Whitehall Diary*, ed. by K. Middlemas, Vol. 1 (London, 1969), p. 57 and Vol. iii, p. 4. See also D. G. Boyce, *How to settle the Irish question: Lloyd George and Ireland 1916–21* in A. J. P. Taylor, *Lloyd George—twelve essays* (London, 1971), pp. 143–5 and generally.
[46] Cab. 23/14.

and Duke and Robinson[47] were present. Wimborne said compulsory service before settlement of the Convention 'would be to cause an explosion in Ireland'. Milner deprecated 'playing with conscription'; once entered upon, it would have to be 'seen through'. The majority, however, remained in favour of taking both together. Smuts thought now was the right time to do so. Bonar Law, having regard to the danger of an explosion in Ulster, guardedly assented, saying that the government would have to stand or fall by both bills. Robinson thought firmness essential, since weakness would provoke resistance to the death and while agreeing with Wimborne on the need for contemporaneous action, nonetheless expected general opposition from Unionists and Sinn Féin, were the two measures to be introduced in conjunction. '. . . However strange it might appear', commented Milner, 'an attack from both sides would not be a bad thing.' He felt also that an Irish settlement must needs be imposed. The fundamental point was the war, remarked Balfour in gloomy philosophic reflection, and the question was whether they would be stronger if they got a few men from Ireland at the risk of disturbances or did nothing. He laid down two policies—all or none. If the second were adopted it would be difficult to persuade England to accept the decision. 'We should have to state' he concluded, 'the naked truth that Ireland is a sheer weakness, but it would be a greater weakness if we did something than it was if we did nothing.'

The package policy was announced in the House of Commons on 9 April[48] with a Military Service Bill on the one hand which, while not extending conscription forthwith to Ireland, empowered the Government to do so by Order in Council and an invitation to Parliament to frame a measure of self-government for Ireland. Carson commended conscription but without concession on the ground that it was either good or bad in itself; the Nationalist members were united in passionate protest against it and next day Lloyd George thought the Irish 'were trying to work themselves up into a frenzy', Tom Jones as a result rather missing 'the buoyant, cheerful note'[49] so characteristic of him. The Cabinet appointed another Committee to draft another Irish Bill, the Chairman being Walter Long, and Curzon, Smuts, Cave, H. A. L. Fisher and Duke being among the members. The first meeting was held on 15 April. On 20 April Tom Jones, after a long discussion, told Hankey that he thought the Government's Irish policy was 'a mad one';[50] on 9 May Chamberlain at a

[47] Sir Henry Robinson, President, Local Government Board for Ireland.
[48] H. of C. Deb. Vol. 104, col. 1364.
[49] Whitehall Diary I, p. 56.
[50] Ibid., p. 61.

meeting of the Irish Committee was contending defensively that
'to withdraw from compulsion was to surrender the unity of the
Imperial Government' in face of a challenge from Irish Nationalists
and he did not see how the government could remain in office
if that were done, while Smuts with the agility for which he was
renowned conceded that 'in abstract principle' Chamberlain was
right, 'conscription and Home Rule were conjoint, associate
measures' but Home Rule might mean 'letting loose forces of
civil war when we are fighting for our life' and should therefore
be held over anyway as 'a big imperial question'—presumably he
was already thinking in terms of a dominion solution—and
conscription, also carrying its own civil war risk, should be
likewise deferred.[51] On 14 June the Irish Committee reported
it was impossible to give effect to the dual policy. Conscription
was tacitly dropped and in Churchill's retrospective verdict the
government was left with 'all the resentment against compulsion
and in the end no law and no men.'[52]

The constitutional discussions in the Irish Committee were
somewhat more illuminating. The Committee, it is true, had here
one essential purpose—to play for time. But its members were
less than content with so self-denying a rôle. They looked for a
more specific *raison d'etre* and found it by seeking to fulfil one
avowed object of their being, namely the drafting of a bill. But
they ran inevitably into difficulties both of principle and of detail.
The Chairman, not unreasonably perhaps, wanted a bill that
might pass through Parliament and he felt that the only hope of
achieving this was by drafting the provisions in such a way that
they would be consistent with federation of the British Isles.
He had strong initial support from Austen Chamberlain, who said
on 16 April, that powers might be given to an Irish parliament
so far as was compatible with a federal constitution. 'I do not
exclude federal reconstruction of [the] United Kingdom—that is
the real test for the Irish Bill.[53] In a later memorandum[54] he
developed the argument, contending that all past attempts at
Home Rule had failed, not because of the incapacity of governments, but because of the impossibility of finding a solution
within the limits they had set themselves. But were the context
to be widened the problem would become more manageable.
He himself believed that, because of the complexity of the issues
and the revolutionary ferment that would arise after the War, it

[51] Cab. 27/46 and *Whitehall Diary*, Vol. I, p. 63.
[52] Cab. 27/46 and W. S. Churchill, *The World Crisis, The Aftermath* (London, 1929),
p. 281.
[53] *Whitehall Diary*, Vol. III, p. 5–6 and Cab. 27/46.
[54] Cab. 24/5, July 14, 1918.

D

would have to be in any case, since one imperial government and parliament could no longer deal with everything, but would find it necessary to devolve a part of its responsibilities on other bodies to set itself free for the work, which it alone could do. If such a scheme of federal devolution were not applied, he surmised, 'We shall be in grave danger of revolution before many years have passed.' Devolution, therefore, was as necessary in English as in Irish interests and the two problems should be run together. That would change the context of the Irish question because while it would, for example, be possible to think of customs and excise in the hands of a Home Rule government, it would be impossible in a federation to conceive of them except in the hands of the federal government. So the Chamberlainite moral was, cease to think of the Irish question in isolation, but enlarge the setting, bearing in mind that the problem of decentralization of government was a general not a particular problem.

The argument was not without consequence on the longer term, but it carried only modest conviction in a disillusioned Committee, from which Cave wished to resign, because he thought it was ploughing the sands and in which Curzon saw no line of advance.[55] An answer of a kind, was later given to Chamberlain's contention in a letter from Lord Hugh Cecil. He recognised, even while deploring, the fact of Irish nationality and he argued that federalism and nationality were contradictory and mutually fatal. 'The truth is,' he wrote, 'that colouring federalism with nationalism is like painting a rat red; it kills the animal.'[56] But while he drew no such inference himself, presumably the federal notion remained relevant where there was no such national sentiment. The strange conclusion that he did draw was that by a process of elimination, nationality and federalism alike having revealed their impracticability, the Irish might eventually be driven towards Union with provincial devolution.

In December 1918 a new balance of political forces emerged to face a new situation. The General Election resulted in an overwhelming victory for the coalition, which returned 478 members on the coalition coupon, as against 29 Liberals, 59 Labour, and no less than 48 Conservatives without it. The Coalition membership of 478 was made up of 333 Coalition Unionists as against 135 Coalition Liberals.[57] There was, because of Sinn Féin abstention, no organized Irish Nationalist vote in

[55] *Whitehall Diary*, Vol. III, pp. 5–6.
[56] *Ibid.*, p. 12.
[57] The results of the election are reviewed in Taylor *op. cit.*, pp. 125–8 and Wilson, *op. cit.*, pp. 89–198. Because of difficulties in identifying allegiance in a few cases the figures do not exactly coincide.

the House of Commons, but the Ulster Unionists remained. Unionist predominance in the House was reflected in a Cabinet, where Lloyd George continued as Prime Minister, with immense prestige, but little personal following; Bonar Law was Lord Privy Seal; Balfour, Lord President; Curzon, Foreign Secretary; Birkenhead, Lord Chancellor; Milner, Colonial Secretary and Churchill, still it is true a Liberal in allegiance, at the War Office. Much, perhaps too much, has been made, by way of explaining the Cabinet's Irish policy, of Lloyd George's isolation, of his comparative impotence as the prisoner of the Coalition.

More important than the change in the balance of political forces at Westminster was the change in the legislative situation. There was now a time-factor tantamount to a time limit. The Home Rule Act was on the Statute book and it was scheduled to come into force automatically when hostilities formally concluded with the signature of the Peace Treaties. The Coalition Cabinet, as the Unionists realised, was no longer playing for time but constricted by time. Either the Home Rule Act, as amended to meet the assurances to Ulster Unionists, was given effect or there was a new Act repealing and replacing it. The Coalition Cabinet decided upon the second course and as a result, the last section, 76 (2) of the 1920 Act was to read, 'The Government of Ireland Act, 1914, is hereby repealed as from the passing of this Act.' A condition of such enactment, however, had been prior Cabinet consensus on Irish policy and if it was reached comparatively quickly that would seem to have been, first because of the statutory need for prompt action, secondly because of the growing realization on the part of party leaders of how few were the options in English political terms, let alone Irish, open to them and last, and probably least, to Lloyd George's ingenuity in negotiation.

The first consideration of policy was left to yet another Irish Committee, under the Chairmanship once again of Walter Long. On 4 November 1919 the Committee in a first Report urged that the Cabinet should make 'a sincere attempt to deal with the Irish question once and for all'.[58] They further reviewed and reached conclusions upon three possibilities. The first to have regard for the conclusions only, was that exclusion from a Home Rule Bill on a basis of county option was unworkable; the second that the idea of an Irish Parliament, at best doubtfully consistent with pledges of non-coercion given by the Prime Minister to the Ulster Unionists was vitiated, as indeed was county option, by the assumption that it was within the power of the Imperial Parliament

[58] Cab. 27/68.

to impose unity upon Ireland; the third was that if alternatively Home Rule were established, not for all Ireland as a unit, but for both parts of Ireland, that would provide for the complete withdrawal of British rule from the whole of Ireland in the sphere of domestic government, be consistent both with the fact that there was a majority in Ulster, as opposed to Dublin rule, as there was a Nationalist majority opposed to British rule in the rest of Ireland and with pledges already given, and finally would 'enormously minimize' the gravity of partition, since there would then be no nationalists under (direct) British rule and both North and South would enjoy immediate state rights with a link between them.

In the course of subsequent Cabinet discussions on the broad issues of policy on 11 November and 3 December[59] onepart of these conclusions especially came in for criticism. While it was accepted that the Ulster Unionists could not be coerced and that their separate status should be recognized, it was urged on 11 November, first, that Ulster had always taken the standpoint of retaining the same position as Great Britain and not, as the Committee contemplated, of being placed under a different régime; second, that the remaining provinces would obtain rather less than under the Home Rule Act and that it was therefore not likely to be acceptable to them, and third, that the three remaining provinces were overwhelmingly in favour of Sinn Féin and that the first action of Sinn Féin in power would be to declare an independent republic unless this was provided against in the Bill in some way. It was, however, also accepted that it was impossible to retreat, that a mere repeal of the Home Rule Act or postponement was probably not acceptable to Parliament and very undesirable from the point of view of the United States and the Dominions. The Committee, taking these views into account, was invited to submit further and more detailed proposals.

At the Cabinet meeting on 3 December discussion centred mainly on three propositions[60] submitted by the committee for consideration; first, that there should be a Parliament for the South and West of Ireland, but that the six counties should be allowed to vote in favour of remaining part of the United Kingdom for all purposes; second, that there should be a Parliament for the South and West and a Parliament for the whole of Ulster and third, that there should be a Parliament for the South and West and a Parliament for the six counties. In favour of the first proposition, that is the six counties remaining an undif-

[59] Cab. 23/18.
[60] Cab. 23/18. The Committee's proposals were attached to the Minutes as Appendix 1.

ferentiated part of the United Kingdom, was a clear basis of principle—so it was claimed—namely that of self-determination to be applied if necessary by plebiscite; against it the assertion that the 'Covenanters' would be opposed, because they had bound themselves to treat Ulster as a unit, that the Nationalists would likewise be opposed and also all moderate elements in the South and West, with the result that the prospect of the eventual unity of Ireland would be 'greatly diminished' by the exclusion of the six counties. There were also practical difficulties.

In the light of objections and difficulties, the Cabinet then ruled out the continued inclusion of the six counties for all purposes in the United Kingdom. There followed an interchange of opinion on policy and while views were expressed in favour of keeping either Ulster or the six counties separate, the general feeling was that the ultimate aim of government policy in Ireland 'was a united Ireland with a separate Parliament of its own, bound by the closest ties with Great Britain, but that this must be achieved with the largest possible support and without offending the Protestants in Ulster; in fact as Sir Edward Carson had put it, 'Ulster must be won by kindness' and this ultimate aim could only be achieved by something like general consent in Ireland.

The assertion of principle did not, however, affect concentration on immediate solutions, which might seem to have rested on the assumption that the longest way round would prove the shortest way home. The reasons for and against a separate Parliament for Ulster or for the six counties were explored in some detail. They were not dissimilar. A significant argument for a six county area was the already higher rate of increase among Catholics, with the danger that in the course of time the Protestants would be 'swamped' if the whole province were the unit. But like so many statistical forecasts this was no sooner advanced than it was refuted. A more acceptable argument for the six county area was the advantage of having people under a Northern Ireland Parliament as homogeneous as possible. Against this, once again, were the sentiments of the 'Convenanters' for the province of Ulster and also its superiority as an administrative unit. In the up-shot the Cabinet agreed that the Bill should be drafted on the basis of a Parliament for Ulster, but reconsidered if it were later found that a six county area was more acceptable. In accord with a recommendation of the Committee it was further agreed that there should be a Council of Ireland with power to bring an Irish Parliament into being and that it should consist of equal numbers of representatives, twenty, from each Parliament.

The most important statement in the records of the Meeting

43

of 3 December, was the enunciation of ultimate aim—a single Parliament for a united country. It came in for subsequent questioning. A week later, on 10 December 1919, when the draft Bill[61] was before the Cabinet, it was stated that life-long Unionists would prefer that there should not be a single Parliament. But it was reiterated that one of the principal aims of government policy was to produce a good effect in the dominions as well as the United States and that this could not be done except by a measure paving the way to unity, if and when both the North and South were willing to accept it. The general trend of Cabinet opinion remained in favour of adhering to the original statement.[62] In a predominantly Unionist Cabinet this was of importance, despite implicit qualifications. At the same time another issue was foreclosing. It was reported that opinion among responsible Ulster politicians was in favour of limiting the excluded area to six counties 'since the idea of governing three Ulster counties which had a Nationalist majority was not relished'.[63] It was noted that such a solution would fit in with any scheme for the creation of a federal system.

On 15 December accounts of further conversations on this, superficially still open, issue with Ulster leaders confirmed doubts as to whether the Northern Parliament would be able effectively to govern the three Ulster counties, where there was a large Nationalist majority. Those leaders, it was reported, 'greatly preferred' that the scheme should be applied only to the six 'Protestant' counties. Sir James Craig had further suggested, in a personal conversation with Sir Laming Worthington-Evans, the establishment of a Boundary Commission to examine the distribution of population along the borders of the whole of the six counties and to take a vote in districts on either side where there was a doubt about allegiance. This proposal was commended as being in accord with the practice and principles adopted in the Peace Treaties and referred to Long's Irish Committee for consideration.[64]

When the Cabinet met on 19 December for the last time before the Government's policy was outlined, in Parliament the Prime Minister reported[65] that he with some colleagues had had a long

[61] C. p. 266.
[62] Cab. 23/18.
[63] Ibid.
[64] Cab. 23/1. The accepted view has been hitherto that expressed by Denis Gwynn *op. cit.*, (p. 202):—'There had been no question of a Boundary Commission . . . until the suggestion was put forward tentatively to Arthur Griffith by Mr. Tom Jones on 8 November [1921], Craig is alleged to have found it "odious", Lyons *op. cit.* p. 432.
[65] Ibid., 19:xii:19.

conference with Sir James Craig that morning and that Craig had expressed his strong opinion in favour of confining the Northern Ireland Parliament to the Six Counties. He was reported to have expressed himself strongly in favour of the proposed Boundary Commission and to be prepared to try to work the new Parliament. One more extended discussion followed in which again it was urged that if the ultimate aim of the Government's policy was a United Ireland, it would be better that the jurisdiction of the Northern Parliament should extend over the whole of Ulster, which included both Roman Catholics and Protestants, both urban and rural districts, and by its size was more suited to possessing a separate Parliament. In favour of the six county scheme was that the Ulster leaders were prepared to work it and that in turn might help towards unity with goodwill, while against the all-Ulster scheme was the difficulty for the Government of trying to force through something unacceptable to friends and critics alike. It was better, such was the general view, to have something theoretically less perfect, if thereby it would secure more general acceptance. The idea of an immediate Boundary Commission, however, met with considerable favour. Its purpose would have been to advise on the precise Boundary to be included in the Bill. It was urged however, that enquiries would produce unrest and the idea was not pressed.

The issue of area was not quite finally disposed of when Lloyd George outlined the Cabinet's Irish policy in the debate on the adjournment on 22 December 1919[66] and the reason was that the Cabinet, partly because of its own uncertainty of mind, desired to leave itself some small freedom of manoeuvre. Lloyd George, who went out of his way once again to underscore heavily the differences between the North-Eastern counties and the rest of Ireland—'a fairly solid population, a homogeneous population —alien in race, alien in sympathy, alien in religion, alien in tradition, alien in outlook from the rest of the population of Ireland . . .', said that in respect of area there were four possibilities: (a) the exclusion of Ulster as a whole, (b) county option, leaving large minorities outside the excluded area, (c) the exclusion of the six counties and (d) the six counties with subsequent adjustments. Policy in fact oscillated between the first and the last two, an excellent device for ensuring attention or, if need be, extracting concessions. But the great concession of separate status was assured in statutory form and Carson, after an initial rhetorical flourish of denunciation, showed his appreciation. Of two cardinal facts mentioned by the Prime Minister, Carson

[66] H. of C. Deb. Vol. 123, col. 1171.

recognized but deplored the first, namely that the Home Rule Act was on the Statute book, but welcomed the second, namely that this was to be the first bill admitting 'Ulster's right to be treated as a separate entity.'[67] Even in respect of the separate Parliament for which Ulster had not asked there was the attraction of security. 'You cannot knock Parliaments up and down as you do a ball, and, once you have planted them there, you cannot get rid of them.'[68] The matter of area was not finally disposed of till 24 February 1920 when the Cabinet decision, after an interposition on the part of Bonar Law for the exclusion of the whole of Ulster, came down finally in favour of the six 'plantation' counties as a bloc, without consultation with the inhabitants on a county or other regional basis. Nor was any boundary commission estad-lished, all of which was reasonable on the basis of temporary, unreasonable on the basis of permanent, separation.[69] In Cabinet terms, however, the Buckingham Palace Conference debates, the 1916 negotiations and the 1918–19 discussions had in effect demonstrated that settlement on such lines was the only outcmoe consistent with semblance of Coalition Cabinet consensus and parliamentary viability. The exclusion of a larger area would have offended some Liberal and doubtless Labour sentiment, the exclusion of a smaller—as contemplated by the Agar-Robartes amendment—would have been unacceptable to the English over and above the Ulster Unionist leadership. But the argument for exclusion of the larger area in the interests of ultimate unity received no convincing answer from any quarter.

The relation between area and form of government was not, however, so clear. The importance of the federal concept, either in its purer form or watered down to devolution, is often over-looked, but was certainly important in some Unionist thinking and in giving shape to the 1920 Act. Federalism in its classic form presupposes the existence of co-ordinate authority as between the centre and the constituent units, not the subordination of the latter to the former. In that form the federal idea was not pursued. The Act of 1920 states explicitly (S.75) that 'notwithstanding the establishment of the Parliaments of Northern and Southern Ireland . . . the supreme authority of the Parliament of the United Kingdom shall remain unaffected and undiminished over all persons, matters and things in Ireland and every part thereof.' So long as that section remains on the Statute book it is, therefore, otiose to talk of a federal, or even quasi-federal, system. On the

[67] *Ibid.*, col. 1197.
[68] *Ibid.*, col. 1202.
[69] *Whitehall Diaries*, Vol. iii, pp. 104 and 106.

other hand the federal concept transmuted into the devolutionary idea, examined by the Speaker's Conference on Devolution in 1919, still carried with it the idea of a separate though subordinate legislature and administrative institutions. To that extent it played an important part in rationalizing the notion of a separate provincial government for the six counties and in so doing had a perceptible influence on the question of area. It was possible to conceive of Ulster as a whole remaining part of a United Kingdom wholly governed from London, but unrealistic to think of it sustaining a separate Parliament on so precarious a balance of political opinion. Equally once the notion of subordinate parliamentary institutions was adopted, it was unrealistic to think of a four county area sustaining them. There was, therefore, a closer correlation between area and form of government than is apt to be recognized. It was implicit but never, so far as I can trace, made explicit in Cabinet discussions.

There is a further point to be noted and this also was clearly a condition of the Cabinet consensus. The partition of Ireland was effected within or upon a concept of continuing unity. The establishment of separate Parliaments in Section 1 of the Act was, on paper, in part counterbalanced by the Constitution of the Council of Ireland in Section 2. 'A fleshless and bloodless skeleton,' Asquith termed it and he appreciated more clearly than any other critic the implications of parity as between North and South, as between minority and majority in the composition of the Council of Ireland. 'It is left,'[70] he said, 'to an Ulster minority for all time to veto, if it pleases, the coming into existence of an Irish Parliament.' None the less this symbolic deference to unity for what it was worth, was also a condition of Coalition consensus and it, too, derived from 1914, 1916 and post-1917 Cabinet or Irish Committee discussions.

Finally, and here I return to the quotation from Professor Lyons with which this paper opened, Cabinet consensus was conditional upon the ignoring on paper of the political realities, not in the whole, but in the greater part of Ireland. Cabinet discussions, beyond the periphery of and therefore not examined in this paper, make it perfectly clear that most members understood that a limited Home Rule measure would not be acceptable in what was termed Southern Ireland any time after 1916 and the reaction to conscription underlined the message for those who had not hitherto received it. More and more there are allusions to dominion status, coupled with a disturbing awareness that dominion status was likely to mean republicanism in two stages

[70] H. of C. Deb. Vol. 127, coll. 1112-3.

instead of one. This was very evident in the debate on the 1920 Bill in the House of Commons, those Labour members who appealed to the principle of self-determination, when confronted with the question, would not self-determination mean a republic, shrinking from an affirmative and taking refuge in federalist generalisations.[71] If, therefore, the Cabinet had sought to conform to Irish realities, it would at once have ceased to conform to those of English politics and in particular those on which two Coalition Cabinets had rested. 'Indirectly,' writes A. J. P. Taylor 'the Government of Ireland Act ended the troubles.' In so doing he had in mind chiefly that it made possible the new initiatives implicit in the King's Speech at the opening of the Northern Ireland Parliament. But his comment has meaning at a deeper level. The enactment of the Bill made possible the consideration of a settlement with Irish nationalism because, and only because, by taking account of English political realities it had reopened options in respect of Irish policy, otherwise foreclosed.

Lloyd George was Prime Minister and Bonar Law the leader of the Unionist party, the one without and the other with strong views on Ulster, but it is a misconception to think of the Act of 1920 as being in any fundamental sense their achievement or the product of Lloyd George's dexterity and still less of his devising. It was on the contrary fashioned in cabinet committee and carried the unmistakable marks of successful committee searching for compromise. It was also and more importantly the outcome of the continually narrowing range of choice, which had confronted each successive British government since the outbreak of War, because of the opinions, prejudices and fears—and there was within the ruling establishment great fear of revolutionary forces, social as well as nationalist—of a succession of secondary figures, Long, Lansdowne, Cecil, Cave, Worthington-Evans, who with an inflexibility deriving from and dependent upon the ground-swell of conservative parliamentary and public opinion,[72] were able to deprive even the most powerful of cabinets of the freedom of manoeuvre that is usually an essential condition of the statesmanslike resolution of complex and intractable issues.

---

[71] H. of C. Deb. Vol. 127, c.f. speeches by Wedgwood Benn coll. 1017–28 and Clynes coll. 944–56.
[72] D. G. Boyce, *British Conservative opinion, the Ulster Question, and the partition of Ireland, 1912-21* in *Irish Historical Studies*, Vol. XXII, pp. 89-112 provides a valuable analysis of developments in Conservative opinion down to the Anglo-Irish Treaty, 1921.

Ireland in the Eighteenth Century British Empire

R. B. McDowell

The expansion of Europe is one of the dominant themes of modern history. During the last four centuries Europeans have gone out and peopled vast stretches in three continents; The European powers have established rule and order over most of the world; European skill and energy have discovered and developed economic resources in every quarter of the globe. European capital has built up great industries overseas, European directed commerce has brought the whole world into profitable association and European intellectual concepts have shaped the thinking of mankind. In this stupendous achievement the maritime powers of western Europe played a major part, building up six overseas empires—the Spanish, the French, the British, the Danish, the Dutch and the Portugese. Ireland of course, in George Macartney's words, formed part of 'the European bottom' of Great Britain's 'vast empire on which the sun never sets and whose bounds nature has not yet ascertained'.[1] Irishmen were very conscious of belonging to the empire. At the close of the seven years war, Dublin and Cork both voted their freedom to the great imperial statesman, William Pitt, and Cork erected a statue to him in the new exchange.[2] Grattan, the voice of liberal Ireland, after making in 1796 a vehement attack on the British cabinet, qualified it by adding: 'whatever feelings the country may have of resentment, let them be directed against the ministers only and not against the people of England; with them we have a common constitution and a common empire'.[3] Again very near the close of his career, Grattan when calling for a great effort to destroy Napoleon's power after his return from Elba, told the house of commons 'your empire cannot be saved by calculation, besides your wealth

[1] *An account of Ireland in 1773*. By a late chief secretary of that kingdom. (London 1773).
[2] R. Caulfield, The council book of the corporation of the city of Cork (Guilford 1876), pp. 754, 808; J. T. Gilbert, *Cal. ancient records of Dublin*, X. 397–8.
[3] *Dublin Evening Post*, 23 January 1796.

is only part of your situation—the name you have established, the deeds you have achieved and the port you have sustained, preclude you from a second place among the nations, and when you cease to be the first you are nothing'.[4] More surprisingly, the Dublin society of United Irishmen, when referring to the catholic relief bill of 1793, congratulated 'the empire that the loss of three millions across the Atlantic is supplied by the timely acquisition of the same number at home'.[5] The Irish house of commons in 1773 spoke of 'the common interest of the whole empire' when attacking trade restrictions 'which, the narrow and short sighted policy of former times, equally injurious to Great Britain and to us enforced upon the manufactures and commerce of this kingdom'. And when a strong and successful drive was being made for the abolition of restrictions on Irish trade the commons voted an address in which they declared that 'with hearts glowing with the warmest wishes for the prosperity and glory of the British empire and full of zeal against the common enemy we have the mortification to find that the limited state of our trade and commerce must be narrowing our resources, set bounds to our liberality'.[6]

It is often stressed that one of the most important political movements in eighteenth century Ireland was the struggle against the trade restrictions. This could be described in another (more correct if more cumbersome form) as an effort to adjust imperial commercial arrangements in a way which would be more profitable to Ireland. Ireland, during the eighteenth century had an important part to play in the imperial economy—sending linen and provisions to the North American colonies and to the West Indies. It may be added that the Irish provision merchants not only supplied the British West Indian islands, but, even in war time, assisted French imperialism by conducting an illicit trade with the French islands—and when in 1777, the embargo on the export of provisions from Ireland, which had been imposed as a war measure, was being attacked, the lord lieutenant suggested a modification which would have allowed Irish provision merchants to export the inferior grades 'not taken up by our contractors but sold to the French for their negroes'.[7] This imperial trade had a most stimulating effect on the Irish livestock and provision industries which, along with the other great eighteenth Irish industry, linen, may be seen as conspicuous benefactories of imperial expansion.

[4] *Hansard*, 1 xxvi, 430.
[5] *Society of United Irishmen of Dublin* (Dublin 1794) p. 82.
[6] *Commons Jn. Ire*. ix, pp. 73–4, x, p. 12.
[7] Buckinghamshire to Weymouth, 30 Oct. 1777 (S.P. 63/458).

Ireland also helped to people the British colonies. The first area of great and profitable imperial development was the West Indies—the sugar islands. And Irishmen played an important part in helping to lay the foundations of the British settlements in these islands. In the early seventeenth century Irishmen went out to Saint Christopher; under the commonwealth Irish prisoners of war were deported to the Barbadoes and arrangements made for sending thousands of Irishmen and women to the West Indies. Later in the century Irish criminals were deported to the West Indies, a traffic which, as time went on, was to be diverted to the American mainland. And well into the eighteenth century Irishmen seem to have been going to the West Indies as indentured labourers. It is impossible to say how great was the emigration from Ireland to the West Indies, but it may be noted that as early as 1643 a Jesuit report estimates that there were 20,000 Irishmen in Saint Christopher (a figure which indicates that at least there was a large number).[8] Twenty years later it was estimated that out of 4,000 men in Barbadoes 2,000 were Irish and reports drawn up in 1677–8 show that of the 11,000 white settlers in the Leeward Islands, over 30 per cent were Irish; in one island, Montserrat, the Irish amounting to over 60 per cent of the white inhabitants. (It may be added that amongst the names given to slaves in Montserrat were 'Kilkenny', 'Tipperary', and 'Galway').[9]

Amongst the more prosperous Irish settlers in the West Indies were families such as Blake, Bodkin, Bolan, Bourke, Birmingham, Daly, Delap, Kirwan, Lynch, Nugent, Perry, Tuite, Scott and Skerrett. Some of these names and other evidence show that during the seventeenth and eighteenth centuries members of well-established catholic families attempted to make a career for themselves in the West Indies, and a group of them were sufficiently powerful to promote a strong Jacobite movement in the Leeward Islands in 1689. There were naturally, then, many ties, social and economic, between Ireland and the West Indies. About the middle of the eighteenth century, Edward Long remarked that 'the national partiality which is made an accusation' against Scottish and Irish gentlemen, was 'attended with good consequences' for many of their young compatriots who came out to seek a fortune in Jamaica.[10] If Lord Carhampton, commander of the forces in Ireland in 1796–8 married a West Indian heiress, Valentine O'Connor, the Dublin radical was part owner of a

[8] J. A. Williamson, *The Caribbean islands* (Oxford 1926), p. 184.
[9] V. T. Harlow, *A history of Barbados 1625–1685* (Oxford 1926), p. 189; P. W. Pitman, *The development of the British West Indies 1700–1763* (Newhaven 1917), p. 54.
[10] (E. Long), *History of Jamaica* (London 1772), ii. 286.

plantation in Saint Vincent. If Patrick Browne of Antigua in 1705 was anxious that his children should go to Galway for their education, Henry Blake of Montserrat, thirty years earlier, had a less pleasant link with Ireland. He was afraid that some of his Irish creditors 'threaten to come hither and discredit me'. Three Irishmen, who had settled in Antigua, Perry, Holmes and French, left legacies for the benefit of the poor in Cork and Youghal, Belfast and Galway respectively, and David Gallway of Montserrat left in 1734 £20 to a catholic church in Ireland.[11] On the other hand when in 1780 a hurricane devastated the West Indies subscriptions for the relief of the sufferers were organized by the citizens of Dublin and Cork and by the catholics of Dublin.[12]

It would be presumptuous to try and summarize the subject of Irish emigration to the north American colonies in a few lines. There is an enormous amount of literature on the subject much of which does not depreciate the Irish contribution to the future United States, but Dickson's *Ulster emigration to colonial America*,[13] with its strict and salutary statistical approach, reminds us that the dimension of flow can be exaggerated. And the bulk of the Irish emigrants being from Ulster, seem to have differed very little from their fellow presbyterians of directly Scottish origin. Nevertheless if Ireland in colonial times did not make a very distinctive cultural contribution to north America, the number of the emigrants from Ireland and their quality was important. It is interesting too that Irish emigrants played a big part in building up an important north American colony which remained part of the second British empire—Newfoundland. There were Irish catholic colonists in Newfoundland in the seventeenth century; Irishmen came out in the annual fishing fleets and often settled permanently on the island, and Irish factors helped to provision the fishing fleets with beef, pork and butter.

The cession of the American colonies from the empire had a serious effect on a depressed sector of Irish society. Transportation had, by the eighteenth century, become an important factor in Irish penal administration, Ireland in the middle of the century sending about 200–300 convicts and vagabonds a year to America. When this outlet was closed the West Indies were used, about 270 prisoners being transported annually.[14] But in 1789 the home

[11] For Irish families in the West Indies see *Caribbean*, V. L. Oliver, History of the island of Antigua, 3 vols. (London 1894–9); and 'Documents relating to the Irish in the West Indies', ed. A. Gwynn, in *Analecta Hib.* IV, pp. 139–286.
[12] *Hibernian Journal*, 15 January, 26 February 1781.
[13] R. J. Dickson, *Ulster emigration to colonial America, 1718–1775* (London 1966).
[14] *Commons Journal Ireland* IV, pp. cclll–ccxiv; xlll, cccil.

secretary informed the Irish government that it was inadvisable to transport criminals to the West Indies. Just before his despatch arrived a boat load of eighty had been sent off by the lord mayor of Dublin. After a long Odyssey, which included an attempt to land them in Newfoundland, which was foiled by the governor, and much legal controversy, the convicts returned to Ireland.[15] With the Irish prisons seriously overcrowded, the Irish government was worried by the prospect of disease and escapes, and naturally was very ready to use the new penal settlements formed in New South Wales.

Professors Shaw's statistics show that of the 16,153 convicts transported to Australia between 1788 and 1815, 3,668 were Irish (25 per cent being women); the Irish forming 21.3 per cent of those transported. Of the Irish convicts, some hundreds—Professor Shaw estimates about 500—were political offenders, sent out between 1795 and 1806. These included Joseph Holt, the Wexford insurgent leader, who worked hard as a farmer; Father James Dixon, who was the first catholic priest to officiate in Australia; James Meehan, who as a surveyor, played a big part in mapping the colony; Michael Hayes, who became a merchant, and Edward Redmond, who prospered as a publican and farmer, and became a leading catholic layman. And the Paramatta rising in 1804, short-lived, ill co-ordinated and quickly suppressed by a blend of discipline, dash and sharp practice, may be regarded as the last reverberation of 1798.

Of the other Irish convicts, many were what Professor Shaw calls 'social rebels', having been convicted of agrarian crimes, others might be called commonplace or routine criminals; for instance Barrington, the celebrated pickpocket, a plausible rogue and a legendary figure in early Australia; George Chartres, convicted of fraud in Dublin, who became one of the first lawyers to engage in private practice in Australia and Sir Henry Hayes who lived in great style in Vaucluse House.

There were too those Irishmen who played a part in the early administration of the colony. Nicholas Devine, the first principal superintendent of convicts, was a County Carlow man; another superintendent of convicts, Andrew Hume, the son of a presbyterian minister from County Down, helped to set up the flax industry (and after being convicted of rape became a successful grazier), and John Marcus Campbell, from Newry, who was secretary to Governor Macquarie. Two of the surgeons in the first fleet were Irishmen, Dennis Considen, who claimed to have discovered the eucalyptus oil plant, and Thomas Jamison, who

[15] *Fortescue MS H.M.C.*, i, pp. 540–55.

carried out the first successful vaccination of small children in the colony. Another Irish medical man, Jacob Mountgarrett, a naval surgeon from County Armagh, was said to have been the first man to grow wheat in the colony (he was also rumoured to be one of the first bush rangers).[16]

Now may I turn to a part of the empire which was not an area of settlement, India, which by the close of the eighteenth century was acknowledged to be the most impressive and romantic of the British possessions beyond the seas—important not only for itself but as the centre of British political and commercial power in the east. From the very beginning of the seventeenth century Ireland was forging links with India or at least with the East Indian company, supplying the company's beef and staves. But very little Irish capital was invested in East Indian company stock. This, of course, is scarcely surprising. The East company proprietors (or stock holders) tended to be concentrated in the metropolitan area and large areas in the provinces were poorly, if at all, represented amongst the stock holders. In 1772 there was only one Irish resident (Peter Hamilton of Fahy) listed among them. In 1798 there were two, Marmaduke Cramer of Dublin, an attorney and lottery commissioner, and Sir Charles Des Voeux of Indiaville, Queen's County. Des Voeux, the son of a distinguished Huguenot refugee, who had settled in Ireland, went to India as a writer in 1762. He became a member of the council at Madras, and on returning to Ireland entered parliament as M.P. for Carlow. By 1805 the number of East Indian proprietors resident in Ireland had risen to nine—including Lord Castlereagh whose great-uncle, Sir John Cowan, the son of a Londonderry alderman, had been governor of Bombay in the first half of the eighteenth century. As the names of Des Voeux and Cowan remind us, a number of Irishmen served with distinction in India— Wellesley, the governor general, and his brother the future duke of Wellington; Macartney, governor of Madras and ambassador to China; Alexander, son of a Londonderry alderman, a servant of the East India company, 'a nabob' who on his return purchased large estates in the north and secured a peerage; Gregory and Sullivan who, after serving in India, rose to be chairmen of the company. Francis, Hasting's unremitting antagonist; Coote, a testy but bold and successful general, a splendid soldier in an emergency; Thomas Maunsel of Limerick, who went out in 1750 as a writer, and on his return founded a bank in Limerick, commanded a yeomanry corps during the '98 rebellion, sat in

[16] A. G. L. Shaw, Convicts and the colonies (London 1966), chapter VIII and pp. 363–5; *Australian dictionary of biography*, 1788–1850 (Melbourne 1966–7).

R. B. McDowell

Parliament and lived in a house appropriately named Plassey;[17] and MacNaghten, chief justice of Madras, and the founder of one of the greatest Irish legal dynasties. MacNaghten's wife was the daughter of a chief justice of Bengal, Sir William Dunkin from Clogher, who, according to Hickey, 'if he had a fault, it was that of being too fond of the pleasures of the table, which was to be accounted for from early habit and having resided the greater part of his life in the country part of Ireland, in the society of men who were all hard drinkers, as was the general practice in those days in the sister kingdom, but now much left off amongst the higher classes'.[18] And it should perhaps be added that Hickey —no anhorite himself—who was the lively chronicler of the society which was settling down in an oriental world with eighteenth century British aplomb, was himself the son of a Dublin man who was a Trinity college graduate.

But a catalogue of names may, by focusing attention on the regional representation in a very large body, give a misleading impression. So it is desirable to try and discover to what extent and in what proportion Irishmen were to be found in the civil and military service of the East India company. Taking the civil administration first: Out of approximately 1690 writers' petitions, which are preserved for the period 1749–1804, 52 are from Irishmen; and out of 491 applications for admission to Haileybury between 1805–1815, only 22 are Irish. It seems therefore that the proportion of Irishmen in the administrative service of the company during the eighteenth century was comparatively small.[19]

For the Indian army *Hobson's List of officers of the Bengal army. 4 vols.* (London 1929–47) gives the names of approximately 6,800 officers. It is impossible to determine the national background of 1,527 of these officers, of the remaining 5,263, 54 per cent were English, 12.7 Scottish, 12.7 Irish and 12.5 from Europe, or British possessions overseas. Perhaps it might be added that of the officers who entered the service up to and including 1815, 14 per cent were Irish, of those who entered after 1815, 10 per cent were Irish.[20]

The company of course maintained European as well as sepoy regiments, and it is possible to ascertain from the embarkation returns the birth places of the recruits sent out by the company from England to these European formations.[21]

[17] *Gent. Mag.*, LXXXIV, Pt. ii, p. 299.
[18] W. Hickey, *Memoirs.* ed. by A. Spencer (London 19132–5), iv p. 25.
[19] Writers' petitions 1749–1805 (India Office library, J/I/I-30).
[20] V. C. P. Hodson, *List of officers of the Bengal Army*, 1758–1834, 4 vols. (London 1927–47).
[21] Embarkation lists (India office library, L/Mil/9/85-106).

E

	Total	Irish	*per centage of Irish*
1740–63 (returns for 14 years available)	7,100	948	13
1792–7	1,964	587	29
1810–15	8,741	4,189	48

Running through the lists of men who embarked, which give not only a recruit's name and birth place, but also his age, height and occupation, it is impossible not to speculate on the circumstances which had led men to enlist in such an arduous and distant service. Many of the Irish recruits, which came from all over the country, were, as might be expected, labourers. But nearly every trade is represented, and one recruit, Thomas Kiernan of Dublin, who enlisted in 1763, is described as a gentleman. The total number of men sent out in any period from the British Isles was of course relatively small, but it is not necessary to emphasise the fighting power and effectiveness of trained European units in the east.

So much for the impact of Ireland on India. But in one respect at least India began to have considerable influence on Irish life during the eighteenth century. In the revenue act of 1727 tea was for the first time taxed in Ireland, by the middle of the century the annual consumption seems to have been about 170,000 lbs per annum, and by the close of the century it had risen to nearly 3,000,000 lbs per annum.[22] Of course it was still an upper and middle class drink, the average consumption being estimated at only ·57 lbs per head (almost certainly an over estimate). The budgets of the poor drawn up by the authors of the statistical survey do not allow for tea, and social reformers were striving to persuade the poor to substitute for whiskey, so destructive of health and morals, that 'wholesome beverage' beer. But tea imports had risen steeply during the eighteenth century, and the great revolution in the pattern of Irish liquid consumption which was to have immeasurable effects on the whole tone of Irish life, was well underway.

The growing importance of the tea trade was partly responsible for making commercial relations with India and the east for a few years a major issue in Irish politics. In 1791 when the convention which ended the Nootka Sound dispute was being debated in the Irish house of commons, the whigs attacked the

[22] *Commons Jn. Ire*, V, p. lxiii and *A return showing the quantity of the following articles: viz. tea, sugar, wine . . . consumed in Great Britain in each of the years 1789, 1799, 1800 . . . and a similar return for Ireland*, H.C. 1865 (14), 1.

East India company's monoply of trade between the British Isles and the East. The opposition argued that by buying its tea through the company rather than by allowing merchants to import it directly, Ireland had to pay higher prices. Furthermore, Ireland was cutting itself off from a market with immense potentialities. 'If gentlemen', George Ponsonby declared, 'say that Ireland was not adapted by nature to trade to any part of Asia, America, Cochin China, or to Japan they discover a gross ignorance not only of these regions but of their own country'. And though it was common ground on both sides of the house that, so far as Ireland was concerned the company's monopoly was secured by the Irish revenue laws, the whigs plainly hinted that Ireland's commercial liberty was being threatened, Grattan denouncing the Irish cabinet for selling the trade of their country. The government's view that the East India company's rights should be respected was urged in a remarkably level-headed speech by the future Lord Castlereagh, who pointed out that if the Irish parliament decided in the future not to sanction the charter, Ireland 'would be made an emporium for English capital to smuggle tea into Great Britain'. The excess of price, which Ireland paid for tea, by taking it through the East India company, was justified by Castlereagh on the grounds that the company, then waging war against Tippo sultan was responsible for maintaining British power in the east.[23] The opposition raised the India trade question several times during the sessions of 1791 and 1792 and the government was seriously worried by the threat to Anglo-Irish relations. 'We have to contend', Beresford gloomily wrote, 'not only with the mistaken notions of the country but with its pride'.[24] Finally when the company's charter came to be renewed in 1793, the Irish parliament confirmed it on the condition that 800 tons of shipping were to be provided annually by the company for carrying Irish goods to the East Indies. And in 1794 an attempt was made to sell Irish linens in China without success.[25]

An empire needs a canapace. The imperial homeland must be guarded, colonies defended and trade protected. At times too, it may seem desirable to extend the bounds of the empire. All these activities require men, money and supplies. It is, therefore, worth asking, what was Ireland's contribution to imperial defence during the eighteenth century. It is of course a very large question, and here can be answered only in part.

During the century Ireland did not maintain its own navy,

[23] *Parl. Reg. Ire.* XI, pp. 197, 246.
[24] J. Beresford to ———— 3 May 1793 (PRO 30/8/325).
[25] *Fourth report of the select committee on the affairs of the East India Company*, H.C. 1812 (148) vi.

though Yelverton in 1781 asked, 'why not an Irish navy, why should not the trade of Ireland be protected by ships under the command of the executive power of Ireland'.[26] The Irish parliament contented itself with voting on occasion, in 1782 and 1795, substantial sums for 'manning the navy'. (Any suggestion that there should be ships earmarked for Irish defence, let alone under Irish control, was regarded in Whitehall with deep disapproval as violating a fundamental principle of imperial strategy—the unified control of the navy). Ireland also contributed to manning the fleet. Professor Michael Lewis has estimated that approximately 12 per cent of officers who joined the fleet between 1793 and 1815 came from Ireland.[27] A return made in 1798 shows that in the 33 ships (20 of the line, 13 frigates) of the channel fleet there were 2,101 Irish sailors and 646 Irish marines (386 of the sailors and 91 of the marines being classified as unreliable). This suggests that the Irish on the lower deck would be then about 13 per cent.[28] On Nelson's ships of the line at Trafalgar about a quarter of the seamen were Irish.[28a]

Towards the army Ireland made a substantial financial contribution—especially in peace time. By the beginning of the eighteenth century there had been in existence for some time the Irish military establishment, that is to say the units, regiments of cavalry and regiments or battalions of infantry maintained out of monies voted by the Irish parliament. These troops were housed by the Irish barrack board, which might be regarded as the biggest business organisation in eighteenth century Ireland, and they were at least partially armed by the Irish ordnance board which was also responsible for constructing fortifications and which supervised the Royal Irish regiment of artillery. Finally there were military pensions to be paid and the Royal Hospital at Kilmainham to be maintained. So it is understandable that by the middle of the century the Irish military budget absorbed about 60 per cent of the government's expenditure (1761–3, 65 per cent; 1771, 62 per cent; 1791–2, 42 per cent.)

Ireland indeed in peace time maintained a high proportion of the British standing army, the force on the Irish establishment between 1715 and 1769 amounting to 12,000 men, of whom about 2,000 were in peacetime stationed overseas. The augmentation act of 1769 raised the force on the establishment to 15,000 but the king's message requesting the increase declared that of the

[26] *Parl. Reg. Ire.* i. p. 7.
[27] M. Lewis, *The navy in transition 1814–1864.* (London 1965), pp. 40–1.
[28] Return, dated September 1798 (Adm I/III).
[28a] Muster rolls in *Adm.* 36. Out of approximately 16,300 seamen there were about 4,500 Irish (27·9 per cent). The nationality of marines is not given.

augmented force 12,000 should be retained in Ireland for its defence. This provision was in fact waived by the Irish parliament during the American war of independence and the home secretary pressed the lord lieutenant to take the first opportunity that 'the good humour or good sense of the Irish may afford' for abrogating this condition, and thereby 'restoring to the crown the full exercise of that great and useful branch of its perogative'.[29]

Ireland, as has been said did not contribute to the navy, and up to the outbreak of the Revolutionary war Irish military finance was characterized by one remarkable feature. As Sir Hercules Langrishe said, 'it is well known that the peace establishment in Ireland is more expensive than the war, the reason is that the troops are all at home and paid for by the country, in war they are abroad and paid for by England'.[30] This is not quite correct. In peace time all the men on the Irish establishment were not stationed in Ireland, a small proportion being sent to imperial garrisons. And in periods of war or acute tension, units had to be brought up to strength, fortifications improved and camps of manoeuvre formed. But even so the Irish military budget did not rise so much as might have been expected, and there were even war years in which it fell, for the reason Langrishe mentions. Therefore the Irish contribution to imperial defence was, until the beginning of the nineties relatively small.

During the Revolutionary and Napoleonic wars the situation was very different. These wars were waged on an unprecedented scale and because of this taken together with the daemonic energy and enterprise displayed by the French, and political and economic discontent in Ireland, it was necessary to provide greatly increased forces for home defence, internal security, and, if any men could be spared, for overseas expeditions. Irish military expenditure (in 1791–2, £576,000) rose rapidly, reaching a peak of four and a half millions in 1799–1800. But taxation did not rise quite so steeply. The Irish taxpayer seems to have contributed to the exchequer in 1800 £3,000,000 compared with £1,638,000 in 1792–3. In tackling the problems of war finance Irish chancellors of the exchequer were, as Corry, with candour, explained in 1800, limited by two factors. It was desirable to avoid laying increased burdens on the poorer classes. And at the same time 'the situation of Ireland was such that they could not consider imposing a land tax or a property tax'.[31] Fifteen years later Grattan, having in glowing terms declared 'that the gentry of Ireland would be ready

[29] Portland to Camden, 13Ap 1795. (H.O. 100/59).
[30] *Parl. Reg. Ire.* x. p. 144.
[31] *Dublin Evening Post*, 1 March 1800.

59

to maintain the British empire with their property and their blood', made very clear that an extension of the income tax to Ireland would be 'injurious to the sensations of Irishmen'.[32] Given these limitations the chancellor had little room for manoeuvre and had to rely for an increased revenue on some cautious increases in customs and excise duties, and on a number of miscellaneous and not very productive expedients—game licences, and taxes on cards, tanned leather, glass, paper hangings, windows, hats, servants, armorial bearings, timber (after the union) and receipts—it being pointed out that a man on being given a receipt is usually in a good humour. The inevitable deficits were met by borrowing. The general view was that Ireland's economic growth should not be checked by taxation; Parnell, the chancellor of the exchequer, stating frankly at the beginning of the war that 'a loan was infinitely preferable to taxes to which it will be at all times disagreeable and painful for me to recur'.[33] Therefore the increased taxation of the war years 1793–1800 seems on the average to have amounted to about £700,000 a year.

After the union Ireland was theoretically expected to meet 2/17ths of the joint expenditure of the United Kingdom. But this soon became a matter of book-keeping, as the British treasury transferred money on loan to Ireland with which the Irish treasury met its obligations. What is, I think, a more realistic approach is to see what was the field from taxation during the Napoleonic war, after the expenses of management and non-military expenditure in Ireland have been deducted. The total yield for the years 1803–15 inclusive was £70,000,000; the cost of management was £12,595,000, and the Irish civil administration and economic development charges absorbed about £12,475,000, leaving an average of about three and a half million a year which might be considered Ireland's contribution to war expenditure. And perhaps it may be added that military expenditure in Ireland during the war amounted to between three and four million per annum. So it could be argued that Ireland was just about paying for the cost of its military defence.

But what about Ireland's national debt. It rose startlingly—from £2,452,000, in 1792 to £27,000,000 at the time of union; and then to £80,500,000 by 1816. Loans, I gather, are to be regarded as voluntary or deferred taxation; the immediate present spending power being transferred to the state by a self selected group and a burden being placed on posterity. So far as this second feature of loan policy is concerned, successive Irish chancellors of the

[32] *Hansard*, 2 series, xxx, p. 712.
[33] *Parl. Reg. Ire.*, x, p. 144.

exchequer postponed the point at which posterity would have to assume the burden by simply continuing to borrow, so that about the middle of the Napoleonic war the yield from Irish taxation was being exceeded by loan charges. And since the Irish and British fiscal systems were merged in 1817 it is difficult to determine the incidence of the Irish debt charge. As regards the first aspect of loan policy, it is worth noting that a very high proportion of Irish wartime borrowing was from British sources. And it may be added, that, according to Foster, half of a loan of two millions raised in 1806 on the Irish market, was in fact supplied by agents from British houses going over and purchasing stock in Dublin.[34] However about £9,000,000 was raised in Dublin between 1793 and 1800 and another £30,000,000 between 1804 and 1815.

When the total British war expenditure between 1793 and 1815 is taken into account, the Irish financial contribution to the war effort may appear to have been relatively small. In respect of man-power the position was very different, Ireland being by the close of the eighteenth century a very important recruiting area. At the beginning of the century it was a rule that Irishmen—that is to say Irish catholics—should not be enlisted in the army. This rule was probably often broken (for instance in 1727 it was discovered that Irishmen had been enlisted in the Royal Scots, the Irish recruits having been sent to Scotland to be sworn and sent back to Ireland wearing Scotch bonnets[35]) and on occasion after the middle of the century officially set aside, and it was finally abrogated in the eighties when in 1784 an inspector of recruiting for Ireland was appointed and in 1787 all regiments were allowed to recruit in Ireland.[36]

Some indication of the extent to which Ireland contributed to the army is afforded by the inspection returns.[37] Returns covering five periods have been consulted and the results tabulated below.

INSPECTION RETURNS

Total number of men included		Country of origin		
		England	Scotland	Ireland
1753–7	20,895	16,870 (80·7)	2,781 (13·3)	1,244 (5·9)
1768	15,935	9,730 (61)	2,982 (18·7)	3,223 (20·2)
1774	19,788	11,938 (60·5)	3,759 (18·1)	4,046 (20·4)
1792	22,102	12,000 (54·2)	3,688 (16·6)	6,414 (29·4)
1812	104,787	55,193 (52·6)	15,651 (14·9)	33,943 (32·3)

[34] *Hansard*, 2 series, vii, p. 42.
[35] J. C. Leask and H. M. McCance. *The records of the Royal Scots regiment* (Dublin 1915), p. 120.
[36] See H.O. 100/28/99, Commander in chief to Rutland, 31 Aug. 1784; H.O. 100/28 f 99.
[37] W.O. 27.

As a check on the last figure we have the numbers added under the Additional Forces act between April 1805 and March 1806. The total number was 12,955, the English contribution amounting to 54 per cent, the Scottish 10.7 and the Irish 35.

Ireland also made a substantial contribution to the commissioned ranks of the army.

	Total number of officers	Country of origin		
		England	*Scotland*	*Ireland*
1753–7	999	534 (53·4)	196 (19·6)	269 (26·9)
1768	1,454	594 (40·8)	315 (21·6)	545 (37·4)
1774	1,715	783 (45·6)	383 (22·1)	549 (31·9)
1792	1,808	857 (47·4)	388 (21·4)	563 (31·1)
1812	5,266	2,102 (30·9)	1230 (23·3)	1,934 (36·7)

It may be added that service returns suggest that at the beginning of the nineteenth century 30 per cent of the army surgeons were Irishmen.[37a]

Until 1793 all commissioned officers had to be protestants and though the relief act of 1793 declared catholics to be eligible for commissions, it was provided in the act that a catholic could not be promoted above the rank of colonel and theoretically he could not hold his commission in Great Britain. Thus in practice Irish officers were bound to drain from a limited area, the protestant upper and middle classes. And the high proportion of commissions they secured shows how strongly a military life appealed to the Irish upper and middle classes—and incidentally how important an element the officer, serving or retired, must have been in Irish society.

There was of course a more humdrum way in which Ireland contributed to the development of British imperial power. It has been said an army marches on its stomach, and Ireland, during the eighteenth century was a victualling centre for the British forces serving in north America.[38] In the great wars between 1793 and 1815 the British forces tended to be provisioned from England or to secure supplies from the areas in which they were campaigning. But in this period Ireland was engaged in an important part in victualling Great Britain itself. Nearly one-third of the vital corn and flour supplies imported into Great Britain during these critical years came from Ireland. In one year (1808) Ireland seems to have met four-fifths of Great Britain's imported cereal requirements and in 1812–13, when the great struggle with France was at

[37a] W.O. 25/3904–3910.
[38] E. E. Curtis, *The organisation of the British army in the American revolution* (New Haven, 1926), pp. 82-3.

62

its height, Ireland supplied over two-thirds of the corn and flour imported into Great Britain.[39]

It is difficult to estimate the value of Ireland's contribution to the growth and protection of the empire during the eighteenth century, and it would also be difficult to gauge the effect that imperial development had on Ireland. An able Irish politician certainly did not deprecate the importance of Ireland's part in building up the British empire when in 1790 he said, 'this I am certain that Britain great as she is among surrounding nations, high in authority, powerful in her resources, knows very well she could not stand firm amidst the revolution of the world, if she did not replenish her vigour and sustain her weight by the strength of Ireland. She is not so confident as to think the time may never come in which even she may feel the infirmities of age and that the growing strength of Ireland may be able to bear her on her shoulders and rescue her from the flames'.[40]

[39] *Corn, grain, meal, flour and rice imported from Ireland and foreign parts, 1792–1812,* H.C. 1812–13 (95), XII; *Corn and grain of all sorts . . . imported into Great Britain from Ireland and foreign countries,* H.C. 1813–14 (159) XII; *Grain, meal and flour imported and exported,* H.C. 1814–15 (87), X; *Grain, meal and flour imported and exported,* H.C. 1816 (379), XIV.
[40] *Parl. Reg. Ire.* X, p. 239.

Encore Une Question: Lucien Febvre, The Reformation and the School of *Annales*

Dermot Fenlon

Few historians of this century have had so remarkable an influence on Reformation studies as the late Lucien Febvre, the co-founder, together with Marc Bloch, of the journal *Annales*. It is now almost fifty years since he published his celebrated essay '*Une question mal posée:* Les origines de la réforme française et le problème des causes de la réforme'; a piece of work which has remained influential to the present day.[1]

Febvre's essay was written in support of a 'history without frontiers' and as it turned out, a history without institutions. In place of a Reformation neatly divided into national units, classified in terms of what he derisively called the problems of *spécificité, priorité, nationalité*, Febvre wrote of an event in the history of Europe as a whole. For years, he maintained, historians had been asking the wrong questions. They had sought to discover whether there had occurred a specifically French Reformation; if so, whether it had started before the German Reformation; and finally, whether it had proceeded without debt to foreign, and more particularly, German, influence. Thus what Febvre called the 'three eternal problems' of *spécificité, priorité, nationalité*, had artificially come to dominate a debate which he considered to be nothing more than a sterile exchange of affirmations and negations.

The problem arose because the historians of the late nineteenth century had taken over an older historiographical tradition reaching back to the Reformation itself, while injecting into it a new preoccupation with national frontiers. This older tradition

[1] *Revue historique*, clxi (1929), pp. 1–73. Reprinted in Lucien Febvre, *Au Coeur Religieux du XVIe Siècle* (2nd ed., Paris, 1968), pp. 3–70 which is the source here cited. An English translation in *A New Kind of History*, a selection of Febvre's essays translated by K. Folca and ed. Peter Burke (London, 1973), pp. 44–107.

had been established by men who were not themselves historians. On the contrary, they had been controversialists: the ministers of the first reformed churches, and their enemies within the church of Rome, alike intent on furnishing themselves with respectable histories to hurl at their antagonists. The history of the Reformation had originally been written in consequence of the fact that a breach with Rome had taken place; and this, according to Febvre, was an 'ecclesiastical', not a 'religious' fact.[2] This rather curious antithesis lay at the root of all Febvre's thinking on the Reformation, and provides a clue to his inability to understand why religious men joined churches in the sixteenth century.

The original protagonists of the religious struggle, wrote Febvre, had sought only to justify or to deplore the breach with Rome. The early chroniclers of these events, ignorant of what Febvre described as 'a history nourished by psychology' had been concerned only to enquire what role had been played by their churches in the political and confessional conflicts of the period. Their question had been echoed mechanically down the centuries. Between the chroniclers and the controversialists, the religious history of the sixteenth century had been reduced to 'two very dry elements: the one ecclesiastical, the other political'. Viewed in this light, the Reformation translated itself into a matter of externals: a schism, caused by Luther's revolt; Luther's revolt caused by abuses in the church. Hence, according to Febvre, the origins of the Reformation became a question of secondary concern: a matter which began to receive scholarly attention only around the middle of the nineteenth century, when historians became aware of developments which they duly began to label 'Pre-Reform'. It was at this point that they discovered the enigmatic figure of Jacques Lefèvre d'Étaples; and, as Febvre had no difficulty in demonstrating, they did not know what to make of him. Lefèvre's importance in the early history of the French Reformation was indisputable. Was it not remarkable, asked the nineteenth century scholars, that this timid, retiring intellectual should have published—five years before Luther launched his protest against Tetzel—a commentary on the epistles of St Paul, in which he claimed that man was justified by faith, and not by works? Was it not equally remarkable that the circle of friends with whom he worked at Meaux, should have devoted themselves so assiduously, in the years before the Reformation, to the study of the Bible, and paid so little explicit attention to the visible church? And what was one to make of his disciples, who remained, some of them, within the Catholic church, but who displayed so

[2] *Au Coeur Religieux*, p. 8.

obvious a sympathy with the doctrine of the early Protestants, while others passed directly into the Protestant camp? Surely Lefèvre, it was argued, stood behind the French Reformation, just as Luther stood behind the German one? But if so, how was one to explain the fact that he never separated himself from the Catholic church; and that he died, in 1536, secure from any more disturbing censures than those directed against him by the uneasy theologians of the Sorbonne? Was he a Catholic? Was he a Protestant? The debate ran round and round; the needle remained jammed firmly in a single groove.

Nevertheless, observed Febvre, one strand of the ancient historiographical tradition had been snapped. It was no longer possible to suppose that the Reformation had 'fallen upon France like a meteorite upon a sterile landscape'; that the French Reformation must be explained exclusively in terms of Luther. But the other strand remained: it was still universally supposed that the Reformation was a reaction against abuses in the church, and this second strand had recently been reinforced by a misleading preoccupation with territorial frontiers. The 'two very dry elements' of ecclesiastical and political history continued to dominate the study of the Reformation.

In the face of all this, Lucien Febvre drew upon his ample reserves of glittering invective, and moved forward to unfold a different landscape. How absurd to imagine that the Reformation had been started by abuses! Had not Michelet long since exposed this myth? One had only to consider the spiritual pilgrimage of Luther, his long struggle for interior security, the blinding illumination which took place in the depths of his own soul, to realize how distant was all this from the external world of ecclesiastical considerations. Or one might reflect upon the charges levelled by Guillaume Farel against the clergy of his day: it was not for their bad lives that he reproached them, but for their bad beliefs. One had only, after all, to know one's Proust; to have read *Du côté de chez Swann* was to realize that 'facts do not penetrate into the world of our beliefs': external realities do not create men's aspirations. But the historians of the Reformation had 'stubbornly refused to admit' this truth, which could be given 'so many applications in their field of activity'. Armed with this somewhat dubious epistemology, Febvre now proceeded to distinguish between 'religious' and 'ecclesiastical' history, and to pit them in opposition to each other. The real question about the origins of the Reformation, the question as it were, *bien posée*, was one which turned upon the history of men's emotions, *l'histoire des sentiments*.

Thus posed, the question disclosed at the beginning of the sixteenth century a revolution in religious sentiment, of which the Reformation was the sign and product. A generation avid for religious certitude had long sought for a religion better adapted to its social needs: a learned and devout religion, epitomised in such figures as Lefèvre d'Étaples, whose thought was nourished by Florentine Platonism, by the traditions deriving from Dionysius the Areopagite, Richard of St Victor, Ruysbroeck and the Brethren of the Common Life, all combined with the teachings of 'un Évangélisme'[3] and 'un Paulinisme' drawn directly from the Biblical sources. In this environment Erasmus produced the first modern critical edition of the New Testament; in this *milieu* his *philosophia Christi* won for him a place of pre-eminence among a generation everywhere seeking new forms of artistic and religious expression. To this generation, the Reformation offered two things: the Bible in the vernacular, and the comfort of being justified by faith alone. It was a generation which attempted 'to break the narrow frameworks of the churches and to build an infinite variety of free religions on their ruins'. The attempt failed. It ended in a multiplication of churches and confessional groupings. A 'long period of magnificent religious anarchy' was succeeded by a 'period of servitude'. But historians must not be deceived into thinking that their task was to explain the development of churches. Unless they abandoned the ground of ecclesiastical history they would miss the real drama of the sixteenth century: the drama of thousands of tormented bourgeois consciences torn between the necessities of social discipline and the aspirations of a personal faith. Their pacifism 'à la suite de leur maître Érasme' reflected their nostalgia for 'cette grande patrie chrétienne' broken into national fragments by the wars of popes and princes. Here was the imposing theme to which future generations of researchers must address themselves. 'C'est à cela, à tout cela que l'historien doit regarder—et non aux petites règles particulières, aux petites convenances des Églises rivales'.[4]

Febvre's rousing appeal received distinctive acknowledgement in 1937, when a work appeared, dedicated to the proposition that the spirit of Erasmus was 'at the heart of the movements which we call the Reformation and Counter-Reformation'.[5] Its author was Marcel Bataillon. Bataillon's work is by any standards a great book. The second, revised edition, which is shortly to appear in

[3] *Ibid.*, p. 61.
[4] *Ibid.*, p. 69.
[5] M. Bataillon, *Érasme et l'Espagne* (Paris, 1937), p.v. A revised Spanish edition (2 vols.) appeared in Mexico in 1950. A second revised French edition is to appear shortly.

France, will doubtless modify a number of assumptions which understandably appeared more plausible in 1937 than they do today. Bataillon was not insensitive to the role of politics in shaping the final outcome of the Reformation. But his concern was to trace the fortunes of the international 'Erasmian' community, encouraged by Charles V, and dedicated to the search for a conciliatory religion, uniting the hostile confessions in agreement around the doctrine of justification by faith alone. Wherever one looked—in Spain, in Germany, in Italy—one found, according to Bataillon, the same eirenic concern among the devotees of Erasmus. It was the concern of Melanchthon as much as of the cardinals of the Catholic reform: of men like Contarini, Morone, and Reginald Pole, whose joint advancement to the college of cardinals Bataillon described as 'la promotion érasmienne'. Again, in a work emanating from the Neapolitan circle of the Spanish humanist Juan de Valdés, a work entitled the *Beneficio di Cristo*, Bataillon saw the epitome of this developed *érasmisme*, organised within what he called 'the neutral country of justification by faith which, for twenty years of religious anarchy' ran like a corridor between Rome and Wittenberg. Bataillon's debt to Febvre is here explicit.[6]

Bataillon's thesis rested upon the fusion of two separate premises, each of them valid, but neither of them dependent in logic or documentary evidence upon the other. The first is that Erasmus, in old age, sought to reconcile the hostile confessions. The second is that a number of European humanists came to believe in the doctrine of justification by faith alone. Some of them hoped to establish confessional reunion on this basis. It is unfortunate that Bataillon, in the first edition of his great work, everywhere substituted the word *érasmisme* for the less restrictive expression Christian humanism. Thus, writing of the Spanish humanists whose conventicles were closed down by the Inquisition in the middle of the century, Bataillon remarked, with what to a sceptical reader might seem like unconscious irony:

> If no attempt has ever been made to relate the movement which they inspired, to the erasmian movement which formed the ambience of their youth, it is, above all, due to lack of documentation.[7]

This admission, startling as it is, not least because it appears on page 556, may have prompted Lucien Febvre to entertain a moment's doubt when he reviewed the work ecstatically in

---

[6] *Ibid.*, p. 550.
[7] *Ibid.*, p. 556.

Annales.[8] If so, he did not allow it unduly to disturb him. Commenting on the failure of the humanists to acknowledge the source of their eirenic inspiration, he explained that it became impossible in Italy and Spain openly to avow the influence of Erasmus after the rise to power of the militant proponents of the Counter Reformation. The humanists therefore discreetly dropped the name of Erasmus from the roll-call of authorities; instead, they pursued his inspiration and his work in secret.[9]

This neat hypothesis, unencumbered by hard evidence, served to propagate the view that everywhere, in the generation that survived Erasmus, his conciliatory influence formed the nucleus of the eirenic policies adopted by a sector of the European humanist community. Slowly this view began to gain acceptance: in the work of the Dutch historian H. O. Enno van Gelder; in the essays of Professor Hugh Trevor-Roper; in the notion of a 'third eirenic party' inspired by Erasmus and spanning the confessional frontiers between 1530 and 1560.[10]

Yet as Bataillon himself acknowledged, the documents do not really point to an uninterrupted connection between the outlook of Erasmus in the *philosophia Christi* and the convictions of the younger generation. What seems to have happened is rather that the *sola fides* of Luther displaced the *philosophia Christi* of Erasmus and forced the humanists to adopt it or oppose it.[11] Others before Luther had raised the question of justification by faith; the epistles of St Paul were not unknown before 1517.[12] Nobody before Luther linked the matter with a question about the nature of the visible church; this was the decisive difference introduced by Luther. The break with Rome carried in its wake a necessary question about the nature of the church. The leading ministers of the first Protestant churches: at Zurich, Zwingli; at Basle, Oecolampadius; at Strasbourg, Bucer; at Geneva, Calvin— were all of them humanists turned Protestant. None of them saw a distinction between 'religious' and 'ecclesiastical' matters. All of them accepted the Lutheran dialectics of sin and faith. All of

[8] *Annales*, I (1939), reprinted in *Au Coeur Religiuex* under the title 'L'Érasme de Marcel Bataillon', pp. 93–111.
[9] *Au Coeur Religieux*, pp. 109–10.
[10] H. O. Enno van Gelder, *The Two Reformations in the Sixteenth Century* (The Hague, 1964, pp. 266–7); H. R. Trevor-Roper, *Historical Essays* (London, 1958), pp. 35–60. 'Erasmianism' in Professor Trevor-Roper's language means something other than the specific doctrines of Erasmus. But he uses it 'for lack of a better word'. *Religion, the Reformation and Social Change* 2nd edn. (London, 1972), p. 24. 'Humanism' is a better word.
[11] A. Dufour 'Humanisme et réformation', *XIIᵉ Congrès International Des Sciences Historiques* (Vienna, 1965), *Rapports*, III, *Commissions*, pp. 57–74.
[12] R. Cessi, 'Paolinismo preluterano', *Rendiconti dell'Accademia nazionale dei Lincei*, Cl. di sc. mor. sto. e filol., ser. VIII, vol XII (1957), pp. 3–30.

them went beyond Luther in the manufacture of church systems designed to be independent of ungodly magistrates or princes.[13] What distinguished these humanists from the older Erasmus was their violent antagonism to the church to which he belonged, and their concern to build the kingdom over and against it. If, like Bucer, they were eirenically disposed, they were so with respect to their differences among themselves, and not in their attitude towards Catholics. Bucer's reputation for ecumenical initative rests upon his mediation between the developing and conflicting doctrines of Wittenberg, Strasbourg, Zurich and Geneva.[14] It did not extend to any desire to build corridors between Wittenberg and Rome. In the cities of southern Germany and Switzerland between 1520 and 1555 a 'second Reformation' came into existence under the leadership of Protestant humanists.

What of Erasmus? Between 1530 and 1541 his eirenic policies won support from Charles V, his ministers, and a number of German princes, bishops and theologians.[15] One of the latter, Johann Gropper, rewrote an Erasmian formula[16] and got it accepted as the basis of the short-lived reunion conference at Regensburg in 1541. But the formula of 'twofold justice' was in reality no more than an epitaph for the 'Erasmianism' of which Gropper, to judge by the most authoritative recent study of the conference, was perhaps the sole representative at Regensburg.[17] It is doubtful whether Erasmus would have regarded Granvelle's attempt to bribe the protestant theologians as compatible with the spirit of the *philosophia Christi*. If Bucer appeared at Regensburg it was as the agent of Philip of Hesse. As Peter Matheson puts it, religious colloquies were for Bucer 'an aggressive weapon to be used for the extension of the Kingdom'; Regensburg was an opportunity for its peaceful extension. Calvin was more perceptive than Luther when he recognised that the Regensburg agreement

---

[13] B. Moeller, *Imperial Cities and the Reformation* ed. and translated by H. C. Erik Midelfort and Mark U. Edwards, Jr. (Philadelphia, 1972); L. Spitz, 'The Third Generation of Renaissance Humanists', in *Aspects of the Renaissance*, ed. Archibald R. Lewis (Austin and London, 1967), pp. 105–121, and the same author's *The Religious Renaissance of the German Humanists* (Cambridge, Mass., 1963). J. Delumeau, *Naissance et Affirmation De La Réforme* 2nd edn. (Paris, 1968).
[14] W. Pauck, *The Heritage of the Reformation*, 2nd revised edition. (London, Oxford, New York, 1968), pp. 73–99.
[15] J. P. Dolan, *The Influence of Erasmus, Witzel and Cassander in the Church Ordinances and Reform Proposals of the United Duchies of Cleve during the Middle Decades of the 16th Century* (Münster, 1959). F. Lau and E. Bizer, *A History of the Reformation in Germany to 1555*, translated by Brian A. Hardy (London, 1969), pp. 153–7.
[16] 'Duplex est iustitia, prior est innocentia cui per fidem ac baptismum restituimur, altera est fidei per dilectionem operantis'. *In Psalmum XXII Ennaratio Triplex* (*Opera* V, p. 325 B).
[17] P. Matheson, *Cardinal Contarini at Regensburg* (Oxford, 1972).

conceded the substance of the Protestant doctrine of justification. 'You will marvel', he wrote to Guillaume Farel, 'that our adversaries have conceded so much'.[18]

The 'adversaries' in question were the cardinals of *'la promotion érasmienne'*: Contarini was the papal delegate at Regensburg. There was nothing Erasmian about the genesis of his interest in *sola fides*.[19] And there was nothing Erasmian about his conviction at Regensburg that the doctrine of justification advanced by Luther was as fundamental to the Catholic faith as the doctrines of transubstantiation and papal primacy. When he found out that the Protestants took a different view of the eucharist and papal primacy the conference collapsed. Regensburg was more significant as a failure than a success. It demonstrated that rival churches (manned by Protestant and Catholic humanists) were already in existence, flatly opposed to each other on grounds of sacramental doctrine and ecclesiastical jurisdiction.[20] After Regensburg, as before (and contrary to Matheson) Contarini continued to regard the *sola fides* of the Protestant reformers as 'vero et catholico'; the 'fundamento della religione Christiana'.[21] His object, like that of Pole and his supporters, was to convert the Curia to *sola fides* and the Protestants to the papacy, recommending in all things submission to the teaching of the church.[22]

Pole and Contarini wanted reunion among European Christians. But they wanted it on grounds distinct from those recommended by Erasmus. Erasmus wanted reunion because he believed that time would settle the points of disagreement; Pole and Contarini wanted it because they believed that the Lutherans were right in their belief in *sola fides*, and wrong in their assault upon the church.[23] It was precisely the first part of this conviction that separated them from any continuous association with the outlook of Erasmus; they had not learned to think thus from Erasmus.[24] And it was precisely on this point that Erasmus had originally taken issue with Luther, when he wrote his *De Libero Arbitrio*—only to find himself so devastatingly rebuffed that he wrote to the young Reginald Pole: 'Luther has written against me in a way that

[18] *Ibid.*, pp. 26, 109.
[19] See his early letters in H. Jedin, ed., 'Contarini und Camaldoli', *Archivio italiano per la storia della pietà* II (1959), pp. 51–117, and my own remarks in *Heresy and Obedience in Tridentine Italy: Cardinal Pole and the Counter Reformation* (Cambridge, 1972), pp. 6–23, and *passim* for the evolution of Pole's interest in justification.
[20] H. Jedin, *A History of the Council of Trent*, translated by Dom Ernest Graf O.S.B., I (London, 1957), pp. 355–409.
[21] Contarini to Pole [July 1542] in F. Dittrich, ed., *Regesten und Briefe des Kardinals Gasparo Contarini* (Braunsberg, 1881), p. 358.
[22] *Ibid.*, p. 355.
[23] *Ibid.*, pp. 353–61.
[24] Above, n. 19.

no one would employ against the Turk'.[25] That sentence, written in 1526, marks a decisive moment in European history: a moment which signalised the ascendancy of Luther, and which imposed upon the humanist community the necessity of adopting or opposing his doctrine of justification, and of considering its implications for the visible church. If they sought a *via media* it was within a confessional setting, and on the doctrinal ground established by Luther, Bucer and Melanchthon, not Erasmus; as Erasmus himself was forced in time to recognise. He moved, in old age, towards an attempt at reconciling the hostile parties, while himself remaining within the fold of the church which Luther had renounced.[26] But in Germany, as beyond, the younger humanists were reading Luther and the Protestant reformers. In Spain the humanist conventicles of Seville and Valladolid were unambiguously classified by their enemies as *luteranos*. It may be that the Inquisitors were by now incapable of distinguishing between 'erasmians' and 'lutherans'. But it seems unlikely. A number of those cross-examined by the Inquisition did not deny the charge of Lutheranism; many who escaped from Spain are known to have been Calvinists; and it is no longer the case that one searches in vain for the growth of an indigenous Protestantism in the countries of the Mediterranean.[27]

In Italy, the cardinals who looked with sympathy at Luther's doctrine of justification sought to curb and channel the demands for local Reformation according to a strategy determined by the norms of Catholic belief and practice.[28] It was this policy which led Pole to shelter in his household at Viterbo a gathering which his antagonist Carafa is said to have described as 'a platoon of heretics'.[29] It was at Viterbo that Marc Antonio Flaminio was brought back to the church of Rome; the author of the final version of that same *Beneficio di Cristo* which Bataillon, in the first edition of his work, quite pardonably regarded as a manifesto of an 'Erasmian' reform group. The same verdict would scarcely pass muster today. The *Beneficio di Cristo* was in reality the first fruit of a transplanted Protestantism on the soil of Italy. Whole pages of it were borrowed directly from the 1539 edition of Calvin's *Institutes*.[30] Pole's associates at Viterbo did not show

---

[25] *Opus Epistolarum Desiderii Erasmi Roterodami* (ed. Allen), VI, p. 283.
[26] *De Amabili Ecclesiae Concordia* (1533), *Opera*, V, pp. 470–506.
[27] Paul J. Hauben, 'Reform and Counter-Reform: the Case of the Spanish Heretics', in *Action and Conviction in Early Modern Europe*, ed. Theodore K. Rabb and Jerrold E. Seigel (Princeton, N.J., 1969), pp. 154–68.
[28] A process which I have described elsewhere (*Heresy and Obedience*, pp. 45–68).
[29] BM Harl, MS 1763, fol. 149v.
[30] V. Vinay, 'Die Schrift "Il Beneficio di Giesu Christo" und ihre Verbreitung in Europa nach der neuen Forschung', *Archiv für Reformationsgeschichte*, LVIII

much interest in Erasmus. Their reading was in Luther, Valdés, Bucer and Melanchthon.[31] Many of them fixed their hopes for reunion on the approaching Council to be held at Trent. Their object was to reconcile the Lutheran dialectics of sin and faith with the church which Luther had repudiated.

The Council of Trent put an end to their ambitions. They had to choose between their opinions and the teaching of the church. Some of them remained within the church. Others departed for Geneva and the north. Some few remained in Italy, secretly adhering to their views. Denounced by Calvin for their cowardice, sporadically persecuted by the Roman Inquisition, they retired into a private world.[32]

The history of the European humanist community in the years which followed the outbreak of the Reformation conclusively demonstrates the overriding importance of what Lucien Febvre so arbitrarily dismissed: the importance of confessional considerations. It is apparent how much the humanists of Europe on all sides of the confessional divide were concerned with the formation and reformation of their churches; how the 'abuses' which Febvre discounted as a significant element in the story provided the occasion and the outrage which drove Luther to make his momentous protest against the sale of indulgences, and the Catholics to take the point in the reforms of Trent. It is hard to escape the conclusion that the 'two very dry elements' of ecclesiastical and political history remain indispensable to any explanation of the Reformation. The historical theme which emerges, clearly from the evidence is the movement of European humanists between 1520 and 1560, into diametrically antagonistic confessional and political groupings. This is not a theme which can be orchestrated by a posthumous conductor into separate 'religious' and 'ecclesiastical' movements; the one played *fortissimo* to drown the echoes of the other. It is a theme which depends for its life on the interplay between the cosmopolitan religious culture of the early sixteenth century, with its strongly Biblical and Pauline orientation, and the political, institutional world of warring states and hostile confessions in which the humanists, like other men,

(1967), Heft I, pp. 29–72. For a further discussion, see my *Heresy and Obedience*, pp. 73–88.
[31] 'Estratto del processo di Mons. Pietro Carnesecchi', ed. G. Manzoni, *Miscellanea di Storia Italiana*, X (1870), pp. 195, 203, 213–4. *Carteggio di Vittoria Colonna*, ed. E. Ferrero and G. Muller (Turin, 1889), pp. 238–40.
[32] D. Cantimori, 'Submission and Conformity: "Nicodemism" and the Expectations of a Conciliar Solution to the Religious Question', translated from the Italian in Eric Cochrane, ed. *The Late Italian Renaissance 1525–1630* (London, 1970), pp. 244–65.

had to find their bearings once the Reformation had emerged as an historical force.

These facts necessitate a fresh evaluation of Febvre's influence as an historian. One may doubt whether his *Une question mal posée* deserved to become a landmark in Reformation studies. One may also doubt whether the landscape which it unfolded was so totally unknown. To read this essay more than forty years on is to arrive at the conclusion that it does a grave injustice to one of the greatest French historians of the present century, Pierre Imbart de la Tour. The four volumes of Imbart's *Les Origines de la Réforme* appeared between 1905 and 1935. The first two volumes were reviled by Febvre on the grounds that they were insufficiently documented; represented the Renaissance as a movement transcending national frontiers; and dealt too lightly with the abuses in the church which were to command so much attention from the Protestant and Catholic reformers.[33] Febvre's objections at this juncture were clearly prompted by questions of *spécificité, nationalité* and the 'very dry' element of ecclesiastical history. This was in 1910. Four years later Imbart's third volume appeared. Its subtitle was *L'Évangelisme.* It was his masterpiece. With this volume Imbart brought to light something which historians had hitherto failed to recognise in the search for Reformation origins: the pre-Lutheran, unTridentine world which had come into existence by the eve of the Reformation; a world which possessed a momentum distinguishable from the Reformation and Counter Reformation, in the sense that these movements became, in the ensuing thirty years, mutually exclusive possibilities.

Already at the outset of the sixteenth century there existed, according to Imbart, a religious world transformed by a new thrust of energy, deriving from the study of the Bible, and in particular the epistles of St Paul. Towards 1520 the currents of Christian humanism and mysticism began to coalesce. The result was what Imbart called *l'Évangelisme:* a new quest for religious assurance, rooted in the rediscovery of the Bible. The emergence of Lutheranism forced *l'Évangelisme* into a crisis from which it never recovered. Instead it broke into conflicting elements. One group detached itself from Rome and from the hierarchical church. Another group reinforced its existing attachments adopting, like the first group, a position of intransigence. Yet another attempted, for a whole generation, to mediate, until mediation proved to be no longer possible.

[33] *Revue de synthèse historique*, t. XII–I, no. 34 (1906), pp. 72–88, for Febvre's review of vol I; and *ibid.*, t. XX (1910), pp. 159–70, for his strictures on vol II.

Imbart had realized that a conceptual error had lodged itself in the historiography of the early Reformation. It consisted in opposing *from the outset* Protestantism and the Counter Reformation—in the manner in which they ultimately ranged themselves into coherent opposition. It ignored the element of confusion. Thus, he explained, between 'these two great masses' every intermediate element had disappeared.[34] It was because they had lacked a conceptual awareness of this possibility that historians of an older tradition had not been able to understand figures like Lefèvre d'Étaples and Guillaume Briconnet: precisely because they did not fit the established categories of early Protestantism, or the forms which Catholicism assumed after Trent. The historically triumphant forces of the century prevented historians from recognising the third world of *l'Évangelisme* which the Reformation and Counter Reformation overwhelmed in establishing themselves. It was this world which Imbart restored to the early history of the Reformation, thereby disclosing a missing dimension which rendered it fully intelligible for the first time.

L'Évangelisme was published in 1914, an unlucky year for everyone, including writers. It was reviewed in the learned journals only twice (in so far as I can determine): once in France, in 1914, and once in Sweden, in 1918.[35] Febvre was busy during the war as a captain of artillery. Life in a machine gun corps is probably not best relieved by an alert eye on the latest scholarly journals; but it taught Febvre something else. He returned to a chair of history at Strasbourg, with a hatred of politics and warfare, and of the kind of history which chose such subjects as its themes. In 1920 he wrote a review which incorporated an attack on Imbart: not on the Imbart of *L'Évangelisme* (which he failed to mention) but on its predecessor, the volume of 1909 which he had earlier reviewed. This time he attacked it on rather different grounds: it ignored the Parisian scholastics and the currents of mysticism in the years before the Reformation.[36] And then in 1929 there appeared '*Une question mal posée*' with its subtitle, 'Les origines de la réforme française'—virtually the same title that Imbart had imparted to his multi-volume study, with the significant omission of the word 'française'. In the course of this essay Febvre remarked upon the importance of Lefèvre d'Étaple's 'Évangelisme' and

[34] *L'Évangelisme* (Paris, 1914), preface.
[35] *Revue d'Histoire de l'Eglise de France*, V (1914), pp. 519–25, an appreciative review by Louis Hogu; *Kyrkohistorisk Aarsskrift*, XLIX (1918), a review by K. B. Westman which I cannot read, being ignorant of Swedish.
[36] 'Quelques Publications Relatives au Séizième Siècle Français', *Revue de synthèse historique*, t. XXXI (1920), pp. 109–19, Cf p. 113.

'Paulinisme' drawn directly from the Biblical sources.[37] Yet we search in vain for any reference in this essay to the third volume of Imbart's *Origines, L'Évangelisme*. All we find is a couple of dismissive footnotes referring to its predecessor, the volume of 1909. By this time one would have expected Febvre to have caught up with the succeeding volume; '*Une question mal posée*' was not the new territory it announced itself to be. Yet again, in 1937, in his review of Bataillon's great work, Febvre once more took occasion to cast his strictures against Imbart's second volume, the predecessor of *L'Évangelisme*.[38] This time he complained that it dealt with a specifically French Reformation. And still he made no mention of *L'Évangelisme;* yet Bataillon's bibliography listed the work.

It is just possible that Febvre never read Imbart's *L'Évangelisme;* that the intellectual revolution which he announced in 1929 proceeded ready armed from his own head and without assistance from the author of *Les Origines de la Réforme* whose work he so obsessively, selectively and repetitiously slighted, while shifting his angle of attack each time, over a period of twenty years. In France, Imbart's great work seems to have passed with little acclaim and virtually without recognition; an effect for which Febvre must bear some measure of responsibility. But in Germany and Italy between the wars, and later in America and Britain, Imbart's third great volume, *L'Évangelisme*, was recognised as a seminal work, and one which slowly transformed the study of the sixteenth century Reformations.[39] Yet even in these countries other historians continued to be hypnotised by the subtly distinct and less reliable directives emanating from Febvre's '*Une question mal posée*'.

Febvre's highly selective and kaleidoscopic criticism of Imbart's work, and the truly staggering *volte-face* which accompanied these attacks, must put us on our guard against his overpowering literary techniques of persuasion. 'Conceptual debts?' he asked rhetorically in an essay of 1933. 'Sometimes. But debts in method and *esprit*, above all'. The essay is entitled *Examen de Conscience*.[40]

Febvre's conceptual debts, his debts of method and *esprit*, are not difficult to isolate. There was Febvre the essayist who wrote an enthusiastic review of Loisy's Memoirs under the revealing

---

[37] *Au Coeur Religieux*, p. 61.
[38] *Ibid.*, p. 110.
[39] E. M. Jung, 'On the Nature of Evangelism in Sixteenth Century Italy', *Journal of the History of Ideas* XIV (1953), pp. 511–27 traces the course of this development, p. 511. For a discussion of 'Evangelism' see my *Heresy and Obedience*, pp. 14–23.
[40] Reprinted in *Combats Pour L'Histoire* (Paris, 1953), p. 14.

title *Du Modernisme de Loisy à l'Érasmisme*.[41] This was an essay in which he declared himself already familiar, as an historian of the sixteenth century, with the recent history of Modernism recounted by Loisy. It may not be unduly rash to surmise that the truth was quite possibly the reverse. There was the teacher who announced that History would in time unravel the laws of human development —when enough research had been done.[42] There was the historian who believed that the past is the property of those who study it: that the social task of the historian is 'to organise the past as a function of the present'.[43] There was the scholar perennially at war with the novelist *manqué;* the admirer of Proust who could recommend the view that 'facts do not penetrate into the world of our beliefs'—an astonishing admission for one who had so many imperative demands to make of history. There was the veteran of the first world war who proclaimed against the history taught by the veterans of the Franco-Prussian war, 'the defeated men of 1870' who taught him.[44] There was the admirer of Jaurès who could quote with approval from the *Histoire Socialiste:* 'Our interpretation of history will be at once materialist with Marx, and mystical with Michelet'.[45] And lastly, there was the friend of Marc Bloch, who helped to found *Annales*.

With the launching of *Annales* Lucien Febvre became the propagandist of a movement which transformed the writing of history in the twentieth century. Where Ranke and the great nineteenth century historians studied the relations between states and nations, the historians of *Annales* turned to the submerged and ever changing world of human communities, in their regional geography, their material and religious environments, their collective *mentalités*, their fortunes and catastrophes. In the pages of *Annales* a new kind of geographical and social history came into existence: Febvre was its propagandist and its pioneer. Yet he did not, after his early incursion into the regional and political history of the Franche-Comté[46] devote himself predominantly to the task of writing social history. The exhaustive research into and recomposition of the social past he left to Marc Bloch and his disciples. Instead, he wrote about how to write it, in *La Terre et l'évolution humaine*[47] and in a glittering array of essays (mostly now collected) which appeared between 1922 and his death in 1956.

[41] Reprinted in *Au Coeur Religieux*, pp. 122–36.
[42] 'L'histoire dans le monde en ruines', *Revue de synthèse historique* t. XXX (1920), pp 1–15.
[43] *Combats Pour L'Histoire*, p. 438.
[44] *Ibid.*, p. vii.
[45] *Ibid.*, p. 109.
[46] *Philippe II et! a Franche-Comté* (Paris, 1912).
[47] Paris, 1922.

For the rest, his books were about *civilisation*, in the French sense of the term: studies in the social and religious sensibility of the sixteenth century. His *Un Destin: Martin Luther*[48] was about a man who provided for the needs of the emerging *bourgeoisie;* a giant who lost his vocation and shrank in stature when he turned to politics. Febvre's analysis did not extend to the political Luther of the years from 1525. The founder of Lutheranism was not allowed to be a Lutheran.

But in what sense were the townsmen really 'emerging'? And why did so many south German cities adopt a Zwinglian, in contrast to a Lutheran Reformation? And why *did* Luther turn to politics and princes? The history of the German Reformation is inseparable from its alignment with political forces and its development into an organised religion. But all this was a closed book to Febvre. He was by now an avowed opponent of political and ecclesiastical history. His historical *civilisation* belonged to a world without the state; his historical religion to a world without the church. But how is it possible to write a history of the sixteenth century with neither? His *Problème de l'incroyance au XVIe siècle; la religion de Rabelais*[49] revealed that atheism was not a sixteenth century phenomenon. Rabelais was a Christian humanist, not an atheist. In its day the book helped to correct some modish nonsense; as a study of Rabelais it has since been superseded.[50] Rabelais belonged to the world of *l'Évangelisme:* a world originally brought to light by Imbart. It did not survive the Lutheran, Calvinist and Tridentine Reformations. Febvre was not unaware of its demise. But his programmatic assault on traditional history precluded him from asking why men wanted to embark upon the destruction, formation and reformation of their churches in the sixteenth century. At this point of tension his mind turned away from explanation to polemic: a polemic against the ecclesiastical, political, military, institutional history of Europe, and against 'the defeated men of 1870', the intellectual avengers of the Franco-Prussian war, the xenophobic nationalist historians of the post-Ranke generation, whose narrow doctrines and political perspectives were to be obliterated by the school of *Annales*. And so they were, or rather simply ignored, in a series of great regional studies which began to emerge after the second war: Braudel's *Mediterranean*, Goubert's *Beauvais*, Le Roy Ladurie's *Paysans de Languedoc*.[51]

[48] Paris, 1928.
[49] Paris, 1947.
[50] M. Screech, *The Rabelaisian Marriage* (London, 1958), and the same author's *L'Évangelisme de Rabelais* (Geneva, 1959).
[51] *The Mediterranean and the Mediterranean World in the Age of Philip II*, 2 vols.

The school of *Annales* still has its giants. But the claim to have arrived at 'une histoire totale' has always looked a little less than convincing in its disregard for political history; it has also bred its opposite. There are signs that the social history of the kind pioneered by the French school of *Annales* is latterly in danger of freezing into a history without humans: a history insensitive to the element of time and the significance of language; a history of tables, pull-out charts and graphs resembling the Manhattan skyline. These developments would scarcely have pleased Febvre. But they are not unrelated to the revolution which he helped to accomplish: a revolution which swept aside the themes dominating nineteenth century historiography, issuing edicts against the study of government in church and state.

A selection of Febvre's essays has recently been translated for English readers under the title 'A New Kind of History'.[52] This is no longer an accurate description. These essays are better read as a collection of manifestoes issuing from the period between and after the two wars. Even in translation they crackle and sparkle with Gallic wizardry and caustic rhetoric. They are lively, unreliable, prejudiced and always readable; they do not justify Febvre's reputation as a great historian. Here, as in other matters, the contrast with Imbart is in every way instructive. Imbart's writing was the product of long years of assiduous study and reflection. His history is all-encompassing; his prose is stately and deliberative. Febvre's history moves always at top speed; his prose charges forward with dramatic rhetoric; his writing is a style of permanent warfare. Everything he wrote after his first book[53] was a manifesto, *un combat*. Such writing does not survive the test of time. He lacked the settled character of mind, the capacity for patient labour, the ultimately contemplative habit of mind which is the hallmark of the truly great historians—Ranke, Mommsen, Marc Bloch. Febvre's essays have pungency and character; read with a mind alert to the polemic which gave rise to them, they retain the flavour of their time and their tradition. The essay on Amiens presents itself characteristically: 'not a complete, painstaking and detailed study' but 'an example' designed to 'suggest . . . a subject of research' to those offering to come forward in the pursuit of 'a truly living history of French

translated by Siân Reynolds (London 1972-3) from the second revised edition (2 vols, Paris, 1966). The first edition appeared in 1949. P. Goubert, *Beauvais et le Beauvaisis de 1600 à 1730* (2 vols, Paris, 1960). E. Le Roy Ladurie, *Les Paysans de Languedoc* (Paris, 1966).
[52] Ed. Peter Burke and translated by K. Folca (London, 1973).
[53] Above, n. 46.

civilization'.[54] The capacity to arouse, prompt, organise, direct: this was the essence of Febvre's genius. He always remained a captain of artillery, directing fire against the enemy and encouraging his troops. Some of his troops went on to become statesmen. Lucien Febvre has his abiding memorial in the dedication of Braudel's *Mediterranean* 'A Lucien Febvre, toujours présent'. *Toujours?* Well, yes, as the acknowledged inspiration of this greatest of all the products of the *Annales* revolution. But that 'wider and more humane history' for which Febvre so eloquently argued, 'the study of man in time' of which Bloch wrote, necessarily compels the reconciliation of the traditions deriving from Ranke and the school of *Annales*. Perhaps it is as well that historians have never completely ceased to recognise that the lives of human communities are decided not only by their geography and environment, but also by their politics, their institutions, their personal and collective initiatives and beliefs, and the movement of events themselves: that whole *histoire événémentielle* so distrusted even by the greatest of the *Annales* historians, Braudel. The best writing of recent years gives ample ground for confidence that the two traditions, the German and French schools of historical analysis, can encounter each other to their mutual advantage, now that the men of 1870 are safely defeated.

[54] *A New Kind of History*, pp. 203–4.

Some Stoic Inspiration in the Thought of J.-J. Rousseau

K. F. Roche

'O, Man, from whatsoever land you are, whatever your opinions, listen! Here is your history as I read it, not in the books of your fellows, who are liars, but in nature, who never deceives. All that will be told you here is true: there will be no falsehood but what I may unwittingly have mixed with it. The times of which I speak are faraway: how you have changed from what you once were! It is, so to speak, the life of your race I shall describe, according to the qualities you have received, which your education and your customs have depraved, but have not been able to destroy. There is, I feel, an age at which the individual man would long to remain: you will see the age at which you would desire that your race had halted. Discontented with your present state for reasons which forbode even greater misery for your unhappy posterity, perhaps you would like to go back: and that sentiment ought to make you sigh for your early days, to loathe your present and to tremble for the unhappy men who will come after you.'[1]

The secret of Rousseau's success was his appeal to our discontents. 'Things were not always thus' is a human reaction to the limitations of life. Whoever tells us this is certain of an audience. If he goes further and sketches a simple plan to restore the happiness of old, he is doubly assured.

The idea that all was once harmonious was far from new: in one form or another, it has been part of the mythology of many peoples; that all would yet become, or could be made, harmonious was familiar to Rousseau's contemporaries of the Enlightenment. What was new in Rousseau was the passionate language and what was relatively new was the romantic conception of the proposed political ideal. He has been called Janus-faced because he at once looked back to the golden legend of a remote past and forward to a great *idée* force of the future: romantic, extreme nationalism.

The ancestry of Rousseau's ideas on man and man's relation

[1] *D. sur l'In des Con.*

83

to his surroundings can be readily traced in large measure to the Stoics and, in an especial manner, to Seneca, while his ideal of political organisation goes clearly back to the ancient conception of the *polis*. The preoccupation of the Aristotelian and the Stoic schools of speculation lay with the conception of 'nature', a preoccupation that descended to Christian Europe and marks all the political doctrine of the great theorists of the seventeenth and eighteenth centuries.

In what senses has the word been used? In a primary sense, *nature* has been used to describe the entire ordered universe, the totality of the created beings and entities that compose it, the laws which govern them and the ends of their specific actions. Metaphysically considered, *nature* embraces the three-fold notion of a specific potentiality, a specific actuality, and the process of becoming by which the specific potentiality becomes a specific actuality: it involves a specific essence, a specific potentiality and the process of becoming by which they are linked. All transcendentalist systems of thought considered Deity as distinct from, as well as immanent in, the universe and thus considered a supernatural as well as a natural order. Pantheistic systems have merged Deity with the universe and have considered but one order: the natural. *Deus sive natura*. Nature, to the Stoics, is God and God is reason, the principle pervading the entire universe and, on the human plane, prescribing the behaviour of man and his relations with his fellows. God, in this pantheistic sense, may be viewed as an idea of reason, a principle which it is necessary to invoke in order to show that there is coherence in life. All classical thought centres around the principle of order. The universe is thought of in terms of a rational, ordered whole. The totality is viewed as a regulated unity, governed by deeply-laid, unerring laws. The Stoics in particular see in it the work of a supreme reason which appoints to all things appropriate functions and purposes, supplying them, in accordance with their needs, with the means of fulfilling their roles and attaining their ends. All reality is an ordered hierarchy, culminating in a rational source, a source which operates, not arbitrarily, but in rigid accordance with fixed and unalterable law. Divine law, Divine reason, is of the nature of Deity itself and, being so, is at once eternal and immutable, since Deity cannot contradict its own nature.[2] Divine reason reflects itself in man. Deity permits man to know something of itself and its workings and equips man to live according to a design of its own making. And this equipment with which Deity endows man is the human reason. Human reason is thus a reflection of and a

[2] Cicero: *De Re Publica*, xxii, III, *De Natura Deorum*, II, xxxv, etc.

participation in the Divine reason. It is that innate and inherent faculty wherewith man is enabled to distinguish between good and evil, between that which the law ordains and that which is opposed to Eternal Justice.[3] All Greek thought found the specific or universal human quality in reason: an innate tendency to categorise in moral terms, to seek truth and practise justice. In this quality of rationality, all men partake.

The law of reason, coming as it does from the principle which regulates all things, is anterior to and takes precedence over all man-made or positive law, and, being common to all humanity, is independent of time and place, of compact and custom. Positive law ought to be designed to give effect to the demands of reason in particular cases. Submission to the wrong decision of an established government is an affair of composition, an imperfect duty that bids us suffer certain evils in order to avert greater.[4]

The elaboration of this theory of a pervading rationality gave the Stoics a lasting influence on European thought. Reality, to the Stoics is pervaded by the divine principle of reason which expresses itself progressively in successive stages or types of existence, namely: in the inanimate, in the brute and in the human. The first, the inanimate, is governed by physical and chemical laws; the second, the brute realm, by fixed laws of instinct which, although necessary, are not as directly and evidently so in their operation as the physical and chemical laws of matter. On the human plane, we come to the highest level of all, in which the divine reason that permeates the universe attains to self-consciousness. Man, then, is essentially rational: the tendency to categorise in moral terms is innate and inherent in all men: consequently, the knowledge of the moral law, the law which the principles of innate and universal reason build up, is attainable to all men who use their reason. Stoicism will have none of the Aristotelian doctrine of inequality, based on the difference in the degrees of rationality. Mankind occupies the highest plane, the plane on which the divine reason attains to self-consciousness. Humanity, then, as an occupant of that one plane, is one: all its individual members, occupying as they do the same plane, are essentially equal, no subdivision in essentials being possible. There exists, therefore, no natural inequality of master and slave: all mankind is a society of equals.[5] By this term, *natural*, the Stoics mean *rational:* that is to say, in accordance with the laws of the universe. Deity, reason and nature are one. Stoicism, hence, issues in a

[3] Cicero: *De Re Publica*, III, xxii; Seneca: *Ep.* 124, etc., etc.
[4] Cicero, *De Legibus*, II, iv.
[5] Seneca, *Ep.* 44, 47, 117, 121, 124; Cicero, *De Legibus*, I, xvi, xvii; *De Natura Deorum*, II, xii, xiii.

panlogism, a rationalistic pantheism, the implications of which were to set Chrysippus on the search for a principle which would serve as a basis for the affirmation of human freedom. A system which identifies God, nature and reason cannot logically avoid materialising reason, or, in the alternative, rationalising matter. By materialising reason, one drags down God to the level of matter; by rationalising matter, one does the same thing. In either case, one ascribes to God the amoralism of the mechanical and historical process. The historical is, hence, the teleogical, the material process is the spiritual and the world is a closed system wherein God is working Himself out from inner necessity. The *natural* is, therefore, the *actual*, as Hobbes and Machiavelli supposed. But this is to deprive the term, *natural*, of any meaning, and to eliminate morality. Yet, Stoicism is concerned throughout with morality. This is the great problem of every form of pantheism: if the Deity is merely immanent, then good and evil are one: there is no objective morality and no personal responsibility. That the Stoics in practice accepted freewill is obvious, but they never solved the problem with which their panlogism left them. The idea of Fate is never far from their thought. Fate is the eternal will of nature, or God, or the universe. It sends disasters and tribulations to us, but these are not moral evils. Moral evil comes from ourselves. There is a law of Necessity, which the Stoics conceive of as something extra-human in origin, over which the individual has no control and submission to which is freedom.[6] To struggle against it is the mark of the slave. *Ducunt volentem fata, nolentem trahunt.* The great soul is the man who gives himself over to Fate; the weakling and degenerate struggles against it and maligns the order of the universe.[7] Everything that is not morally evil is sent by providence and is therefore in accordance with divine reason. It is intrinsically good, coming as it does from nature or God. This conception of Necessity, a divine or an impersonal force, figures prominently in Rousseau's *Émile* and in Godwin's 'Political Justice' and indeed in the literature of anarchism generally.

> 'Spirit of Nature, all sufficing Power,
> Necessity, Thou mother of the World . . .'

It has an apparent clarity, until we recall that many occurrences that seem at first sight the product of non-human forces are contributed to (even if very indirectly) by human will. Complementary to the duty of accepting what providence sends is the duty of obeying the dictates of 'right reason', which is also of the

[6] Seneca: Naturales Quaestiones, II, xxxv–xxxviii.
[7] Seneca: *Ep*. 107.

nature of the universe or God, and therefore of man (since man is but part of the universe or God). The world is entirely perfect: its laws lie in impersonal necessity and 'right reason'. He who obeys both is free. What is freedom, asks Seneca? And he answers that it is 'not fearing either men or gods', 'not craving wickedness or excess' and 'possessing supreme power over oneself'. *Non homines timere, non deos; nec turpia velle nec nimia; in se ipsum habere maximam potestatem.*[8] It is true that in the *Naturales Quaestiones* Seneca says: 'When I shall treat of that question (destiny), I shall show how one can, without diminishing the power of destiny, accord something to the freewill of man'. It is equally true that he did not achieve his purpose.

The world is entirely perfect; yet, man is not perfect, but can become so.[9] The actual is the ideal, then, only in so far as men are purely rational. Man is rational, but men misuse their reason. The late eighteenth century, following the Stoic tradition, allowed the term, *natural*, to all those states or conditions the contrary of which the cosmic laws (as the thinker conceived them) do not enjoin. According to this usage, the products of human art are 'unnatural'—or, at any rate, those products which are not necessary to our conservation. Unthinking instinct and spontaneous emotion are 'natural'. The word, *natural*, when employed in this sense, signifies the primitive: that which exists anterior to civilisation, that which stands in contrast to the works of human art. In the making of this distinction, the Cynics were perhaps more extreme than the leading Stoics. The practice of making this contrast, so dear to the Stoics and to Rousseau, is a legacy of the cyclic theory of history, according to which mankind in its earliest days lived in happy simplicity, spontaneously obeying the laws of divine reason or providence which permeated the entire universe. These laws, on the human plane, were moral laws and obedience to them supplied man with all the requirements of happiness. All else is vanity. 'Inventions', says Seneca, 'come from reason of a sort, but not right reason': *Omina ista ratio quidem, sed non recta ratio commenta est.*[10] The true role of philosophy is the discernment of moral truth; this is the only thing 'right reason' is concerned with; all the rest is the work of 'reason of a sort' and its effects have led to the deterioration of the human race. To both Seneca and Cicero, the liberal arts with which the savants occupy themselves are, at best, mental sharpeners or preliminary exercises for the great work of pursuing true wisdom (which is the knowledge and practice of morality); they are a mere apprentice-

[8] *Ep.* 76.
[9] Cicero: *De natura Deorum*, II, xiv.
[10] *Ep.* 90.

G

ship to the real work. In themselves, they are *istaeque quidem artes, pusilla et puerilia*.[11] The true purpose of philosophy is the cultivation of good morals and not the enjoyment of intellectual adventure; intellectual activity is justifiable only in so far as it conduces to virtue; the calamitous effects of 'vain learning' and technology or 'inventions' the latter pandering to luxury, bodily ease and pleasure seemed as clear to Seneca as it did to Rousseau when he wrote his Discourse to the Academy of Dijon. Hence, the Stoic distinction between 'right reason' (*recta ratio*) and 'reason of a sort' (*ratio quidem*). The former is natural, the latter is debased and productive of evil. 'The voice of nature and that of reason', said Rousseau, 'never find themselves in contradiction, if man does not impose on himself needs which he is subsequently forced to prefer always to natural impulsion'. (Sur la Luxe, le Commerce et les Arts). 'Right reason', which is the law of all entitles in the universe, governing and regulating the ends of the specific actions and processes of everything, is intended by providence to govern man. It is a law of strict duty, a law which prescribes action untainted by suspicion of unworthy motive. Yet, it is broken by the mass of men. Rousseau found himself in a difficulty akin to that of the Stoics. He, like them, found a benevolent providence whose laws are calculated to keep the world in harmony. He, like them, found the world was not in harmony. At one time, it must have been. There must have been a Golden Age. Why did we leave it? It must have been due to Fate or to some initial human mistake. Some hypothesis must be found, to account for evil.

Faced as they were by this contradiction between the intention of a benevolent nature or immanent deity and the unhappy reality, it is not surprising that the Stoics resorted to the myth of the Golden Age. The world is in decline and has been so for ages past, ever since man disobeyed the law by seeking to make himself richer, more comfortable, more powerful. To do these things, he invented property, which gave rise to inequality, avarice, ambition; vice begot vice and the disorder which ensued made coercive government necessary. Hence, the degeneration of the present which stands out in such sad contrast to the goodness and happiness of an age long left behind. The idea of the Golden Age, in which the ideal natural law prevailed in all its completeness, securing the spontaneous and joyful obedience of all, so that the ideal justice was the actual in human interrelationships and the ideal harmony was the actual in society, is one of the most important of the legacies that Stoicism has left the world. It would

---

[11] *De Re Publica*, I, viii; *Ep.* 88.

not be too much to say that this myth has provided the exemplar of all the humanitarian utopias of western history: there was no evil and therefore no need for constraint, no coercive government, no private property, no envy, no friction.

Precise ideas of the human condition in that age of happiness varied somewhat among the Stoic writers. To Seneca, it was an age of childlike innocence in which reason was not needed. In the early days of man, there was no philosophy: it was unnecessary, for men obeyed instinctively the promptings of nature or providence. Those happy people held all things in common: there was therefore no scope for avarice. The earth was more productive, since it was used in the interests of all. There were no rich and no poor: all was divided in friendly fashion. Such being the spirit, there were no wars. All was safe and tranquil. Men did not huddle in luxurious houses, but lived where they chose under the trees or the open sky. They knew nothing of wealth and inflicted no needless cares on themselves. They freely accepted the leadership of the best among them. *Sed primi mortalium quique ex his geniti naturam incorrupti sequebantur, eundem habebant et ducem et legem, commissi melioris arbitrio.*[12] For these leaders, 'ruling was a service, not an exercise of royalty'; they owed their power to the people and never tried to use it against them. *Nemo quantum posset, adversus eos experiebatur, per quos coeperat posse, nec erat cuiquam aut animus in iniuriam aut causa, cum bene imperanti bene paretur nihilque rex maius minari male parentibus posset, quam ut abiret a regno.*[13] Seneca disagrees with Posidonius that wisdom was used in those remote times to promote comfort or develop the arts: the cult of comfort, science and art belongs to a later age and originated, not in philosophy, but in ingenuity. These matters are the body's business. The business of philosophy is with the soul: that is to say, with right living, the pursuit of morality, which nature dictates to us and from which these things are a distraction. *Non desiderabis artifices; sequere naturam. Illa noluit esse districtos.* The earliest men knew nothing of artifice, beyond the simplest. Their lives were excellent and guileless; they were 'fresh from the gods'—*a dis recentes.*[14] But although they followed the dictates of eternal reason in all things, they did so instinctively and without study. They were not virtuous, for virtue proceeds from the study and practice of morality, from the conscious and purposeful following of the precepts of 'right reason'. These happy people were merely innocent: they had never encountered evil.

Such was the life of the Golden Age, as Seneca conceived it.

[12] *Ep.* 90, 4.
[13] *Ibid.*, 5.
[14] *Ibid.*, 16, 44.

He does not indulge in any contemplation of that figment of Rousseau's imagination, the isolated man in the 'state of Nature'; but for Rousseau, too, the real Golden Age does appear to be the age of earliest society which immediately succeeded isolation. It is most remarkable that this ancient Stoic view should have been given by Rousseau with such memorable vehemence within two lifetimes of the theory of evolution, its very antithesis.

The ancient harmony came to an end when avarice broke in. *Inrupit in res optime positas avaritia et, dum seducere aliquid cupit atque in suum vertere, omnia fecit aliena et in angustum se ex immenso redigit.*[15] With avarice came private property; with property came inequality, poverty, luxury, vice and dissension. Vice and dissension created a need for laws and coercive government; government transformed itself into tyranny. So, having broken with Nature, mankind took its downward path.

Stoicism, because of its cyclic theory and its belief that mankind was on the decline, made of itself a socially conservative force: the immensity of present evil it regarded with a sense of impotence; the world being on a downward slope, a career whose progress human effort cannot stop, it is idle to think of general fundamental amelioration. The most that can be done in the conduct of public affairs is to check this downward rush in some measure by adapting positive enactment as far as possible to the demands of the ideal natural law (that is, the law of right reason). In order that the process of decline may be, as far as is humanly possible, arrested, coercive institutions are needed. To Cicero, the enlightened and virtuous mind 'is born to take part in the life of the State' (*cumque se ad civilem societatem natum senserit*) in order to promote what is honourable and check the wicked; to Seneca, 'the advantage of the State and that of the individual are yoked together' (*iuncta est privata et publica utilitas*) and the wise, who profit most by the security which the State gives them, 'must needs cherish as a father the author of this good' (*Necesse est auctorem huius boni ut parentem colant.*[16] Yet, rational as the coercive State may be, it owes its degree of rationality to corruption: it bears a taint. When the natural law reigned in all its fulness, the coercive State did not exist. Neither did private property nor the other artificial restrictions of contemporary fallen society. There was material in Stoicism that could be made explosive.

If the Stoics had, by assuming that the world was on an upward curve, transposed the Golden Age to the future, how different a force would the doctrine have become, politically and socially?

[15] *Ep.* 90, 38.
[16] Cicero: *De Legibus*, I., xxiv; *De Re Publica*, I, xx., etc.; Seneca, *Ep.* 66, 73.

Then, one might think, in place of the sense of impotence, there
would reign the exaltation of mind that distinguishes the revolutionary, the sense of complete certainty that the millenium
lay around the corner and the savage impatience with the human
shortcomings that delay its advent. Old Rome might have had her
Robespierres, St Justs and Bakunins, had her Stoics placed the
Golden Age in the future. But the old pagan world was incapable
of doing this. Its millenia all lay in the past: to die young was good,
not be born was best. Even to the deeply religious-minded Seneca,
who clung tightly to the consolations of philosophy, the world
was a darkening place.

> In nos aetas ultima venit;
> O, nos dura sorte creatos.[17]

The infinite sadness that underlies so much of ancient thought,
the daily experience of squalid evil, unrelieved by a supernatural
religion of hope, made exaltation of mind impossible. Furthermore,
the Stoics placed the Golden Age in the past and adopted their
semi-cyclic theory of history in order to account for the origin
and progress of evil. It remained to the post-Christian world,
with its distant recollections of the doctrine of the brotherhood of
man and the idea of future blessedness, to transpose the Golden
Age to the future. The ancient world had its palace-revolutions
and, in places, its ideas of social justice which sometimes issued in
class struggle, but it knew nothing of revolution in the modern
sense of the word, based on political or social doctrine: progress
in the sense of a continually ascending process of amelioration was
foreign to it. 'Christianity grown wild' combined with ancient
ideals to make the revolutionary creeds of the modern world,
every one of which has based itself ultimately on an optimistic
naturalism, a theory of progress, of evolution either of rationalised
matter or of materialised reason towards ever higher forms of life.

The pervading evil of the world drove the Stoic in upon himself.
The law of reason, no longer generally accepted, still existed and
could be discerned and followed by the individual who was
prepared to seek it. This entailed constant self-denial and self-
examination in the light of rational precepts. Philosophy, which is
essentially a guide to right conduct, has to be learned laboriously
in the decadent world in which we live; good conduct no longer
comes to us through our instincts, which are now corrupted; it is
no longer made easy by social pressures. But it is possible for
the individual to find wisdom and to live by it. Sanabilimus
aegrotamus malis; ipsaque nos in rectum natura genitos si emendari

17 Thyestes, in Thyestes-Phaedra, 877-9.

velimus, iuvat.[18] A man can be stronger than the world. The great mystification of all fatalistic systems has been the co-existence of fixed laws that determine the behaviour of the generality of mankind and of individuals who persist in defying these laws by exercising free choice. Mankind, according to the Stoics, is condemned by the historic process to deterioration. Yet, the Stoics remained, continuing to maintain the primitive values and to show how nature intended all men to live. The development of the intelligence and of the vices takes place, according to Rousseau, 'in direct proportion, the one to the other, not in the individuals, but in the peoples'.[19] This is the assumption on which the whole of *Émile* is based. Émile and Sophie were to be the exceptions from the lot of mankind and were to prove that the development of individual intelligence and sensibility is not necessarily accompanied by moral deterioration. The distinction between the individuals and the peoples is characteristically Stoic. The degeneration of mankind in general is explained in terms of the cyclic theory of history, but the existence of exceptions cannot, save on manichaean premises. God, nature and reason are one; the trilogy attains to self-consciousness in man.[20] But man, the highest manifestation of Deity, is deteriorating and increasingly defying the laws of Deity. The laws are eternal, but between them and the historic process there is perpetual conflict, a conflict which the laws are losing on the human plane. The logic of the system would seem to be that Deity embraces two conflicting principles: good and evil.

The Stoic response to the riddle which their beliefs set them was a mixed one: despair of the world and hope for the individual. In relation to the masses, the Stoic was the *Promeneur Solitaire* ('more alone than Robinson on his island'), for the masses have nothing to teach one. *Immo vero crudelior et inhumanior, quia inter homines fui*.[21] Yet, every man is rational and can follow the path of wisdom if he determines to do so. Chrysippus and other Stoics maintained that 'there is no root of evil in human nature' and that moral evil in each individual is due 'to the bad influence of society'.[22] Nature (that is to say, our rationality) gives each one of us the power to recognise true wisdom and to practise virtue, if only we would bend our wills that way. *Satis natura dedit roboris si illo utamur*.[23] Man is a social being and is consequently bound

---

[18] Seneca; *De Ira*, I., II., Ch. XIII, quoted as epigraph to *Émile*.
[19] Lettre à Christophe de Beaumont.
[20] Cicero: *De Natura Deorum*, II., liii.
[21] *Ep.* 7.
[22] Bevan: *Stoics and Sceptics*, p. 104.
[23] *Ep.* 104, etc.

by his nature to help others. The duty of self-conservation, which is the first and holiest of all, entails continual effort at moral self-improvement and moral self-improvement entails active benevolence towards others. *Alteri vivas oportet, si vis tibi viere.*[24] It is true that the 'natural man' of Rousseau's *Discours sur l'Origine de l'Inégalité* can scarcely be described as social, for he lives in virtually complete isolation and complete self-sufficiency. Yet, even in this extravaganza, Rousseau endows him with a 'natural pity which takes the place of laws' and goes on to transport him into the simple and innocent society described by Seneca in his picture of the Golden Age. Both Seneca and Rousseau more-over agree that the age of innocence can never be recalled and that the virtuous man is better off than the merely innocent. For both the virtuous man is social. For both, the pursuit of virtue lies along the path of self-conquest, the eschewing of vanities such as speculation for its own sake, the shunning of luxuries (for luxury enslaves the mind to the body), the practice of simple living. The sage does not need much. In their mistrust of speculation and their contempt for technological progress ('inventions'), Seneca and Rousseau are remarkably conservative. *Ommia ista ratio quidem, sed non recta ratio commenta est.*[25] 'I have made him feel that all the ideas which are wholesome and truly useful to men are the first that were known, that they have ever constituted the true bonds of society, and that all that is left for transcendent minds to do is to distinguish themselves by ideas which are pernicious and dangerous to the human race'.[26] And again, to the Academy of Dijon: 'See how luxury, debauchery and slavery have at all times been the chastisement of the proud efforts we have made to break out from the happy ignorance where the eternal wisdom placed us. The thick veil with which she covered all her operations seemed to turn us away, as if we were never destined for vain researches. But is it one of her lessons from which we have been able to profit, or one which we have been able to neglect with impunity. Peoples! Know that nature once wished to preserve you from science, as a mother snatches a dangerous firearm from the hands of her child; that all the secrets she hides from you are so many evils from which she keeps you, and that the trouble you find in instructing yourselves is not the least of her benefits. Men are per-verse; they would be worse still if they had the misfortune to be born learned.'[27] The notion, so fashionable in the days of the Enlighten-ment, that man could be trained to see what his 'true self-interest'

[24] *Ep.* 48.
[25] *Ep.* 90.
[26] *Emile.*
[27] *Discours a l'A. de Dijon.*

required and that knowledge of this requirement would necessarily ensure universal, indefinite progress in all spheres of life, moral, intellectual and technological, was rejected by Rousseau. Not for him the visions of a Condorcet or a Godwin. The role of 'right reason', Rousseau would agree with Seneca in asserting, is to discern moral truths; it shuns the vanities of speculation for its own sake and the base pandering to comfort and ambition in which a *ratio quidem* ('reason of a sort.') has been employed throughout the ages of decadence. Truly enlightened self-interest, Rousseau would agree, would dictate the same course as 'right reason', but mankind, having put itself under the dominion of the debased *ratio quidem*, cannot be relied on to discover the requirements of true self-interest. 'Human reason', he says, 'is in my eyes by this time so feeble and so miserable that I do not think it possible to demonstrate its proper feebleness'.[28] The dreams of the Enlightenment are delusory. If a future of happiness is to be sought for mankind, it must be one in which morality will reign throughout the whole of society, to the exclusion of all vanities. The wise man can achieve happiness for himself by following the promptings of 'right reason', but the generality of mankind is incapable of doing this unless it auto-limits itself: that is to say, unless it places itself in a position in which the demands of 'right reason' are enforced upon it and in which it comes to love them and obey them freely in course of time. Men can auto-limit themselves to the practice of virtue (compliance with the demands of 'right reason') only be placing themselves under an infallible authority upon which no restriction is imposed, for infallibility should not be restricted. *Tuto enim quantum vult potest, qui se nisi quod debet non putat posse.*[29] The readiness to submit to such an authority can be brought about only by the sentiment of sociability, the only true guide to virtue left to the generality of men, and the submission is achieved by the Social Contract, which sets up the Sovereign People as the infallible lawmaker. The Contract can be made only where the social sense of men is strongest and where the associates can gather together to make laws: that is to say, in the small region. The generality of men recognise justice only when its demands are supported by the sentiment of sociability: they do not see it in the abstract. 'All justice comes from God: He alone is its source. But, if we knew how to receive it from so high a source, we should need neither government nor laws. Without doubt, there is a universal justice, emanating from reason alone: but that justice, to be admitted

[28] Pensées Detachés.
[29] *Ep.* 90.

among us, should be reciprocal. Humanly speaking, the laws of justice, failing a natural sanction, are vain among men; they wreak only the advantage of the wicked and the misfortune of the just, since the latter observes them in his relations with everyone, while no one observes them towards him.'[30] The generality does not recognise the demands of justice because they have been corrupted by the *ratio quidem*, the debased 'reason of a sort', which promotes selfishness and the pursuit of the private or particular interest. The greater the number of men, the greater the sway of corrupting influences: the less chance of the operation of justice. The will of the majority, therefore, is not always necessarily right; even the will of all is not necessarily so. There has been much mystification on the subject of Rousseau's conception of the General Will. It is not necessarily the will of the majority, nor even the will of all. Only when corrupting influences are absent, or only in so far as they are absent, does the General Will emerge. And it can do this unfailingly only in a small, homogeneous community of simple and uncorrupted people, a people so devoted to the welfare of the group, that that group constitutes a *moi commun*, a moral person. In these circumstances, justice will always emerge: 'it is necessary only to be just in order to follow the General Will.'[31] The General Will, then, is the expression of 'right reason' (*recta ratio*), in the Stoic sense: that is to say, reason untinged in its operation by any unworthy motive. This, in turn, is 'the voice of Nature', since Nature and reason 'never find themselves in contradiction'.[32] This, then, is how we 'receive justice from so high a source'. 'The voice of the People is the voice of God.' In these circumstances, the lawmaker, the Sovereign People, needs no restriction: the infallible should not be restricted. In the ideal State, the sovereignty of the People is absolute. It can harm none of its members, because in doing so, it would harm itself, which is impossible. It would, of its nature, enforce only the demands of 'right reason', and in enforcing them, it would cause men to love these demands, through their experience of the happiness that follows compliance. Living under the rule of 'right reason' would be truly living according to Nature, since 'right reason' comes from Nature.

Both as to the goal of humanity and as to the means of reaching it, Rousseau is at variance with the Enlightenment. The goal is not mastery of the universe, but mastery of the self. The future of humanity is not to be a race of gods, but one of virtuous, undemanding men. And the means of reaching it is to shun the

[30] *Contrat Social*, 1. II, ch. VI.
[31] *Economie Politique*, p. 184.
[32] *Ibid.*, 177.

allurements of debased reason and follow the sentiment of sociability, that instinct which has come down to us with the least corruption from the early days of man.

In discussing Rousseau's debt to the Stoics, one is concerned with his ideas, as distinct from his life, which was not remarkably stoical. He was a man of acute tension: his mind partly formed in the calvinistic atmosphere of the city of Geneva to which he and his forbears belonged and by his absorption of stoical ideas in various modifications, which would have been congenial to the puritanically-formed:

> 'D'Epictète asservi la stoique fierte
> M'apprend a supporter les maux, la pauvreté'[33]

His nature was weak, his imagination lively, and the result was a heavy sentimentality. Everything had to be excused: evey situation had to have its ingredients of modesty, purity and innocence; every misfortune to the hero had to be due to external circumstances. It is not surprising, then, that his moral ideals should have been pitched very high and that the professors of these ideals in their severest form, the Stoics, should have had a special attraction for Rousseau. Their austerity, their integrity and their personal independence were the things he envied most. The attainment of perfect morality without effort, as in the state of innocence, or as part of the collectivity, was a dream which was certain to attract him. A Stoic would have abhorred the notion of absorption in the mass as an abdication of personal responsibility and might well have argued, as Godwin did, that there is no easy, automatic coincidence of absolute moral excellence with the decisions of any collectivity, however well-intentioned and homogeneous. For the Stoic, the romantic dream of the Golden Age was over and life was a stern test. Rousseau agreed, and could speak as eloquently as any Stoic of the beauty of virtue: the *Émile* is a prescription for the education of a Stoic of the Senecan stamp, combining absolute rectitude with a high degree of sensibility; the picture of the Man of Nature, withdrawn from and independent of externals, might well have been drawn in part from Seneca; the despair of reforming a corrupt world, the very definition of Nature (short of identifying God with the universe, although the overtones are sometimes pantheistic) and the dichotomy of its benevolent laws and the course of criminal folly which mankind has pursued: these outstanding features of Stoic thought formed the inspiration of Rousseau's themes. Indeed, as early as 1766, Dom Cajot hastily concluded that Rousseau was

[33] Oeuvres, VI.

only 'a shameless and unskilful plagiarist of Seneca'.[34] And Diderot says: 'If we dare to prefer the manner of the philosopher to that of the orator, this is less the fault of the author of the *Essais* (Diderot): it is that of Jean-Jacques, who recalls Seneca to us at a hundred points, and who does not owe Cicero a line.'[35]

To trace briefly the ancestry of Rousseaus' outstanding ideas from external evidence, one might quote, first, the same Diderot: 'I shall cite only one of them (the French authors): it is M. Rousseau of Geneva. It would be easy to prove that he owes to Seneca, to Plutarch, to Montaigne, to Locke and to Sidney the greatest part of the philosophical ideas and the principles of morality and politics which have been most praised in his writings: he even owes to Seneca some of his sophisms and of his strangest paradoxes; that is a source from which, if I may use the expression of Montaigne, he has drawn like the Danaids, filling and pouring without cease.'[36] Next, one might cite Montaigne: 'As for my other reading, in which the pleasure is more tinged with profit and whereby I learn to order my opinions and behaviour, the books which serve me best are Plutarch—now that he is translated into French—and Seneca. I never seriously settled myself to any works of solid learning except these. Like the Danaids, I am forever filling and pouring from them. . . . Plutarch and Seneca agree in most of their soundest opinions. . . . Their teachings are the cream of philosophy—at once simple and pertinent.'[37]

It is true that Plutarch does not belong to the Stoic school; indeed, he rejected the elements of determinism in the system and reacted against the excessive severity of its ideas of virtue; nevertheless, he accepted the Stoic belief in a particular Providence and always emphasised personal responsibility, which the Stoics (despite their fundamental determinism) never ceased to do, and he shared with them their cult of fortitude and nobility of character. In practical matters, his attitude might be described as modifiedly Stoic; his insight on human nature is as remarkable as Seneca's. It is not surprising, then, that the success of Plutarch should have been linked with that of Seneca and that the term, 'plutarchian stoicism' should have been used.[38] Even after his reaction against the severities ('the arrogance of Stoicism, which developed in the 1560's. Montaigne continued to hold Seneca in affection and to think of him, less as a master of Stoicism than

---

[34] *Les Plagiats de M. J.-J. Rousseau de Genève sur l'Education.*
[35] *Essais sur les Règnes de Claude et de Neron.*
[36] *Essais sur les R. de C. et de N.*
[37] Autobiography.
[38] Ernest Seillière: *Les Origines Romanesques de la Morale et de la Politique Romantiques.*

as a *médecin des ames*.') This role of guide and counsellor to friends is one which M. Thomas sees Seneca and Rousseau both filling.[39] The charm of Seneca seems to stem from his kindliness and his sureness of touch in penetrating the heart: so it seemed to the eighteenth century, when his vogue, a little diminished in the late seventeenth, revived and assumed great proportions. Montaigne's 'retreat from Stoicism' brought with it a decline of faith in reason, a pessimistic view of the sciences and philosophy (even moral philosophy), an envy of the happiness of the ignorant and the tranquil patience of the poor. *Nature* is all that which has not been contaminated by human art, but right reason is natural, since it comes from Nature.[40] The happy man follows Nature and has no pretensions to science or philosophy. The noble savage is free from the diseases of our civilisation. ('A Man from the New World'). This is a deviation from Stoicism; yet, the points from which the deviation was made are clearly recognisable. Equally clearly is Rousseau's indebtedness: 'Rousseau', says Faguet, 'is an unbalanced Montaigne'.[41]

It is true that Rousseau is more explicit in acknowledging his debt to Plutarch than to Seneca. This is clearly due to the similarity of the political antecedents of Plutarch and Rousseau: they were both the products of small communities—Plutarch of Chaeronea, Rousseau of Geneva. Municipal life still flourished in Greece and Plutarch spent most of his life in his native town, to the affairs of which he gave a whole lifetime's devoted service. The tone of his writings is municipal: he was imbued with a very strong local patriotism, which could not but make its mark on his political philosophy. The contemporary Roman Stoic—such as Seneca—lived in a great cosmopolis, the centre of a vast empire in which nationalist prejudices were disappearing. The developing cosmopolitanism inevitably reinforced the basic universalism of Roman Stoicism. Rousseau's forbears had been prominent in the affairs of the city-state of Geneva and he never lost his local patriotism. 'That news', he wrote of the announcement of the award of the Academy of Dijon, 'reawoke all the ideas that had been dictated to me, it animated me with a new force and put in fermentation in my heart that first leaven of heroism and of virtue which my father and my country and Plutarch had put there in my childhood'.[42] The patriot-hero, austere, devoted and generous, would appeal to both Stoic and Romantic. Furthermore, Plutarch himself was, like Seneca, a merciful and kindly man.

[39] P. Thomas: *Senèque et Rousseau.*
[40] *Les Sources et l'Evolution des Essais de Montaigne:* Pierre Villey.
[41] *Rousseau Penseur.*
[42] Rousseau: *Confessions.*

The Church in Italy in the Fifteenth Century

Denys Hay

I propose in this paper to give a synoptic view of my subject, hoping that I may one day have an opportunity for a more detailed analysis. I shall concentrate on those features which I believe may be less familiar to you, but nevertheless I fear that what follows may be criticised for being too descriptive. We are in the depths of the examination season and it strikes me that the question I have set myself can only be too readily answered, not by an argument, but by 'writing down all I know about the matter'—a horrid sort of question, which all good examiners try to avoid. Yet its avoidance depends on the subject having been so studied and discussed in the past that one can profitably be argumentative about it. Such is, unfortunately, not the case with the history of the Church in Italy.

My interest in the church and clergy of Italy goes back for some years and originated in a desire to isolate a large literate class (or a class which ought to have been literate) and see how it reacted to the new values of the humanists. In fact it has gradually been borne in on me that this involves a major effort at understanding the church and the clergy in the peninsula since there is no adequate up-to-date account on which to rely. Italy lacks a Hamilton Thompson and a Knowles. There are, of course, good reasons why this is the case. The first is the facile identification of the Italian church with the papacy. In the general histories of the church, such as that edited by Fliche and Martin, while there are sections on the church in France, Germany, Spain and so on, there is no account of the church in Italy—only of the vicissitudes of popes and curia. Now popes and curia are important, and perhaps especially so to the Italian clergy, but they are not to be identified with the *ecclesia italica* as such, with the church of the 'Italian nation', so feared by other 'nations' during the general councils of the early fifteenth century. Certainly the 'Italic church' (if I may invent some jargon) is not the same

99

sort of creature as the Gallican church at this time, nor as the Anglican church.[1] Both these churches may be regarded as expressions, in the ecclesiastical field, of the strong monarchy which was found in these two countries—in despite sometimes of weak kings. In the political sense, there was no Italy until the nineteenth century. In so far as the popes resolutely resisted all attempts at unification they had, it is true, a negative influence on the whole Italian scene, but it would be absurd to equate the history of the one with the history of the other. Even at the end of the fifteenth century there was much curial business concerning, much papal involvement in, matters to do with Christendom at large. Problems of documentations also make it difficult to investigate the structure and personnel of the Italic Church. The great archives of the Vatican are accessible but—so far as Italy is concerned—very imperfectly studied for later medieval times. Teams of scholars have tried to gut the main series for material bearing on Britain, but no-one has done the same for any significant diocese or group of dioceses in Italy.[2] Much of this work could be done readily enough, for the documents often indicate the diocese in the margin, and some of the great indices are arranged by dioceses.[3] But there are so many dioceses that it would be an extremely long if not a hard task.

The multiplicity of dioceses constitutes a further impediment. There were between 285 and 289 bishoprics in mainland Italy in the fifteenth century—almost as many as in the countries of western Christendom put together. Most of these still exist, but the state of their archives is known only in part, and there is some evidence that for this period there is nothing of value surviving in about half the total. Beyond that, many of the diocesan acts which in an English see were conveniently registered and preserved in the bishop's chancery, were in Italy attested by notaries and may have to be hunted down in notarial archives. The overall view of the clergy which is possible in pre-Reformation England through bishops' registers is, therefore, hardly to be attained in Italy—or at any rate will never be as securely founded on a wide range of factual information, even if a determined effort was made to investigate local ecclesiastical archives.[4]

[1] For the sake of brevity I refer to my discussion in *History*, liii (1968), 35–50 where a fuller bibliography will be found.
[2] See the bibliography (which in the nature of things has become out of date) in Fliche et Martin (eds.), *Histoire de l'Église*, vols. xiv, xv (Paris, 1962–4) and that in G. Mollat, *Les Papes d'Avignon*, 9th ed. (Paris, 1949).
[3] E.g. the *Schedario* of Cardinal Garampi.
[4] For some reflections on the episcopal archives in England and Italy see R. Bretano, *Two Churches: England and Italy in the Thirteenth Century* (Princeton, 1968) and the same author's 'Bishops' Books of Città di Castello', *Traditio* 16 (1960), 241–254.

The state of these archives—so imperfectly preserved if compared with those of the Vatican itself or of the Italian States—has long given cause for concern. The canonical obligation to keep records carefully is ancient and was explicitly rehearsed in the *Codex* of 1917-8.[5] Long before this popes and their advisers tried to apply stricter procedures to the archives of the bishoprics of Italy. That their efforts met with little response may be inferred from the need to repeat the orders and exhortations and from the establishment in 1955 of a papal commission charged with the supervision of local ecclesiastical archives in Italy.[6] It remains to be seen what effect this will have.

In view of the scattered sources, even less well catalogued and even less accessible in earlier centuries than in our own, the achievement of the Cistercian abbot Ferdinand Ughelli in publishing his *Italia Sacra* (Rome, 1643-62) deserves the highest praise. It was an astonishing performance, which did something to foster Italian self-consciousness, though this was not Ughelli's aim; and of course it led to similar books being compiled for every other large country in Europe. Ughelli's work was republished, extended in time to his own day, but not otherwise much improved, by Nicola Coleti (Venice, 1717-22). Since then, although the early history of some of the dioceses has been reinvestigated in a thoroughly scholarly way, nothing of a general kind has been attempted. G. Moroni in his dictionary (Venice, 1840-61) is entirely dependent on Ughelli when traversing similar territory; G. Cappelletti's *Le chiese d'Italia* (Venice, 1844-79) paraphrases Ughelli in Italian and for all practical purposes may be forgotten. I said that Italians neglect the history of their own church. Nothing illustrates this better than their neglect, at any rate until recently,[7] of Ughelli himself. Centenary conferences are a great feature of the Italian scene. Muratori, who was a very great man, had the anniversary of his death celebrated in a conference in 1950, and in 1972 another gathering saluted his birth with further oratory and erudition. Yet the three hundredth centenary of Ughelli's death in 1670 passed unobserved and his tomb at the Tre Fontane is hard to find.[8] We shall have to wait until the anniversary of his birth in 1595 to do him honour.

Some steps have been taken to remedy this situation. In 1946

---

[5] The present pope, when Cardinal Montini, provided an authoritative statement in *Archiva Ecclesiae* ii (1959), 43–55.

[6] For a description of these attempts see the account of the present prefect of the Vatican Archives, Mons. M. Giusti, *ibid.*, 149–157.

[7] Some welcome interest in Ughelli is now evident; his letters have been indexed by Dr. G. Morelli.

[8] A draft for the inscription is in Vat. Lib., MS. Barberini 3239, fo. lll. Cf. Ughelli-Coleti, i. sig.** [3].

the *Rivista della storia della chiesa in Italia* made its appearance. From the group of friends who inspired and collaborated in this venture other related activities have sprung—a series of conferences dealing with major problems of Italian church history, and a series of books under the general heading, reminiscent of Ughelli, 'Italia Sacra'.[9] All of this, one may hope, will in the end make it possible to generalise with greater security regarding Italian church history, and will enable the many valuable regional studies, the many researches promoted by religious orders on their own history, to be absorbed with a wide pattern of description, analysis and narrative. Some of the present difficulties will emerge in what follows.

The popes and the papal curia of the fifteenth century have been much studied since the time when Pastor published his first volume in 1886. And yet much remains to be done, not least from the point of view of the Italian church. The popes were Italians after 1417,[10] when the Schism ended, and, especially after Pius II, their public interests were largely bounded by Italian dynastic policies. Yet the Italian side of papal activity in the XV century has not been sufficiently analysed, and we have little save a few works bearing on diplomatic activity.[11] This is a pity. There is little doubt that the persistent activity in the field of church reform of Eugenius IV was more effective than is often supposed; and there is no doubt that this reform was restricted to Italy. One might go further and note that Eugenius IV had been a protegé of another Venetian pope, Gregory XII; and that Eugenius promoted the Venetian Barbo who was to become Pope Paul II, another man of principle. Venetian popes in the fifteenth century had certainly a more beneficial influence on the Italian clergy than the Tuscans, the Ligurians, or the Catalans.

As for the central offices of the Church, chancery, camera, Rota, and the rest, they were certainly not staffed exclusively by Italians, but Italians monopolised them.[12] This had a marked influence on the Italian church. It meant that Italians regarded the curia as their personal preserve, which was, of course, another reason for Rome being hated in trans-Alpine lands. It meant that the sale of offices, that new fiscal device pioneered by the

[9] Cf. Paolo Sambin, 'Nuove iniziative di pubblicazioni di storia della chiesa in Italia', *Archiva Ecclesiae, ubi supra*, 179–188.
[10] Except for Calixtus III (Borja, 1455–8) and Adrian VI (Dedel, 1522–3).
[11] Fifteenth century popes have not attracted the biographer, save for an extensive literature dealing with Pius II and—very recently—the work on Eugenius IV by Father J. Gill, S. J. (London, 1961).
[12] See the lists in W. v. Hofmann, *Forschungen zur Geschichte der Kurialen Behörden vom Schisma bis zur Reformation*, ii (Rome, 1914).

papacy, produced a breed of bureaucrats who hungered for the fruits of proximity to the plenitude of power—men who wanted for themselves and their relatives the comfortable prelacies of the Italian church. Even the uncomfortable and penurious sees were worth having for they enabled their possessors to parade with enhanced grandeur down the corridors of Vatican power. So a very large proportion of the senior church appointments in all parts of Italy, but especially in the so-called 'Roman' province itself and the Papal States, went to clergymen who were papal servants and sometimes never saw their sees from beginning to end.

The bishoprics of Italy were extremely thick on the ground, as I have said. They were not only numerous, but they were, partly because they were small in extent, especially in south Italy, poor by comparison with those in Northern Europe. Two fifths of them were assessed for common services at less than 100 florins, another two fifths were assessed between 100 and 500 florins and only a fifth had assessments higher than that.[13] This is even lower than the assessments in Ireland, where the average was 227 florins, if only because Armagh, Meath and Dublin were judged to be relatively rich. But the churches of Ireland were both numerous and poor by comparison with the rest of North Europe; the average assessment of sees in England and Wales were over 4000 florins.

However poor, these Italian churches never lacked aspirants; since residence was not required the poorer sees were treated as being almost *in partibus* and the mendicants who often held them acted as vicars in spirituals for their better off brethren in the north of Italy. Of course the assessed revenue is only a rough indication of the real revenue of a bishop's *mensa*. Since the camera seldom varied its assessments it was possible to find a bargain and this no doubt explains some of the mysterious chopping about one can find recorded in Eubel's *Hierarchia catholica* for the fifteenth century. There are some remarkable examples of exchanges, unparalleled, so far as I know, elsewhere in Christendom. Let me give two of the score of examples that I have noted. Dr Agnese Troilo, nephew of a cardinal and bishop of Penne and Atri since October 1482, in December 1483 exchanged his see with Dr Matteo Giudici, bishop of Telese since 1464. Agnese Troilo is at it again in 1487, when he exchanges Telese for the threadbare bishopric of Lavello, whose bishop, a Franciscan theologian called Pietro Pallargio, must have enjoyed the greater

[13] H. Hoberg, *Taxae pro communibus servitiis . . . ab anno 1295 usque ad annum 1455 . . .*, Città del Vaticano, 'Studi e Testi' 144, 1949. Note that these assessments were originally made in the XIII century and were seldom revised later.

H

revenues of his new diocese. Here is the episcopal career of Nicolò Ippolito, who became bishop of Ariano (prov. Benevento) in 1480; the next year he was translated to the penurious archbishopric of Rossano (assessed at 25 florins, and with no suffragans in his so-called province); thence he went in 1493 to the lusher living of Città di Castello, being compensated for the loss of his southern archbishopric by promotion at the same time to the titular metropolitan dignity of Caesarea. Finally our archbishop *in partibus* lost this honour in 1496 and, stranger still, returned to his first bishopric in 1498, holding it until his death in 1511.[14] I believe such goings on are uniquely Italian. Doubtless an encouragement to these practices was the extreme unimportance of the metropolitan in the Italian church—an archbishop had no significant power, only grandeur. Another encouragement was the very large number of bishoprics in Italy which were immediately subject to the Holy See, almost a third of the total.[15] To many Italian sees the pope nominated freely but those immediately subject were especially at his disposal.

The question of papal provision raises another Italian phenomenon: the tangled relationship between pope and lay power in a land where, since the pope was resident, the rapacious legislation of the Avignon period had more bearing than elsewhere. Kings outside Italy secured the bishops of their choice without real papal interference, as they had done for centuries; the pope in compensation was allowed to collect common services. In Italy the case was different. Here the pope was a political force and bishops were often pawns in a political game. Likewise the curia and, by the second half of the fifteenth century, the college of cardinals had attracted the ambitions of the leading Italian political powers, republics and principalities. There was no overt challenge to the papal right to reservation and provision. But as the century went on it became increasingly hard for the pope to get his own way in the case of sees situated in the lands of the tougher republics such as Venice or the tougher princes such as the Sforza rulers of Milan. It was not always a case of the state simply brushing aside a papal nominee; that the pope had provided a man was recognised in Milan or Venice as constituting a very real problem; the prelate so provided did not always wish to withdraw, even when the pope had agreed to a change. Sometimes a long period went by before the prelate would be found an alternative promotion to his liking. Often the most elaborate negotiations dragged on for years—the state refusing to admit

[14] See C. Eubel, *Hierarchia catholica* ii. (Munster, 1914), under relevant dioceses.
[15] See the Provinciale in Hoberg, which is more accurate that that in Eubel.

the papally-provided candidate to get at his revenues, the pope trying to offer inducements to make the government pliant.[16] One example must suffice. In March 1471, towards the end of his pontificate, the Venetian Paul II gave the bishopric of Verona *in commendam* to Cardinal Giovanni Michiel; the patriarchate of Aquileia to Cardinal Marco Barbo; and the bishopric of Vicenza to Cardinal Battista Zeno. All the recipients were Venetians, nephews of the pope, promoted to the red hat by Paul, and none met with favour in Venice. The Senate at first refused to allow possession to all three. It relented in the case of Barbo, after six months, but at the same time the Dieci ordered the sequestration of all Zeno's benefices. Some years of tortured negotiation followed. Finally, in April 1476, five years after the papal provision, the Senate finally accepted the bulls for Michiel and Zeno—but only as of that moment. That is to say the temporal revenues of the bishoprics of Verona and Vicenza had been confiscated by the Signory and (it was claimed) spent on the war against the Turks.[17] I can think of no northern parallel to this type of tug-of-war. Nor outside Italy do we find many capitular elections at this late date. They are certainly not excessively rare in Italy, even if they sometimes occur because the local power found it a useful way of bringing pressure to bear on the pope, or—when political control of a town had changed hands—on the bishop who had been the nominee of the discomfited party.[18]

This brief discussion of one aspect of the relations of Church and State in the peninsula has brought us to the bishops and I propose now to consider the clergy in Italy beginning with their pastors. Their pastors, as I have indicated, were extremely numerous. Who were they? The answer depends partly on the richness and political sensitivity of the see and on the region involved. In the larger dioceses of the north—Milan is the main example— the local prince ensured the appointment of a member of his family or of some other client. Likewise the Visconti and later

---

[16] This kind of transaction has been much studied. See, for instance, Luigi Fumi, 'Chiesa e stato nel dominio di Francesco I Sforza', *Arch. stor. Lombardo*, li (1924), 1–74, and C. Cenci, 'Senato Veneto—"Probae" ai benefizi ecclesiastici', *Spicilegium Bonaventurianum* iii. (1968), 313–454.

[17] Cenci, *op. cit.*, 401–2.

[18] Capitular elections are prescribed in the bulls establishing the unions of dioceses Nepe and Sutri in 1435 (Ughelli ii. 202) and of Città Castellana with Orte in 1439 (Ughelli ii. 166) and there is much scattered evidence for actual elections. At Chiusi in 1410 the canons asked for a *congé d'élire* from the magistrates at Siena, Ughelli iii. 642–3. Nicolò Albergati was elected by the citizens of Bologna on the death of the previous bishop, 3 January 1417; two days later he was elected by the canons in chapter, who sought and obtained confirmation from the archbishop of Ravenna. P. de Töth, *Il beato cardinale N. Albergati e i suoi tempi 1375–1444* 2 vols. (Viterbo? 1934?), i. 99–152. There was, of course, no pope at this particular moment. Martin V was elected at Constance on 11 November 1417.

the Sforza did their best to have their nominees placed in subject cities as the frontiers of their dominions fluctuated. And their servants at the Roman curia were not entirely forgotten, though they were never remembered sufficiently to satisfy them. The result of this was the provision by the pope of many scores of bishops who were political placemen, many of whom were non-resident. This together with the bishops provided from the ranks of the curia, meant that a very large number of Italian sees were occupied by extremely able men, who had climbed to promotion through their wits, and by well-connected men, also for the most part well-enough educated. But the point is fairly academic, since they merely drew revenues from their sees and did not serve in person. The shepherds actually visible to the Italian flock were the vicars in spirituals of these successful operators—the bishops *in partibus* and bishops of miserable south Italian sees, who earned their living by doing the jobs that only a bishop could do. These men were overwhelmingly members of the mendicant orders, mainly Franciscans. Usually they are shadowy figures, glimpsed only in some notarial instrument as they ordain clergy, or act as proctors in litigation concerning their masters.

In these circumstances the average Italian bishopric of the fifteenth century was deprived of real leadership and some—especially in the south—must have had virtually no episcopal control whatever. The consequences were that visitations seldom took place and the quality of clergy steadily declined. Some visitations there were, which I shall mention in a moment. But in general the cathedral clergy went on their quarrelsome way, the parishes in the towns developed or decayed, and rural clergy behaved as they pleased, without much interference by the ordinary. As for preparing clergy for ordination, the prescriptions of the Lateran council of 1215 had never meant much in Italy, where theology only gradually enters the indifferent universities towards the end of the fifteenth century. Most priests were educated by being apprenticed to a local parson, often a relative, and were presented for ordination—usually to an auxiliary bishop who did not conduct a real examination, or to the officials of the curia where large numbers of Italians and foreigners were ordained in the most perfunctory way down to 1510.[19] Something was being done to remedy this state of affairs—some seminaries were founded in Italy after the Schism, of which the most famous was the Collegio Capranica in Rome which still exists and still trains

---

[19] This is to be justified by a study of the fourteen volumes (1425–1524) of the 'libri formatorum' in the Secret Vatican Archives, which I plan shortly to publish. Meanwhile see L. Schmitz in *Römische Quartalschrift* viii (1894), 451–472.

priests.[20] But Cardinal Capranica was no ordinary prelate and few bishops followed his lead until Trent made such institutions obligatory. As for the laity, what did they know of their bishop? Episcopal confirmation seems to have been erratic and rare everywhere in medieval Christendom. Usually the laymen only saw his pastor in the bigger towns where it was customary, even for a bishop with no intention of residing, to make a ceremonial entry into his diocese and into his cathedral. Such occasions were moments of great civic rejoicing and panoply, regulated by minutely prescribed traditions, marked by elaborate processions involving clergy, magistrates and guilds.[21] But then the great man went away again—back to the curia, or on an embassy for his prince.

Chapter organisation was also disrupted by absenteeism, since the lusher canonries went to successful clerical opportunists. The matter is complicated and, since chapter organisation was very different from northern Europe, it is not easy to generalise. It seems certain that the hold of noble families on specific prebends and dignities was growing at this time;[22] it seems certain that absenteeism involved greater importance for the lesser cathedral clergy, often present in the flesh unlike their betters;[23] and—for reasons already mentioned—there are moments when the chapter acts with unaccustomed energy to elect a bishop, or at any rate to act as though this was spontaneous assertion of canonical independence. Much work, however, will have to be done before the role of canons and other cathedral dignitaries emerges distinctly for this period.[24] We may note that many chapters at this time embarked on major architectural innovations in all parts of Italy. The *opera del duomo* has been studied in very few centres as yet.

When we turn from the cathedral to the parishes we do not experience (as we do in England) the same sense of sharp distinction between large and smaller churches. Parish structure in Italy had followed a very different path from that found in the North. The cathedral itself in theory and often still in practice dominated the parishes of its own town and its *contado*. The

[20] On Capranica the only (but unsatisfactory) study remains, M. Morpurgo-Castelnuovo, 'Il Cardinale Domenico Capranica', *Archivio della R. Soc. Romana di Storia Patria*, lii. (1929), 1–146.
[21] Often, especially in smaller sees, the new bishop took possession through a proctor.
[22] Cf. Ughelli iii. 284 (Pistoia); iv. 731 (Forlì).
[23] Cf. Ughelli iii. 682–9 (Grosseto).
[24] For details of chapters see e.g. Ughelli ii. 515 (Ferrara), iv. 521 (Brescia); and for Milan, C. Castiglioni, 'Gli ordinari della metropolitana attraverso i secoli', *Memorie storiche della diocesi di Milano*, i (1954), 11–56.

visible sign of this was the baptistery. Only in the cathedral and its baptistery could the infants of the area be baptised—and only at certain defined periods of the year.[25] This situation changed slowly in some centres and by the fifteenth centuries many chapters had become parish churches in the full sense (with a font) and their chaplains were parish priests, able to baptise and hear confessions, as well as say mass. It seems likely that the main pressure behind the securing of independence was popular sentiment.[26] The development of town parishes is paralleled in rural areas, where the typical organisation of an earlier period was a *pieve*, organised as a chapter composed of clergy serving dependent chapelries. We again see the emergence of separate parishes, under the impulse of the *filii ecclesiae*, the lay sons of the church.[27] Two points should be borne in mind regarding parochial organisation in Italy: the dominant position of the cathedral as mother church was in part a function of the relatively small size of the diocese: sometimes the areas were minute.[28] And the number of 'churches', in both town and county was very high. There were 52 'parish churches' in Verona,[29] at the end of the fourteenth century there were 260 'churches' in Bologna itself (not including convents) and in the diocese of Bologna there were 648 'churches' in 44 parishes.[30] It would, of course, be wrong to imagine that these many churches were all served by fully ordained priests. When we can glimpse the real situation we find a pullulating mass of undifferentiated 'clerks', *chiericati*, some resident in capitular parish churches, others non-resident; churches are often without a priest, or share a priest with other churches; there is evidence of churches becoming so dilapidated as to be useless; there is evidence of gross superstition and ignorance among so-called clergy and people.

The training and promotion of the clergy was fitful, and as already noted, was commonly by apprenticeship. Ordination was often by a bishop *in partibus*, or by a complacent and busy prelate

[25] P. Sambin, *L'ordinamento parrochiale di Padova nel medio evo*, R. Università di Padova, Pubblicazioni della facoltà di lettere e filosofia xx. (Padua, 1941), p. 85.
[26] *Id.*, 'Studi di storia ecclesiastica medioevale', Dep. di storia patria per le Venezie, *Miscellanea di studi e memorie* ix.1. (Venice, 1954), pp. 1–60.
[27] *Ibid.*, p. 15.
[28] For most of Italy one can now consult the maps associated with the *Rationes decimae* volumes published in the 'Studi e Testi' series.
[29] Maria Billi, 'Origine e sviluppo delle parrochie di Verona e variazione nelle relative circonscrizioni territoriali', *Archivio Veneto*, ser. 5, xxix. (1941), 1–61.
[30] Tommaso Casini, 'Sulla costituzione ecclesiastica del Bolognese: I. L'elenco nonantolana del 1366', *Atti e memorie della R. Deputazione di storia patria per Romagna*, ser. 4, vi. (1916), 94–134; 'II. Il campione vescovile del 1378', *ibid.*, 361–402.

at the Roman curia.[31] As for the gift of a benefice, bishops were obtaining more and more patronage in the later Middle Ages,[32] though there were still many parishes where patronage lay in the hands of the parishioners—and this was notably the case in Venice.[33] It is the case that in ordination lists (and a good many of these have survived) the 'title', which was canonically required before major orders could be conferred, is often not recorded, even in the case of ordinations to the priesthood.[34]

We may guess that, by comparison with many other parts of Christendom, the number of secular clergy in Italy was very high—the number of men, that is to say, who were technically and for certain legal or social or economic reasons *clerks* as well as those fully ordained and with a proper benefice, with or without cure of souls. Similarly one has the impression that the number of religious was probably a good deal higher in Italy than it was in other areas.[35] The history of religious Orders in Italy has been much more fully written about than the history of the secular churches. This is because, while only a few dioceses have any adequate programme of historical research or publication, all the main orders maintain historical scholarship at a very high standard, much of it directly bearing on the Italian scene and the later Middle Ages. Sometimes, indeed, the ransacking of archives results only in biographical studies which lack (so it seems to me) much significance, showing a modest enough return for so much labour. One would welcome more general impressions of a larger kind from scholars whose work must enable them to have a remarkable birds-eye view of the church and the clergy as a whole. Such generalisations would, I suppose, seem a betrayal of the interests of each Order; at any rate they are hardly to be found.

Despite this great amount of research, despite one's hunch that the friars certainly and the monks probably were very numerous, it would be hard to establish significant trends as to recruitment or to answer this question: proportionately to population as a whole, did the religious constitute a bigger or a smaller percentage in the fifteenth century than they had constituted in the thirteenth

[31] See the ordinations, for example, printed in R. Maiocchi and N. Casacca, *Codex diplomaticus Ordinis E. S. Augustini Papiae*, ii. (Pavia, 1906). And cf. above n. 19.
[32] This tended to happen because of the many unions of poor parishes.
[33] N. Caturegli, 'Le condizioni della chiesa di Pisa, nella seconda metà del secolo XV', *Bolletino storico pisano* xix. (1950), 17–124, at pp. 57–9; B. Cecchetti, *La repubblica de Venezia e la corte di Roma nei rapporti della religione*, 2 vols. (Venice, 1874), i. 165–6.
[34] It was, of course, not needed when members of a religious order were ordained.
[35] Cf. J. Beloch, *Bevölkerungsgeschichte Italiens* ii. (rev. ed. Berlin, 1965), pp. 3–4 (Rome), 131–2 (Florence).

or fourteenth? For what it is worth, one's hunch suggests that the answer is No. There can be no doubt that the effects of the schism had badly disturbed the internal organisations of many, perhaps all, the Orders (save for the big independent Benedictine houses). Many convents seem to have been in great disarray and dilapidation,[36] with lazy abbots, who insisted on retaining control *ad vitam*,[37] and sometimes few monks—or few properly professed monks. The mendicants, all of whom experienced an Observant movement at this time, attracted much popular support and their recruitment was such that, in default of secular priests, they were often to be found supplying parishes.[38] Yet Observant-Conventual contradictions must have sometimes discouraged the devout. The violence of the tensions in the Franciscan Order in the fifteenth century is well known.[39] The Dominicans in Italy also went through a time of trouble.[40] In such rivalries it was a temptation to reinforce numbers by admitting poorly qualified candidates. The Observant Dominicans of the Lombard Congregation legislated in 1483 'to preclude the multiplication of useless brethren'. In future no one was to be given the habit 'nisi fuerit in grammaticalibus sufficienter instructus'.[41] Perhaps a final guess would be that numbers of religious were beginning to rise towards the end of the fifteenth century.[42] This would be in line with what happened in England.[43]

From the friars it is an easy step and a logical one to the Third Orders and the lay confraternities of Italy. Of the third orders of Francis and Dominic a good deal has been written, for their prominence as influences in lay piety on the Continent is obvious, however hard it is to see it at work in England.[44] But recently there has been a great concentration of effort by Italian historians on the penitential and charitable confraternities of the late Middle Ages. These were, of course, often affiliated to or descended from the Tertiaries of an earlier day, and they were in

---

[36] Cf. Caturegli, *ubi supra* n. 33, at pp. 81–8.
[37] N. Widloecher, *La congregazione dei canonici regolari Lateranensi: periodo di formazione: 1402–1483* (Gubbio, 1929), *passim*.
[38] Caturegli, *ubi supra*, p. 53 and n.
[39] Cf. John Moorman, *A History of the Franciscan Order . . . to 1517* (Oxford, 1968), pp. 441–585 and refs.
[40] R. Creytens O.P. and A. D'Amato O.P., 'Les actes capitulaires de la congrégation dominicaine de Lombardie, 1482–1531', *Arch. Frat. Praed.*, xxxi. (1961), 213–306.
[41] *Op cit.*, 254.
[42] Maiocchi and Casacca, *supra* n. 31, pp. 369–90.
[43] See the table in David Knowles and R. Neville Hadcock, *Medieval Religious Houses: England and Wales* (London, 1953), p. 364.
[44] Cf. Moorman , *op. cit.*, p. 560.

turn to lead to the 'oratories of divine love', and the Oratory.[45]
Their aims sometimes had an educational emphasis: the regular
instruction of children in the basic elements of religion. But more
often they were designed to act as societies for the relief of distress
among gentlefolk. Nowadays we regard such activity as fairly
marginal, even a little comic. It was far from this in a society
where only the humble could beg and where the well-bred were
precluded from working. Many of the confraternities were also
organised to provide occasions for penitential exercises—for
flagellation sometimes in public, more often now in private.[46]
At first confraternities, especially those for discipline, had seemed
a danger to established authority; by the fifteenth century they
were under episcopal control and acting as a support for bishop
and parish priest.[47] We are at the end of the evolution neatly
described by Delaruelle: 'from crusade to pilgrimage, from
pilgrimage to the Stations of the Cross'. Devotion was becoming
easier for men who described themselves in a Bolognese statute
as 'men of the world who have charge of property and a family,
who cannot always be occupied in the service of God like men of
religion'.[48]

It will be evident from this last quotation that the Italian laity
had moved a considerable way from the fierce austerities and the
high hopes of St Francis. What was the quality of the clergy
whose structure I have tried briefly to sketch? Was the tepid
character of lay piety a reflection of a corrupt or an indifferent
hierarchy?

A lack of spiritual fervour characterises the clergy of so many
parts of Christendom in the fifteenth century that it would be
surprising if Italy were exempt from the trend. The absenteeism
of many bishops—perhaps of most—has already been noted and
it naturally often led to a slatternly supervision of clergy. This
must not be exaggerated, however. Just as there were fewer
episcopal visitations in England than there had been of old, so
in Italy they were undoubtedly less common than they should
have been and did not happen at all (it seems) in very many

[45] Gennaro Maria Monti, *Le confraternite medievali dell'Alta Media Italia*, 2 vols.
(Venice, 1927) remains the only general book. See also Pio Paschini, *La benificenza
in Italia e le compagnie del Divino Amore . . . Note Storiche.* (Rome, 1925). Of
recent work I instance only *Il movimento dei Disciplinati nel settimo centenario del
suo inizio (Perugia, 1260)* Dep. di storia patria per l'Umbria, appendice al *Bolletino*
no. 9 (Perugia, 1962).
[46] Antonio Niero, 'Statuti della confraternità di Santa Maria della Misericordia di
Chirignago (Venezia)', *Rev. di storia della chiesa in Italia*, 20 (1966), 389–409.
[47] G. Alberigo, 'Contributi alla storia delle confraternite dei disciplinati e della
spiritualità laicale nei secc. XV e XVI', *Il movimento dei disciplinati, cit.*, p. 191.
[48] *Id., loc. cit.*, pp. 176–9.

dioceses. But some there were. Naturally the active and spiritually-concerned prelates—men like Antonino at Florence and Albergati at Bologna—were thorough and conducted visitations personally.[49] But so did some more perfunctory prelates. For instance Fabrizio Marliani, bishop of Piacenza from 1478 to 1508, was in no sense a reformer. He was the nephew of Michele Marliano, a Milanese curialist who had served Paul II as governor of Foligno; with papal and Milanese support he succeeded Michele first as bishop of Tortona and then of Piacenza. He acted as the envoy of the duke of Milan at Rome, made a lot of money, did some building at Piacenza and died in Milan.[50] A very uninspiring careerist, one might judge, yet he held one personal visitation of his diocese and celebrated one synod of its clergy. The visitation occurred in 1492-4 and it seems not to have been very penetrating; largely concerned with the city churches, he only attended to the *chiese plebane* in the country, not the *filiales* which were rapidly becoming parish churches themselves—that is only about 10% of the total 400 churches were visited.[51] The synod (sometime between 1477 and 1481) was content to rehearse the enactments of earlier assemblies (the last had been 70 odd years earlier).[52]

Such visitations were, it would appear, rather mechanical, insisting on the observance of the letter of the law, content when the letter of the law was discovered to have been observed: for example in the Piacenza situation authority insisted that baptism should only be conferred in the *pieve*, and in the city only in the cathedral itself. But occasionally the record, however much it betrays a lack of fire and conviction on the part of the visitor, does shed light on the state of the clergy and the laity. At Pisa visitation records survive for the second half of the fifteenth century; it appears that a church in this diocese could expect to undergo a visitation about once in every ten year period.[53] The visitors found a fairly dismal state of affairs, partly at any rate the result of the occupation of the territory by Florence. Many rural churches were ruinous and were getting more tumble-down as the century went on. Pisa itself suffered some depopulation and one of its churches was deserted. In the rural areas of the diocese one could only rely on a Sunday mass in the *pieve*, not in its dependent chapels; some *pieve* occasionally had a weekday

[49] Stefano Orlandi, O.P., *S. Antonino*, 2 vols. (Florence, 1959–60); Paolo de Töth, *ubi supra*, n. 18.
[50] Ughelli, ii. 232–3; Eubel ii. 216, 247.
[51] Franco Molinari, 'Visite e sinodi pretredentini a Piacenza', *Problemi di vita religiosa in Italia nel cinquecento*, 'Italia Sacra 2' (Padua, 1960), pp. 241–279, esp. 248–9.
[52] *Id.*, *op. cit.*, pp. 263–68.
[53] Caturegli, *ubi supra*, 17–20.

mass, some even a sung mass, though such splendour was rare. Far commoner were churches where no services took place because no rector could live on the miserable stipend. The worst case was one 'Presbyter Albertus' who was *pievano* at one church and rector of seven other chapelries at each of which there were a few parishioners: his week was a perpetual journey from one shabby church to another. Such men were poverty-stricken and not unnaturally devoted their exiguous funds to themselves rather than the fabric of the buildings. They were also not well-trained. Pisa, relatively rich though it was and the head of a province,[54] had no episcopal school and the local priests were the apprentices of other local priests, ordained by the bishop or his vicar and elected into their benefices by the parishioners, the bishop only confirming. As for the laity it would be surprising if the documents did not suggest their apathy, not to say cynicism. No visitor enquired whether priests instructed their flocks in Christian doctrine (nor, indeed, was this a canonical requirement then). The priests often complained to the visitor that the people did not come to church or take Communion at Easter; the people complained that the priest did not say mass. Many of the rural churches which were seldom used for services were regularly used as granaries. Tithes and burial dues were a frequent cause of recrimination. Some of the evidence suggests that couples were not bothering to get properly married and, of course, there is no evidence of any bishops performing the confirmation service. A dreary picture: but one which could have been paralleled in many other parts of Europe.[55]

The Pisan visitations also covered four of the 30 monasteries in the diocese, none of which was very old or very significant. Concerning the exempt Vallombrosan house of S. Paolo a Ripa d'Arno, held *in commendam* from 1457 to 1483, the scandal was such that, armed with a special papal authority, a visitation was conducted by the archbishop *in propria persona* accompanied by three Benedictine abbots. They were kept waiting in the rain for a long time and when finally admitted found none of the monks properly professed and a general local contempt for the abbot and his convent. The other three houses visited were nunneries—

---

[54] The province of Pisa, with two suffragan bishops in Corsica, and the diocese of Massa Maritima in Tuscany, lost the latter to Siena in 1459 when it was made suffragan to the newly erected archbishopric of Siena. Ughelli iii. 575–7. Pisa was assessed at 800 florins, Hoberg, p. 95.

[55] The unedifying picture revealed by the Pisan records is paralleled in the even grimmer account of the metropolitan visitation conducted by Archbishop Antonino in Fiesole and Pistoia and here one cannot urge that Florentine attacks were responsible, as at Pisa. See Raoul Morçay, *Saint Antonin: fondateur du convent de Saint-Marc, archevêque de Florence 1389–1459* (Paris, 1914), pp. 156–9.

in bad shape economically and with a sluttish air about them, except the one where the ladies came from good Pisan families, which was quite well conducted.[56] Two other visitations of monasteries have justifiably attracted more attention. In 1431 Ambrogio Traversari was appointed general of the Order of Camaldoli. He then embarked on a tour of the houses of the order which he described in his *Hodoeporicon*.[57] There are not many records of humanists conducting visitations. This one, with a good deal of supporting correspondence, was exploited to the full by G. G. Coulton, so that there is no need to repeat the stories of slack nunneries, ruthless commendators, grasping cardinals and a pope too easily misinformed.[58] The other remarkable visitation record refers to the monasteries of the Greek rite in southern Italy.[59] Under the impulse of Cardinal Bessarion an attempt had been made in 1446 to bring the Basilian monks of Sicily, Calabria and Apulia into a Congregation observing certain agreed canons. The visitation of 1457–8 shows how imperfectly earlier legislation was observed. We read of monasteries deserted save for one or two monks; of an abbot who already had six children 'and said he could not desert the woman because he loved the children she had borne him and because his doctor advised sex as a treatment for the stone, and so he had got her with child and she had had a daughter three weeks ago'.[60] Candour like this has its pathetic side. But what could Bessarion's visitor Athanasius do with the fighting abbot he encountered? He was, in effect, powerless.[61] All visitors, as Coulton tirelessly pointed out, were ineffective when they lacked armed force provided by a resolute government.

The south—the Abruzzi, Apulia and Calabria, where political disorder was endemic in the later Middle Ages—have received even less attention from ecclesiastical historians than the better documented centre and north of the peninsula.[62] Perhaps in these areas conditions were worse, deserving of that phrase used

[56] Caturegli, *ubi supra*, pp. 84–8.

[57] A. Dini-Traversari, *Ambrogio Traversari e i suoi tempi* (Florence, 1912). The *Hodoeporicon* is in appendix 3, separately paged.

[58] *Five Centuries of Religion*, iv. (Cambridge, 1950), pp. 269–310; Dini-Traversari's commentary, pp. 149–194 with references to Mehus's edition (Florence, 1759) of Traversari's letters.

[59] *Le 'Liber visitationis' d'Athanase Chalkéopoulos (1457–1458). Contributions à l'histoire du monachisme grec en Italie méridionale*, ed. M.-H. Laurent and André Guillon, 'Studi e Testi,' 206 (Città del Vaticano, 1960).

[60] *Op. cit.*, p. 51.

[61] *Op. cit.*, pp. 161–7.

[62] There has been much loss of ecclesiastical archives: cf. V.-M. Egidi, 'Il "diplomatico" dell'Archivio capitolare di Cosenza, *Calabria Nobilissima* ix. (1955), 8–25. The history of this diocese was written in a queer mixture of scholarship and tactful piety, by Francesco Russo, *Storia del arcidiocesi di Cosenza* (Naples, c. 1956), but

of them by the early Jesuits: 'the India of Italy, *India Italiana*'.[63]
Yet it was at Paolo that another St Francis was born in 1416
who established his Order of Minims in 1435. Their rigorous
rule is worth remembering, for it was the only religious order of
the later Middle Ages which spread a little beyond the native
land of its founder.[64]

St Francis of Paola is, of course, not the only devout man to
come out of fifteenth century Italy and it is tempting to go on to
a survey of the efforts at systematic renewal and discipline then
made—to the preachers from Bernardino down to Savanarola, to
the men who saw the need for an educated priesthood (one
thinks of Albergati, Bessarion, Capranica, Nardini), to the
organisers of what one might term the 'congregational' movements, even to the fitful interest of some popes in supporting
reform of local churches (like Eugenius IV) or in 'head and member'
reform (Pius II, Sixtus IV and Alexander VI, in that moment
when the murder of his son made him repent for a few weeks).[65]
Such a survey would, however, take us too far afield and I shall
conclude with some observations on the role of the papacy in
Italian church government and discipline—the topic with which
I began.

For good and for ill the plentitude of power bore more directly
on Italian church affairs than it did elsewhere in Christendom.
The effects of this were manifold. For example the disruption in
Italy, especially in north Italy, of the Schism was intensified by
the draconic actions taken after 1409 by two sets of Italian popes,
those called of Rome and those called of Pisa. It took Martin V
twenty years to unscramble the mess produced by two rival sets
of *motu proprios*, if one can produce such a plural; and Martin
did this, of course, by a further set of injunctions not all of which
were acceptable to the clergy and the governments involved.
But even in times of relative ecclesiastical peace, it is extraordinary
how carelessly the popes intervened in the due processes of
clerical administration. I shall give as an example the experiences
of the reformed Dominicans of the Lombard congregation.[66]
This turned on the ambiguous nature of the relations between

few other southern dioceses have been the subject of recent work. Not much can
be gleaned, despite its promising title, from D. Taccone Galucci, *I Regesti dei
Romani Pontefici per le chiese della Calabria* (Città del Vaticano, 1902).
[63] Pietro Tacchi Venturi, S. J., *Storia della compagnia di Gesu in Italia*. i. *La vita
religiosa in Italia durante il primordi dell'ordine*. 2nd ed. repr. (Rome, 1950), p. 327.
[64] *Acta Sanctorum*, 1 April, pp. 103–234.
[65] These are discussed at appropriate points in L. Pastor, *History of the Popes*;
trans. Antrobus, i–vi. (London, 1891–8); see too L. Celier, 'Alexandre VI et la
réforme de l'église', *Mélanges d'archéologie et d'histoire*, xxvii. (1907), 65–124.
[66] Creytens and D'Amato, *ubi supra* n. 39, pp. 213–244.

the reformed houses and the rest of the province. Raymond of Capua in November 1390 had envisaged the establishment of a reformed house in each province (under the provincial) while existing Observant communities would come under the vicar general. When Boniface IX confirmed this arrangement in January 1391 the reference to the vicar general was omitted and a series of battles was fought during the next century to secure advantages from the *intentions* of Boniface IX's bull or from its *actual terms*. Popes issued documents giving the edge now to one party and then to the other. Boniface IX gave the reformer Dominici his support in 1399 but withdrew it, under pressure from provincials, the next year. Similar upheavals occurred in 1417, 1421, 1426, 1428. In 1436 a vicariate gave independence to the reformers— for six months. Nicholas V supported reform, but issued contradictory documents under the influence of the French Minister-General. Pius II's influence lay with the Observants, but in 1470 Paul II was persuaded to overthrow all reforming legislation. These are the highlights of a tangled story. In the sixteenth century the two sides were still wrangling, still getting popes to upset earlier papal decisions. Much the same sort of capricious papal intervention can be observed when a church or a convent was being reformed: the abbot *ad vitam* appealed against displacement and a brief enjoined the bishop to hold his hand—there was then need for the bishop to explain to the curia the true facts of the case. Years might pass in this way before a definitive decision was reached.

Tiresome and unpredictable papal action often was—a striking consequence of an almost total failure to delegate proper authority to the active and resident members of the Italian episcopate. But, quite apart from the rival pressures of powerful persons, the plenitude could be powerless on occasions, for instance if it encountered genuine popular resistance. Such resistance was provoked by the laudable attempt of several popes to introduce into the Lateran basilica reformed canons, at that time called 'of Fregionaia' (near Lucca). It is a long story and begins with Eugenius IV, as so many worthy developments do.[67] Such efforts were in vain. The reformed canons were not anxious to send a colony to live in Rome, which was not only troubled politically, but immoral and unhealthy as well. They bowed to the papal commands, but the seculars in possession of the Lateran prevaricated, demanded that only Romans should enjoy Roman benefices, and staged a wild rumpus in May 1440 when the old canons and the new fought over the Corpus Christi procession.

[67] Widloecher, *ubi supra* n. 36, at p. 74 n.l, for the canons of S. Giorgio in Alga.

It needed the Castellan from S. Angelo with troops to give possession to the reformers, who had been ousted by the mob. After this Eugenius allowed them to depart, but in 1443 and 1446 he tried again—and by now he himself resided in Rome— without much effect. Under Nicholas V for a time the Lateran Canons (as they were now officially called) actually seem to have controlled the Lateran. But the unregenerate seculars refused to hand over endowment income, and made an unseemly fracas when the Emperor Frederick III visited the Basilica in March 1452, and they had their rivals expelled by Calixtus III in 1455. Paul II, who as cardinal Barbo had been protector of the Congregation, restored them to the Lateran in 1464 but on his death the old seculars forcibly ejected the reformed canons and Sixtus IV finally agreed to their eviction. Who (one may ask) had the whip hand in these Roman transactions? Certainly not the pope who, on his own doorstep, was compelled to cede to local pressure. We may add that it was from the ranks of the Lateran Canons, who were not in the Lateran, that one or two Italian reformers were to be drawn in the early sixteenth-century, and notably Peter Martyr Vermigli.[68]

I began by complaining that the history of the church in Italy in the later Middle Ages has been too readily identified with the history of the papacy. And you will have observed how I have, in the last few moments, seemed to accept that this identification is unavoidable. I do not, although, as I have said, the existence of Italian popes in the fifteenth century exercised an influence on the clergy of the peninsula which has to be remembered, an influence which was peculiarly oppressive when the Italian princes and republics began, as they did with the pontificate of Nicholas V, to realise how important the pope was in the Italian political game. But below the popes there was an Italian ecclesiastical evolution in process which, in the end of the day, was itself to affect papal policy—affect it, some might think, in a very critical fashion in the decade which followed Luther's challenge and culminated in the Sack of Rome of 1527. So that if we are to understand the Italian church and clergy from the Great Schism to the Council of Trent we must understand the actions of the popes. And if we are to understand the role of popes in Christendom at large we should study carefully the Italian environment from which they nearly all sprang, and in which they all had to operate.

[68] Cf. Philip McNair, *Peter Martyr in Italy* (Oxford, 1967).

Addendum: Since this lecture was given in May 1971 I have dealt further with the subject in the Birkbeck lectures which I was privileged to give at Trinity College,

Cambridge in November 1972; I hope to publish these in due course. There is also some relevant material in my Renaissance Society Lecture (January, 1973) on *Italian Clergy and Italian Culture in the Fifteenth Century*.

The Catholic Clergy and Irish Politics in the Eighteen Thirties and Forties

Kevin B. Nowlan

I have taken as the period for this paper roughly the era of parliamentary reform, of the Grey, Melbourne, Peel and Russell administrations. In terms of British history, this forms a convenient unit and, for Ireland, it spans the years between the triumph of O'Connell's emancipation campaign and the end of the repeal movement in the difficult famine years after 1846.

The Catholic emancipation campaign, though it may have achieved only limited ends, in strictly legal terms, was one of the earliest and most dramatic illustrations of how organised public opinion could compel an unreformed parliament to make what was, in fact, a major decision in terms of principle. In the latter stages of the emancipation agitation, there was a close identification between the interests of the ecclesiastical and political leaders of the Catholic people which made the Irish movement so remarkable in the early history of popular liberalism in the nineteenth century—a striking indication for contemporaries that liberal ideas and Catholicism were not of necessity completely alien one to another. But the question that emancipation helped to formulate was: would the Irish Catholic clergy continue to be politically involved after emancipation as before it? To some extent, perhaps, this is the same as saying would Ireland from 1830 onwards be increasingly integrated into the overall pattern of British society, economically, politically and socially—and could a place be found for a large, localised Roman Catholic community within the Protestant United Kingdom?

In the immediate post-emancipation months, there seems to have been a certain optimism on this point among the Irish Catholic hierarchy, or at least a willingness to withdraw the clergy from the political scene in the hope of better things. In February 1830, the Irish bishops issued a statement, drafted by Dr Doyle,

119

the bishop of Kildare and Leighlin, in which, having thanked Crown and Parliament for emancipation, they went on to say that '. . . . we rejoiced at that result . . . . because we found ourselves discharged from a duty which necessity alone had allied to our ministry—a duty imposed on us by a state of things which has passed, but a duty which we have gladly relinquished, in the fervent hope that by us, or by our successors, it may not be resumed. These are the sentiments which the spirit of our calling inspires . . . . and which our clergy, always obedient to our voice, will cherish all with us . . . .'[1] This statement and two resolutions adopted by the bishops in January 1834 might well have provided the basis for a firm disciplinary practice to keep the Irish priests out of politics. The effect of the two resolutions was to prohibit the use of chapels for meetings unconnected with religious or charitable purposes, and the clergy were reminded of the terms of the February 1830 address and advised to refrain from connecting themselves with political clubs.[2]

The public statements of the hierarchy were further strengthened by the attitude of Rome, where the British government carried on, from time to time, throughout the eighteen-thirties and -forties, a campaign aimed at influencing the policies of the Holy See. Cardinal Fransoni's letter to the Irish Primate, in March 1839, was a typical expression of the circumspect approach of Rome to the dangerous subject of the Irish priest in politics: 'Once again this Sacred Congregation [Propaganda] with greatest sorrow has been informed that the Archbishop of Tuam and also one of the bishops of this kingdom do not hesitate to hold the first place at civic banquets, and to speak imprudently about the Government . . . . Although I am myself persuaded that imputations of this kind have perhaps been exaggerated . . . . nevertheless, in a matter of such great moment, I am forced to inquire of your Excellency whether or not the stories are true . . . .'[3] This can stand for many such inquiries. And yet, the remarkable thing is that, throughout the whole of the eighteen-thirties and -forties, Catholic priests and bishops did become involved, in varying degrees, in activities of a political nature.[4]

Though the fortunes of political parties, Irish and British, might vary throughout our period, there is nevertheless a remarkably constant element in the issues at stake. In Britain, questions

---

[1] *Dublin Evening Post*, 16 Feb. 1830.
[2] John F. Broderick, *The Holy See and the Irish movement for the repeal of the union with England 1829–47*, p. 59.
[3] *Ibid.*, p. 102.
[4] Kevin B. Nowlan, 'The relations between Church and State in the age of emancipation', in *Proceedings of the Irish Catholic Historical Committee 1960*, pp. 25–31.

such as the Corn Laws and Free Trade could be argued out divorced from religious considerations. But in Ireland, a striking feature of the politics of the mid-nineteenth century was how deeply interlocked sectarian issues remained with what might otherwise have been political questions, and this was as true of the eighteen-forties as of the eighteen-thirties. Catholic emancipation had left unresolved the problem of how to emancipate the Irish Catholic socially, especially the rural poor. It left unresolved the problem of a Protestant state church in a fundamentally Catholic community. The 1831 arrangements about National Education by no means pleased all Catholics. The Ascendancy remained in control of public office and in control of much private wealth. Again, the tithe question and the strains between landlords and tenants had strong religious undertones and the difficulties were further heightened by the growing intensity of the Protestant evangelical revival, a certain renewal of Orangeism and, on the other hand, a new confidence in some Catholic circles. Politics remained sectarian and the chances of the clergy withdrawing from politics remained rather theoretical. Indeed, even those who sought most effectively to do so, like Archbishop Daniel Murray of Dublin, found themselves drifting into the rôle of advisers to the government by the eighteen-forties, if not earlier.

Already before the resolutions had been adopted by the hierarchy in 1834, the priests were back in politics. The clergy, for example, in Wicklow and Monaghan, appear to have been active in the election campaigns of 1832. The divisions were clearly drawn: a Protestant candidate could be commended to the electors at this time in the following terms: 'Born and educated a Protestant and a Protestant from conviction, he will stand by that Church . . . . he will use his best efforts to strengthen the connection between the British islands'.[5]

A factor of some importance in keeping the clergy involved in politics in the eighteen-thirties was, of course, the tithe issue. The degree of clerical involvement is hard to determine, but the dislike of the tithes was widespread among all classes of Catholics and among many Protestants too. The clashes between their people and the armed police and military caused dismay and anger in clerical circles, though it should be added that this unease did not of necessity involve approval of violent resistance to the authorities. In January 1835, for instance, a group of senior priests in Co. Wexford decided to join the Anti-Tory Association. Because of the state of the country, they felt 'the

[5] *Dublin Evening Mail*, 10 Dec. 1832.

necessity of laying aside their natural reluctance to mingling in the battle of worldly politics and of joining the ranks of the people and their patriotic representatives. . . . The late carnage at Rathcormac has struck such a thrill of horror through human nature of every age, that it has aroused both myself and brother elders to come forward. . . . This is a sacred duty which we now feel that we owe to our country, the people and ourselves'.[6] At much the same time (January, 1835), and in much the same tone, Dr Edward Nolan, the bishop of Kildare and Leighlin, wrote to his clergy: 'I am decidedly of opinion that the present critical and most important juncture of public affairs not only justifies, but imperatively calls for our most active and energetic exertions'. And having deplored the 'sanguinary tithe massacres', he went on to specifically urge the priests to instruct their parishioners 'in the conscientious obligations of electors' and to advise them not to vote for candidates of conservative principles alien to the interests of the Catholic people.[7]

Dr Nolan and Archbishop John MacHale in Tuam were probably the most outspoken politically among the bishops, but Daniel O'Connell's strategic retreat from repeal, after 1834, helped to make political activity easier for the more cautious-minded among the clergy. Indeed, I am left with the impression that in 1836–37 the clergy, including the higher clergy were probably more involved in popular politics than at any time since the emancipation period—and possibly even more so than during the great repeal agitation in 1843–44.

In the late summer of 1836, O'Connell, by now a master in the art of launching and, when necessary, of sinking political associations, founded a new one attuned to the spirit of the Lichfield House compact: the General, or as it was sometimes called, the National Association. Its aims were to end the tithes, to reform the municipal corporations, to organise the people to oppose injustice and to put down faction fighting. From the outset, from August 1836, large numbers of Catholic priests applied for admission to membership and O'Connell's address to the people of Ireland, at this time, was well-calculated to please the most moderate of ecclesiastics. The Association thoughtfully provided the bishops with bundles of printed copies of the address for distribution, counselling the people to moderation but emphasising their grievances. Not merely did the more radical among the bishops, such as Higgins of Ardagh and Dr MacHale, join the Association but so did moderates like Dr Kennedy of Killaloe.[8]

[6] *Pilot*, 5 Jan. 1835.
[7] *Ibid.*, 12 Jan. 1835.
[8] *Ibid.*, 19, 31 Aug., 14 Oct. 1836.

122

Even Dr Murray, of Dublin, wrote to the Association, on his return from the continent in October 1836, that 'I avail myself, therefore, of the first moment after my arrival in Dublin to forward my humble offering to the fund to be employed for obtaining justice for Ireland'.[9] Archbishop Crolly of Armagh was another subscriber to the 'justice rent'.[10]

The General Association was, however, a short-lived affair. In September 1837, O'Connell recommended that it should be dissolved on the interesting grounds that to do so would be 'proof of our satisfaction at the improved state of the administration of the government of Ireland'.[11] His satisfaction was not to last very long. O'Connell's apparently harmonious association with the Melbourne administration was soon to be followed by something like a withdrawal from the alliance with the British Whigs, culminating in the formation of the Precursor Society in August 1838. As an astute politician, O'Connell may well have realised, by 1838, that the whigs' prospects were dim, and that the Tory, Sir Robert Peel would soon again be in office.

Though the clergy of the Dublin diocese appear to have played only a limited part in politics in our period, those in many of the other dioceses were less inhibited and their activities, as organisers in the General Association, were paralleled by their presence, though in limited numbers at anti-tithe meetings in 1838.

The year 1838 was a turning point in the history of popular Irish politics. It saw the beginnings of what proved to be the repeal movement of the eighteen-forties and the tentative return of O'Connell to the politics he had, in effect, abandoned in 1834. I say tentative because the Precursors did not give up hope of obtaining redress for Irish grievances within the constitutional structure of the United Kingdom. The organization was, in fact, pledged to make one last attempt 'to procure from the British legislature full justice to Ireland'. If that attempt failed, then the repeal agitation was to be resumed.[12]

As in the case of the General Association, the foundation of the Precursor Society was a signal for renewed political activity among what appears to have been a sizeable section of the Catholic clergy. As in the earlier O'Connellite organisations, they seem to have played a key rôle in the work of recruitment, of collecting funds and of communicating with the central organisation in Dublin. As early as October 1838, the priests were busy with the

[9] *Ibid.*, 7 Oct. 1836.
[10] *Ibid.*, 14 Oct. 1836.
[11] *Freeman's Journal*, 25 Oct. 1837.
[12] *Pilot*, 20 Aug. 1838.

formation of the society in Tipperary town and in Fethard, where the first meeting was actually held in the chapel yard. A number of bishops joined. George Browne of Galway and at least three or four others; and the cautious Primate, in January 1839, went so far as to say that though he seldom took part in public proceedings, 'agitation will not cease for it will not be unnecessary till all Irishmen stand upon a platform of justice, equal. . . .'[13] But the Primate was not destined to go much beyond this point, and he, along with Archbishop Murray and Dr Cornelius Denvir, the bishop of Down, were to form the nucleus of a rather influential minority group of bishops who were prepared to co-operate with, or at least facilitate a 'dialogue' with the government of the United Kingdom.

The Precursors gave way, in April 1840, to the 'National Association of Ireland for full and prompt justice or repeal'—an appallingly cumbersome title which suggested O'Connell's dwindling hopes of securing some remedial measures from the Whigs. The name was soon changed to the Loyal National Repeal Association—a title equally revealing of the working of O'Connell's mind at this time. It is generally agreed, I think, that in 1840–41, Daniel O'Connell had a hard task in stirring up enthusiasm for the cause of the repeal of the Union. He had aroused only a limited response in the early eighteen-thirties for repeal and O'Connell in 1840 again encountered, initially, much apathy. But, though bishops such as Murray and Crolly avoided the repeal movement, I think it fair to say that, yet again, the clergy proved of enormous importance in the hard slogging work of organising the people, collecting funds, arranging meetings and acting as the literate interpreters of O'Connell's mass following.[14] The decision of the formidable Archbishop of Tuam to join the Association, in August 1840, was the beginning and, though ultimately fourteen members of the Catholic hierarchy joined the Association, it was the rank and file of the ordinary clergy who helped to give coherence to the movement in many rural areas.

The involvement of the clergy in the Association brought with it obvious advantages for O'Connell and he was fully aware of this. But it brought with it certain disadvantages too. It proved increasingly difficult to give the Repeal Association that all-embracing, as distant from Catholic, character that O'Connell wished to give it—or, perhaps better, would have liked it to

[13] *Ibid.*, 26 Oct. 1838.
[14] Kevin B. Nowlan, *The politics of repeal*, pp. 21–3; Lawrence J. McCaffrey, *Daniel O'Connell and the repeal year*, pp. 11–14.

possess without having to make too many concessions to Protestant opinion.[15]

The rôle of the clergy during the Repeal year 1843, was striking
and, as we shall see, it gave rise yet again to much concern in
government circles. Early in May 1843, for example, we find the
bishops of Meath and Ardagh attending the great repeal rally at
Mullingar. And, at the subsequent banquet, the Bishop of Ardagh,
in his enthusiasm, went so far as to say that all the bishops of
Ireland were repealers and 'have all declared themselves as such'.
Almost at once Dr Murray of Dublin, on 22 May, hastened to
assure his clergy in an open letter that 'in no instance did I give
to any human being' the slightest reason to suppose that he
subscribed to the movement, rather he concurred in the 1830
resolution of the hierarchy that the clergy should refrain from
taking any prominent part in political proceedings.[16] Dr Murray's
rebuke in no way discomposed the Bishop of Ardagh, who, with
somewhat elaborate courtesy, replied that 'The Most Rev. Dr
Murray is a man whose piety, whose learning and whose every
good quality, I have had too many opportunities of admiring
and though, in his own wisdom . . . . he may frequent the Castle,
I believe . . . . that he goes there for charitable and noble purposes
alone. I do not go to the Castle. . . .'[17]

The Catholic bishop of Killaloe, Dr P. Kennedy, would have
been satisfied with a measure of political autonomy short of full
repeal and joined the Association, in March 1843, with this
reservation, which O'Connell accepted. But he expressed in May
1843 in very emphatic terms the case why the Irish clergy were
justified in concerning themselves with political issues. Attacking
conservative critics of the priest in politics, he was reported as
saying: 'Now when they expressed that sanctimonious concern
for the sacredness of their clergy [i.e. the Catholics] . . . . let them
at once dismiss their own bishops from the House of Lords . . . .
let their injured and oppressed people be only treated with common
justice and humanity and he would answer for it that the Catholic
clergy, priests and prelates, would gladly retire from political
agitation'.[18] But, as against such episcopal statements and the
regular attendance of Catholic clergy at repeal banquets in
1843–44, must be set the refusal of the Bishop of Ossory, Dr
William Kinsella, to sign a requisition for a repeal meeting on
the grounds that his professional duties left him little time for

[15] Kevin B. Nowlan, 'The meaning of repeal in Irish history', in G. A. Hayes-
McCoy (ed.), *Historical Studies IV*, pp. 4–5.
[16] *Nation*, 14, 20, 27 May 1843.
[17] *Ibid*. 3 June 1843.
[18] *Ibid*.

political matters—though he added that he believed a domestic legislature was the best means of promoting the happiness of a nation.[19] Again, the Bishop of Cork, in May 1843, indicated that 'it is not my habit to interfere in political matters' and his neighbour, the Bishop of Cloyne, was not 'altogether so sanguine as to the belief that the repeal of the Union would prove a panacea for all our sufferings'.[20] Crolly of Armagh and Murray of Dublin were by no means alone in their attitude towards the repeal agitation. There were differences of opinion within Irish clerical circles and they were expressed in public with vigour and often with a stimulating lack of reserve.

The link, however, between a wide sector of the Catholic clergy and the repeal movement is evident and well established. Yet, I think, it would be a mistake to describe the O'Connellite movement of the eighteen-forties as being dominated by clerical interests. Priests and prelates, we know, were prominent in the Association and helped the repeal cause at election time. But O'Connell was not afraid to attack clerics when political considerations made it appear necessary to do so. And, though he did denounce the entrenched attitudes and power of the Protestant Ascendancy, he was equally quick to stress the point that repeal of the Union was not a sectarian issue. As he put it, in September 1843, 'There never was a political question having in it so little of sectarian tendency as the repeal question'.[21] Protestants would gain equally with Catholics, he argued, once legislative independence was restored to Ireland. Again, O'Connell's initial welcome for William Smith O'Brien, Thomas Davis and the other Protestant repealers may reasonably be seen in the context of this attempt to make the movement attractive to at least a section of the Irish Protestant community.

The response to such gestures was, however, very limited and within a short time, too, Davis and his friends became increasingly critical of the weight of clerical influence within the Repeal Association. There was no easy solution to the difficult task of disentangling political from religious issues in the given condition of Ireland in the eighteen-forties. The close identification of Daniel O'Connell with Catholic emancipation and mass agitation and his dominant place in the Repeal Association made no easier the work of winning converts to repeal in Protestant circles. No matter how O'Connell and the Young Irelanders, in their different ways, might seek to convince Irish Protestants of the advantages

[19] *Ibid.*, 6 May 1843.
[20] *Ibid.*, 27 May 1843.
[21] *Ibid.*, 16 Sept. 1843.

of repeal, in fact, Tory power and Protestant interests were to remain in close alliance throughout our period. Sir Robert Peel's tentative attempts, in 1844–45, to widen the basis of government support in Ireland, through concessions to the Catholics, brought few results, so that the Tory connection was destined to remain associated with the major Ascendancy groupings.[22] Some Catholic clerics did move further away from the O'Connellite camp towards what might be described as a Whig position, but their following remained small and the majority of Irish priests continued to be regarded with suspicion by successive British governments as a potentially dangerous political factor.

In the wake of the set-backs suffered by the repeal agitation in 1843–44, Sir Robert Peel was resolved to introduce remedial measures which, as he put it, in February 1844, would serve to detach 'a considerable portion of the moderate Roman Catholics' from the O'Connellite party. He considered that more than additional funds for the National Schools was necessary and to the doubters among his political friends he put the question— what other courses could be followed? If they acted on the assumption that there would be no favourable Catholic reaction and so did nothing to meet Catholic grievances in Ireland, then, 'you have the whole Roman Catholic population banded against you (and with such a union trial by jury will be impossible)'.[23] From the beginning, a not unimportant consideration in the pro- posals to improve the laws relating to charities in Ireland and to increase the parliamentary grant to Maynooth College was that such reforms would help both to improve clerical education and, by facilitating the transfer of property by landlords to the Church, would make the clergy less dependent on their flocks. This concern about the influence of the people on the attitudes of their priests was to be a recurring theme in official comments on the Church in high politics.

It is not necessary for our purpose to examine the provisions of the Charitable Donations and Bequests Act and the provincial colleges measure beyond saying that, with the Devon Commission, a feeble and unsuccessful attempt to provide compensation for tenants' improvements to farms and the Maynooth Act, we have the full range of the conservatives programme for Ireland. The limited scope of the proposals was an indication of their ultimately

[22] 'We cannot abandon the Protestant Church in Ireland; tho' I am most anxious to remove any remnant of abuse . . . We cannot give to the Roman Catholics an establishment . . . but no opportunity should be omitted of winning them to the State . . .', Sir James Graham to Sir Robert Peel, 18 June 1843, Peel papers, BM Add.MS 40448, ff. 328–31.

[23] Memorandum by Peel [Feb., 1844], Peel papers, Add.MS 40540, ff. 40–5.

very limited impact on political attitudes. But the controversies, often spirited, which surrounded the ecclesiastical measures are interesting in revealing the scope for debate in Ireland at this time.

O'Connell's concern about the efforts to detach moderate Catholic, including clerical, support from his organisation was understandable. As early as the summer of 1843, Metternich, the Austrian Chancellor, had used his influence at Rome to try to restrain the activities of the Irish clergy in the repeal campaign and, to the same end, in November 1843, a 'nosegay' of political speeches and writings of Irish priests was prepared by the British authorities and forwarded to Rome by way of Vienna.[24]

Behind the parliamentary proposals, lay a certain measure of diplomatic activity—moves which inevitably created in Ireland the fear of a bargain between London and Rome: of a concordat which might effectively curb the political activities of the Irish clergy and bring the Church under a measure of state control. And though the Lord Lieutenant, Lord Heytesbury, in January 1845, informed Archbishops Murray and Crolly, with the 'strongest assurances', as he put it, that no concordat was contemplated, the suspicions were to last long in Ireland on this point. The only concrete results of the negotiations with Rome was a very cautious papal rescript addressed to Dr Crolly which simply conveyed Rome's disapproval of clerical involvement in political matters. Little notice was taken in either clerical or lay circles of the admonition which came as something of an anticlimax to the rumours and tensions of 1844.[25]

It was against a background, therefore, of unease that the assault on the Charitable Donations measure began. Certain clauses were considered to be a reflection on the honesty of the Irish clergy and O'Connell did not mince his words in attacking the Act. He claimed that the 'real intention of the Act was and is to limit and to restrict the power of endowing Catholic charities'—which, in fact, was the very opposite to the intentions of the Peel ministry in introducing the measure.[26] O'Connell's ally, John MacHale, the Archbishop of Tuam, described the new legislation as being designed 'to corrupt its [the Church's] pastors, to alienate from them the affections of their beloved flocks'.[27] Public meetings against the measure were held, as for example

---

[24] John F. Broderick, *op. cit.*, pp. 163–71; Peel to Graham, 27 Nov. 1843, Peel papers, Add.MS 40449, ff. 233–4; Aberdeen to Peel, 30 Dec. 1843, Peel papers, Add.MS 40454, f. 78.
[25] *Nation*, 18 Jan. 1845.
[26] Kevin B. Nowlan, *The politics of repeal*, pp. 66–8.
[27] *Nation*, 14 Dec. 1844.

in Waterford Cathedral, in December 1844.[28] The pressure
exerted was strong on those Catholics who were tempted to
cooperate with the government in the administration of the Act.
Yet the significant fact remains that sufficient clerical support
was found to make the legislation on charities a modest success.[29]
Somewhat reluctantly, as they too had some reservations about
details of the Act, two archbishops, Crolly and Murray, along
with Bishop Denvir, agreed to join the new charities' board.

The tangled controversy surrounding the 'Godless colleges'
question, in 1845–46, did little to alter the political balance in
Catholic clerical circles: the moderate prelates giving the measure
a cautious initial approval, provided it was amended in certain
respects, the radical majority, some 17 bishops in all, protesting,
in September 1845, that the colleges would prove dangerous to
the faith and morals of the people. Daniel O'Connell, after some
hesitation to begin with, came out in criticism of the measure
and his son, John, even more strongly.[30] And, it was against the
background of the colleges dispute that the Young Irelanders
became involved with the O'Connells on the issue of clerical
influence within the Association. Davis, concerned lest a Catholic
ascendancy, as he saw it, might replace a Protestant one in Ireland,
was inclined to see in the O'Connellite attitude the makings of a
priests' party. As early as 1844, he had warned William Smith
O'Brien that 'it behoves all Protestants to insist on education,
it will be our guarantee against a Browne and MacHale government'.[31] And it was a reflection of the tensions within the Repeal
Association by mid-June 1845, that Davis could write: 'We had
a most serious affair in *committee* yesterday in which all Protestants who interfered in the education question were denounced
in the strongest courteous language by O'Connell and his son
and by other parties in rougher fashion'.[32]

The educational question was one of the factors which contributed to the estrangement between the Old and Young Irelanders
and I think it fair to say that John O'Connell, in particular,
helped to create a feeling of tension within the Association which
was, perhaps, the counterpoint to Davis's sharp criticisms of the

[28] *Ibid.*, 21 Dec. 1844.
[29] 'His [O'Connell's] allusions to our proceedings at Rome, his reference to the
veto, his denunciation of "the adulterous connexion" between the Roman Catholic
Church and the State—all mark his deep sense of the advantage we have gained . . .',
Lord Heytesbury (lord lieutenant) to Peel, 20 Dec. 1844, Peel papers, Add.MS
40479, ff. 216–7.
[30] Repeal Assoc. meeting, 12 May, *Nation*, 17 May 1845.
[31] Thomas Davis to William Smith O'Brien [1844], N. Lib. Ir. MS, Smith O'Brien
papers, vol. 434, no. 1293.
[32] Davis to Smith O'Brien, 15 June [1845], Smith O'Brien papers, vol. 432, no. 884.

Association's leadership. But it would be an over-simplification of the problem to see in the disputes a clear-cut issue between a clerical and a lay party, though there were, no doubt, elements of this present. It must be remembered that there was a lack of agreement in high ecclesiastical quarters about the merits of the Colleges Bill. Indeed, a few years were to pass before a reasonably clear and definitive stand was taken by Rome, in 1847 and '48, on the unacceptability of the Colleges. It would be more accurate to say that, in coming to the decision to finally oppose the Bill, O'Connell was influenced by the opinions of his clerical supporters —a support which was of the highest importance as a link between the Association and the people. But there was also present the overriding political consideration of frustrating Peel's efforts to 'detach' moderate Catholics from repeal. O'Connell did not take the risk of making the course an easy one for Peel and certainly the conservative gestures of conciliation to the Irish Catholics appear to have had the minimum political effect. Political allegiances in 1846 were much as they had been in 1844 among the Irish clergy. When the split came between Old and Young Irelanders, in the summer of 1846, on political and tactical issues, there can be no doubt that the great bulk of the clergy and their congregations stood by O'Connell and the Repeal Association. As *The Times* rather succinctly put it, in August 1846, 'Old Ireland has beaten its young rival. The priests have done it'.[33]

An examination of the proceedings of the Repeal Association and of its Young Ireland opponent, the Irish Confederation, in 1847, suggests that insofar as the clergy were actively involved in politics in those difficult famine months, when the structure of the Repeal movement was disintegrating, their sympathy was with the Association, both before and after O'Connell's death. There were exceptions, like Fr John Kenyon and Rev James Birmingham, the parish priest of Borrisokane, who was replaced, in April 1848, by his bishop for 'inciting to war'—to which the priest replied that he only took part in politics because he saw 'thousands consigned to famine with all its horrors'.[34] In the elections of 1847, the clergy in general supported the O'Connellite candidates and were most certainly a moderating force in 1848–49, insofar as any clerical intervention was needed to restrain armed insurrection. And yet, despite the relatively moderate course adopted by the Irish clergy, both before and after the advent of the famine, both the Peel and Russell ministries and the Irish Tory connection continued to regard, if for sometimes different

[33] *The Times*, 13 Aug. 1846.
[34] *Nation*, 29 April 1848.

reasons, the Catholic clergy as a force which had to be neutralised in political terms.[35] It was an element to be regarded very narrowly and closely at all times. It might be said that this preoccupation with the Irish Church in politics was yet another expression of the failure of British legislators to find a place for the Roman Catholic Church and its priests in a state where the Reformation had provided the inheritance of political and social respectability.

Already during the tithe agitation of the eighteen-thirties the attitude of the Catholic clergy in many areas had given rise to alarm in Dublin and London. Again, as we have seen, the Peel administration, especially in 1843-44, regarded the political activities of the Catholic clergy with sufficient concern as to take the matter up with Rome. Yet the correspondence of the time reveals, in official circles, an interesting conflict of motives—on the one hand, a growing desire to see more Catholics in the public service and, on the other, an enduring suspicion and even dislike of the influence of the Catholic priest. Peel put the first consideration clearly to the ultra-Tory Lord Lieutenant, De Grey, in August 1843, when he wrote: 'What is the advantage to the Roman Catholics of having removed their legal disabilities if, somehow or other, they are constantly met by a preferable claim on the part of the Protestants, and if they do not practically reap the advantages of their nominal equality as to civil privilege?'— a view which his Home Secretary, Sir James Graham shared, if in a slightly more muted way.[36] Yet, in October 1843, Graham could make the comment that, 'All the authorities begin to converge towards the admssion of the necessity of obtaining some influence, direct or indirect, over that priesthood which holds in subjection seven-eighths of the Irish people'.[37]

In the summer of 1846, the Peel administration gave way to that of the Whigs under the rather indecisive leadership of Lord John Russell. The question of the rôle of the Catholic Church in the United Kingdom had been, as we have already seen, a source of concern to Peel and it is not surprising that the Whigs saw in the contrast between the Established Church in Ireland and the Catholic Church a source of injustice. They were, however, to prove no more successful than their predecessors in solving the Church problem in Ireland as the events leading up to the Ecclesiastical Titles Bill dispute were to show so clearly. They, too, were preoccupied by a nagging apprehension about the power of the priests in the political and social life of Ireland.

This conflict of feelings emerges again from the correspondence

[35] Kevin B. Nowlan, *The politics of repeal*, pp. 227–9.
[36] Peel to De Grey, 22 Aug. 1843, Peel papers, Add.MS 40478, ff. 160–7.
[37] Graham to Peel, 30 Oct. 1843, Peel papers, Add.MS 40449, ff. 166–9.

of Lord Clarendon, who became Lord Lieutenant in May 1847, with members of the Russell ministry in London. The involvement of many priests in the tenant-right movement from 1847 onwards, the active participation of the clergy in the 1847 general election in support of the Repeal interest, were considerations which exercised the Lord Lieutenant a great deal, but so did the consideration that, 'The priests are everywhere behaving ill and are bitterly hostile to the Government whom they accuse of starving the people. . . .' There was always the danger or the fear that the priests would take over the political leadership now that Daniel O'Connell was dead—an ill-educated clergy who shared, it was claimed, the political passions of their flocks: 'The clergy have thus become the slaves of the people'.[38] The Whigs, however, tended to the view that if somehow the dependence of the clergy on the people could be broken, the position would be improved; and Archbishop Murray assured Lord Clarendon, in October 1848, that 'if the vote of the clergy could be taken by ballot, the question [state payment of the clergy] would be carried by an immense majority though they will not dare express themselves favourably to it in the dioceses of opposing bishops'.[39]

In practice, the Dublin Castle authorities sought to widen their contacts with the Catholic hierarchy beyond the 'whig' bishops such as Dr Murray, or, as Clarendon put it to Dr Foran, the Catholic bishop of Waterford, in July 1847: 'I have long regretted that between the Roman Catholic hierarchy and the Government there should not exist those friendly relations which, without in any way affecting the independence of either, might manifestly be for the advantage of both'.[40] This approach only met with limited success, but the attempt to establish a closer accord with the Catholic Church was made on another and higher level as well.

We have seen how the Peel administration sought to secure the active support of the Holy See in its efforts to contain the political influence of the Irish clergy. Its successor, the Russell ministry, brought the process a stage further, but its efforts were to be hampered both by the traditional caution of the Holy See and by the emergence of a very influential Irish clerical 'lobby' in Rome. This latter was quickly recognised as being in many ways hostile by the British Government, but the British representatives did not succeed in defeating the influence of men of the quality of Dr Paul Cullen (then of the Irish College) who were imbued perhaps with both a distaste for Protestant power and something of a

[38] Clarendon to Russell, 12 July 1847, Bodleian Lib. MS, Clarendon papers, letterbook I; Memorandum for Lord Minto [Oct., 1847], *ibid.*
[39] Clarendon to Russell, 4 Oct. 1848, Clarendon papers, letterbook III.
[40] Clarendon to Foran, 28 July 1847, Clarendon papers, letterbook I.

new confidence in an uncompromising, independent Catholicism.[41]
Here was an approach which certainly contrasted with the dis-
creet policies of Dr Murray in his dealings with government.

The Russell administration, however, did meet with some
initial success. As a result of rather secret negotiations conducted
through the papal nuncio in Vienna, who advised the British to
negotiate always directly with the Court of Rome and *not* with
the rival factions in the Irish Church, a private letter was sent, on
10 April 1847, by Pope Pius IX to the four Irish Archbishops,
advising them to work for the preservation of peace. In discussing
this fairly satisfactory outcome, the British ambassador in Vienna
made the interesting comment that the Holy See would be satisfied
simply with a legal recognition of the Catholic Church as a legal
institution in Ireland and an assurance that there would be no
interference by the state in ecclesiastical matters. The ambassador
added hopefully that Rome, he believed, had more confidence in
the British government than in any continental power.[42]

A few months later, he was not so sure of all this—thanks to
the intervention of the Catholic lobby in Rome. In August 1847,
Lord Palmerston, the foreign secretary, made clear his annoyance
to Russell that, as a result of the political activities of the Irish
priests, 'I see that almost all the Irish elections have gone in
favour of repeal candidates; and this just after two or three
million of Irish have been saved from famine and pestilence by
money which, if the Union had not existed, their own Parliament
would never have been able to raise'.[43] An effective diplomatic
representation at Rome, he considered, was essential in the
circumstances.

The insufficiency of the lines of communication between
London and Rome was underlined by the issue of a papal rescript,
in October 1847, condemning the provincial colleges because
there was not sufficient provision for the religious instruction of
the student body. It was a reminder, too, of the influence of the
more uncompromising sector of the Irish Church in Rome. The
Minto mission, at the end of 1847, to Rome had wider political
implications than the Irish problem—but it was of central importance in the negotiations. The representations, backed by Dr
Murray, covered old ground—the trouble caused by the confusion
of political and religious issues in Ireland, that the clergy under

[41] Kevin B. Nowlan, *The politics of repeal*, pp. 174–9. See further, John H. Whyte,
'Political problems', in Patrick J. Corish (ed.), *A History of Irish Catholicism*, vol.
v. (fascicule), sect. i. 1–12.
[42] Lord Ponsonby (British ambassador at Vienna) to Russell, 3 May 1847, Russell
papers, P.R.O. 30/22/6.
[43] Palmerston to Russell, 19 Aug. 1847, Russell papers, P.R.O. 30/22/6.

pressure were becoming 'the slaves of the people'. Only Rome could provide a remedy.[44] Torn between British representations and Irish replies, Rome compromised, yet again, with a rescript of January 1848, which said that, while the Congregation of Propaganda could not believe that the Irish priests would condone murder, to avoid any such allegations, the clergy should confine themselves to the spiritual sphere alone. The situation, in effect, remained unchanged and Rome was not prepared to risk a full confrontation with the Irish radicals.[45] The Russell administration was to receive no further practical comfort from Rome.

There remained one other possibility of neutralising the Catholic clergy in politics: to somehow find a place for the Roman Catholic Church in the constitutional scene—to create, in some form, a second establishment. This would both free the churchmen from dependence financially on their flocks and link the Catholic Church with a state, albeit still a Protestant state. There were memories here of the proposals made before 1828–29 to meet Catholic claims—and neither Peel in a tentative way, nor Russell in a more consequential way, were able to discover a formula which would overcome the deep suspicions in Ireland to state endowment—an interesting combination of O'Connellite liberalism and historic experience may have been at work here. The contrast with the continental pattern of Church-state relations is obvious.[46]

It would lie outside the scope of this paper to develop the theme of the efforts made by the Russell administration to give the Catholic Church some legal status within the United Kingdom. A measure was passed—which proved abortive—to establish diplomatic relations with Rome; and, as late as November 1849, Russell was still raising, in Cabinet circles, the question of an endowment for the Catholic Church in Ireland. But the times were unfavourable. Sectarian feeling was rising in Britain and Ireland, hostility to Ireland and Roman Catholicism was growing, and Russell had regretfully to write to Lord Clarendon: 'I consulted Tufnell [chief whip] yesterday as to the probable fate of any proposal to pay the Catholic priests. His opinion is that it would upset the Government and that the measure would fail, so we must put it off for another year'—an optimistic estimate as it proved.[47]

[44] Clarendon to Russell, 1 Oct. 1847, Clarendon papers, letterbook I.
[45] *Dublin Evening Post*, 5 Feb. 1848.
[46] Kennedy F. Roche, 'The relations of the Catholic Church and the State in England and Ireland, 1800–52', in James Hogan (ed.), *Historical Studies III*, pp. 9–24.
[47] Russell to Clarendon, 22 Nov. 1849, Clarendon papers, Ir. box 26, bundle 34.

Kevin B. Nowlan

Already with the activities of the clergy in the Repeal Association and especially from 1847–48 onwards in the tenant-right movement could be recognised symptoms of the rôle which the Catholic clergy in the post-O'Connell era were to play in Irish politics. The grievances of the people, nationalism, the reality of the Ascendancy, the unsatisfactory status of the Church and the religious tensions of the time combined to keep a very significant sector of the clergy in politics and no government found an answer. One distinguished public servant, Sir Randolph Routh, in a memorandum to Lord Clarendon, at the end of 1847, put the challenge facing the state when he said: 'The measure which of all others would produce the greatest moral effect in Ireland is exactly the one which it is to be feared no ministry has now the power to carry out . . . . the recognition by the Government of the religion of the Irish people. I do not mean by this simple toleration nor the removal even of every existing disability, but the frank adoption by the state of the Roman Catholic religion as part of itself'.[48]

[48] Routh to Clarendon [Dec., 1847], Sir William Somerville's letterbook, ff. 27–34. (In the possession of Q.C. Agnew Somerville, Esq., Navan, Co. Meath).

K

Senchas: The Nature of Gaelic Historical Tradition

Francis John Byrne

Imprudens Scottorum gens, rerum suarum obliuiscens, acta quasi inaudita siue nullo modo facta uindicat, quoniam minus tribuere litteris aliquid operum suorum praecurat, et ob hoc genealogias Scotigenae gentis litteris tribuam: primo gentis Ebir, secundo gentis Herimon, tertio gentis Hir, quarto gentis Lugdach meic Itha.

'The foolish Irish nation, forgetful of its history, boasts of incredible or completely fabulous deeds, since it has been careless about committing to writing any of its achievements. Therefore I propose to write down the genealogies of the Irish race: firstly the race of Éber, secondly the race of Éremón, thirdly the race of Ír, and fourthly the race of Lugaid son of Íth'.[1]

These words were most probably written in the late ninth or early tenth century by a scholar whom it is tempting to identify with Cormac mac Cuilennáin, the famous king and bishop of Cashel who fell at the battle of Belach Mugna in 908. They remind us of the complaint voiced by the Welshman Nennius a century earlier: *aliqua excerpta scribere curaui quae hebetudo gentis Britanniae deiecerat, quia nullam peritiam habuerunt neque ullam commemorationem in libris posuerunt doctores illius insulae Britanniae*; 'I have gone to the trouble of recording certain fragments which the slothful nature of the British race had cast aside in neglect, because the scholars of that same island of Britain had no knowledge of tradition, neither did they keep any written records'.[2] Such remarks were in fact commonplace among medieval historians since the time of Gregory of Tours: *Decedente atque immo potius pereunte in urbibus Gallicanis liberalium cultura*

---

[1] M. A. O'Brien, *Corpus geneal. Hib.*, i. (1962), p. 192; cf. Paul Walsh, *Irish men of learning* (1947), p. 112, and F. J. Byrne in *Z.C.P.*, xxix. (1964), p. 384.
[2] For this passage see Ifor Williams, *Bull. Board Celt. Studies*, ix. (1937-9), pp. 342-4; *Z.C.P.*, xxv. (1956), p. 157; N. K. Chadwick, *Studies in the early British church* (1958), p. 45; Bieler, *Scriptorium* xiii. (1959), p. 118.

137

litterarum . . . ingemiscebant saepius plerique, dicentes: Vae diebus nostris, quia periit studium litterarum a nobis, nec repperitur in populis qui gesta praesencia promulgare possit in paginis! 'With the decay and indeed destruction of liberal education in the cities of Gaul many people complained repeatedly, lamenting the conditions of the time, the death of learning, and the absence of any writer capable of recording contemporary events'.[3]

Such admirable sentiments echoed by our genealogist stand in odd contrast to his placid acceptance of the pseudo-historical descent of the Irish noble families from the sons of Míl. The truth is that Gaelic Ireland never produced a Bede or a Gregory of Tours. The muse of history here never escaped from the swaddling bands of *senchas*. *Senchas* was the traditional lore of Irish culture: topographical (*dindshenchas*—an essential part of the poet's repertoire),[4] legal (the most ambitious attempt to compile an authoritative corpus of law texts was known as the *Senchas Már*, 'the great tradition'),[5] and genealogical. In this last sense it comprised tribal history and origin legends, and was the preserve of the *senchaid* or 'chronicler' as the Elizabethans were to call him. In modern Irish the *seanchaí* is the custodian of oral lore and folk tradition.

Latin *peritia* acquired a specialised meaning in Ireland, corresponding to historical and genealogical *senchas*. It is interesting to see Nennius also using it in this sense. In the late seventh century Muirchú says, in the preface to his Life of St Patrick: *pauca haec de multis sancti Patricii gestis parua peritia . . . explicare aggrediar*; 'these few from among the many deeds of Saint Patrick shall I attempt to narrate, although my historical learning is small'.[6] *Peritia* occurs frequently in the genealogical manuscripts as the exact equivalent of *senchas*: *De peritia et de genelogis Dál Niad-*

---

[3] *Historia Francorum, praefatio.* For the medieval *topos* or commonplace see Ernst Curtius, *Europäische Literatur und lateinisches Mittelalter* (zweite Auflage, 1954), chapter 5, especially pp. 93 ff.; and for a warning against taking this passage at its face value, *ibid.*, p. 159.

[4] The Middle Irish topographical poems are edited by Edward Gwynn, *The metrical Dindshenchas* in five volumes with translation and commentary, R.I.A. Todd lecture series, viii.–xii. (1903–35).

[5] For the dating and original state of this compilation see Thurneysen, 'Aus dem irischen Recht IV. 6. Zu den bisherigen Ausgaben der irischen Rechtstexte. I Ancient Laws of Ireland und Senchas Már,' *Z.C.P.*, xvi. (1926), pp. 167–96; 'Zum ursprünglichen Umfang des Senchas Már,' *ibid.*, xviii. (1930), pp. 355–64; MacNeill, 'Prolegomena to a study of the *Ancient Laws of Ireland*,' published with notes and introduction by Dr. Binchy in *The Irish Jurist*, (new series), ii. (1967), 106–15. Binchy describes the *Senchas Már* as 'in no sense a "code", but simply a collection of tracts made about 700 A.D.' (loc. cit., p. 108).

[6] *Bk. Arm.*, fo. 20ra 21–7; cf. Stokes, *Vita Tripartita*, ii. (1887), p. 269. The whole of this elaborately written preface is a veritable tissue of *topoi* and deserves further study.

Cuirp; De peritia et genelogis Loĭchsi; Alia peritia de genelogis et de generibus Hibernensium[7]—examples could be multiplied indefinitely. The *senchaide* are styled *periti: In Cathaĭr Mār immorro xxx.iii. meic [lais] ut periti dicunt;* 'this Cathaĭr Már had thirty-three sons according to the genealogists'.[8] Variant traditions which do not accord with the *senchas coitchenn* or accepted teaching of the schools are dismissed by ascription to *imperiti:* *Dā brāthair didiu Eochaid 7 Conn Cĕtchathach, dā mac Feidelmid Rechtada 7 nĭ hEochaid mac Airtt m. Cuind ut imperiti dicunt;* 'Eochaid and Conn of the Hundred Battles were two brothers then, the two sons of Feidelmid Rechtaid, and not "Eochaid son of Art son of Conn" as the unlearned say'.[9] *Aliter: Eochaid Liathān m. Maine Cherbba m. Cirbb m. Ailella Flaind Bic m. Fiachach Fir-dā-liach, sed tamen hoc non probabile est quia Fiachaich Mullethan 7 Fiachu Fer-dā-liach duo nomina unius hominis sunt quamuis imperiti aliter putant;* 'Otherwise: Eochaid Liathán son of Maine etc. . . . —however, this is unlikely because Fiachu Mullethan and Fiachu Fer-dá-liach are two names for the one man, although the unlearned think otherwise'.[10]

We have much reason to be grateful to the men of learning who guarded so jealously the mystery of their art. They have preserved for us a mass of detailed information thanks to which we can draw up tables of dynastic succession for every important kingdom in Ireland as well as for many of the multiplicity of petty *tuatha*. The first volume of O'Brien's *Corpus genealogiarum Hiberniae* contains close on 13,000 names, the bulk of which refer to historical personages who lived between the fifth and twelfth centuries.[11] Only a small proportion of these names are identifiable from other records, and the dearth of early southern annals has left many of the Munster pedigrees without an adequate chronological framework.

The genealogies are fullest for the three hundred years between c.450 and 750 A.D. A fairly comprehensive compilation covering the whole of Ireland seems to have been composed in the eighth century and to have been brought up to date from time to time in subsequent generations with varying degrees of consistency. The earliest manuscripts both date from the twelfth century—

---

[7] Rawlinson B. 502, ff. 120b 46, 126b 13, 142a 10; O'Brien, *Corpus geneal. Hib.*, pp. 42, 87, 147. The manuscript Laud Misc. 610 reads for the last example *Senchas Airgiall inso.*
[8] R 120b 51; O'Brien, p. 42.
[9] R 125a 55/b 1; O'Brien, p. 79.
[10] R 151a 51–4; O'Brien, p. 225.
[11] See my review in *Z.C.P.*, xxix. (1964), pp. 381–5, and J. V. Kelleher, 'The pre-Norman Irish genealogies,' *I.H.S.*, xvi. (1968), pp. 138–53.

Rawlinson B 502 and the Book of Leinster.[12] But oddly enough they devote considerably more space to petty tribes of no political significance and to antiquarian traditions than to the dynasties whose kings strode so forcefully across the 'trembling sod' of twelfth-century Ireland. Professor Kelleher has suggested, I think quite rightly, that 'by the twelfth century the corpus was already in a state of partial desuetude and considerable disrepair. It may be that already the chief motive for making these collections was historical, not to say antiquarian'.[13] For the kings of the twelfth century based their new powers on wealth and military prowess, fortified by the ecclesiastical reformers of the day, and kinship was a dying force in politics: the great provincial kings all participated in the partition of Mide and sought to depose sub-kings, intruding themselves or their sons into their place as 'strangers in sovereignty'. Toirrdelbach ua Briain and his son Muirchertach took the foreign city of Limerick as their true capital; Toirrdelbach Ua Conchobair carved out a centre of power in Connacht based on Tuam and Dunmore, ringing it around with castles and strategic bridges; and all claimants to the high-kingship saw Dublin rather than Tara as the symbol of monarchy.

This process, it is true, was rendered abortive by the Anglo-Norman invasions which achieved the conquest of precisely those areas which were most advanced politically and economically. The history of Gaelic Ireland after 1169 is in many ways regressive. The backward regions became the most typically Gaelic, and pedigrees once more became important. But it would be a grave mistake to base our picture of pre-Norman Ireland too closely on the detailed information we have, for instance, of sixteenth-century Ulster. Archaic though that society was, it represented the end-product of a long evolution. Ulster was but a single region then of a culturally fragmented country, and its society but a maimed limb. It had incorporated many features of bastard feudalism and was approaching the 'clan system' of eighteenth-century Scotland. The latter, so far from being a survival of a pure Celtic polity, was in effect a simplification (resulting both

[12] These form the basis of O'Brien's first volume, published posthumously; O'Brien's transcript of the genealogies in the fourteenth-century Trinity College manuscript H.2.7 is being prepared for publication as the second volume of the *Corpus*.
[13] *I.H.S.*, xvi, p. 139. It is perhaps revealing that the two twelfth-century genealogical manuscripts, viz., Rawlinson B 502 and the Book of Leinster, disagree totally as to the pedigree of the chief family of the Northern Uí Néill of their time—Mac or Ua Lochlainn. For this problem see James Hogan, 'The Irish law of kingship,' *R.I.A. Proc.*, xl. (1932), pp. 210f.; id., 'The Ua Briain kingship in Telach óc,' *Féilsgríbhinn Eóin Mhic Néill*, ed. Ryan (Dublin, 1940), pp. 425f.; and Séamus ó Ceallaigh, *Gleanings from Ulster history* (Cork, 1951), pp. 73–87.

from internal evolution and external pressure) of what had once been a complex structure.[14]

Equally mistaken is the assumption that Irish society was static. This illusion indeed is fostered by the documents, which, emanating as they do from a privileged learned class with vested interests both in preserving the status quo and in claiming that the structure they found so satisfactory dated from time immemorial, display a total lack of historical perspective. A prime example are the law tracts, fossilised in the early eighth century: the archaic and obscure texts studied in the schools down to the seventeenth century ignored the changes that had actually taken place in Irish society well before the Norman invasion. The glossators and commentators of the Middle Irish period help little in the elucidation of the sacred text: rather do they reveal by their incomprehension that, for instance, the elaborate ramifications of the *fine* or joint-family, were already obsolete.[15] In the eleventh century ruling dynasties resorted to the device of adopting a surname: thus the common descendants of a relatively recent king were marked off from their more distant relatives as alone constituting the royal *derbfhine*. Needless to say, this process lost its usefulness after a few generations, and sometimes a new surname was adopted by the inner circle of the royal heirs.[16] But the tendency was for all members of the 'name' to feel a common relationship long after they had ceased to be legally bound together, thus paving the way for a fully fledged 'clan system'.

For the earlier history of Irish society the laws are our primary source. Taken together with the archaeological evidence they provide much information on the economy. But their excessive schematisation does not allow us to differentiate between one part of the country and another. Obviously the economy cannot have been identical everywhere. Some areas no doubt, then as now, had more tillage, while others were predominantly pastoral. Only in certain *tuatha* can summer pasturage on the mountains have been a practical proposition.

The genealogies too are reticent on many points where we

---

[14] Cf. Binchy's remarks, 'The passing of the old order,' in *Proceedings of the International Congress of Celtic Studies, Dublin 1959*, ed. Ó Cuív. (Dublin, 1962), p. 132.
[15] *Ibid.*
[16] For example, the descendants of Eochaid mac Ardgail, king of Ulaid (972–1004), took the surname Mac or Ua Eochada, but when after 1137 the kingship became confined to the descendants of Donnsléibe Mac Eochada (+1091) the *rígdamnai* set themselves apart from the rest of the family by adopting the new surname of Mac Duinnsléibe; similarly in the neighbouring kingdom of Airgialla the family of Mac Mathgamna traced their descent to Mathgamain (+1022) mac Laidgnén meic Cerbaill and so are an off-shoot of the surname Ua Cerbaill.

should like to question them. Anyone who reads through a genealogical tract will be struck by the immense number of families mentioned. But we are not told whether all or any of these groups formed actual *tuatha*. Often they can have been little more than families living in a certain area, claiming a common descent that distinguished them from their neighbours (either to their advantage or disadvantage), but hardly forming separate political entities. Sometimes they may have had memories of a former tribal status, and one is left with the distinct impression when attempting to draw detailed maps that in some regions a form of tribalism persisted well into the historical period among the *aithechthuatha* or subject peoples. In other words these may not always have formed a coherent grouping that can neatly be shown on a map, but lived intermingled with their neighbours (on the poorer land perhaps) while having a king who represented them as a people (in the original sense of the word *tuath*) rather than as a territorial unit.[17] Even where a definite territory was recognised, as it was for the dynastic kingdoms by the seventh century at latest, the boundaries may not have been such as would lend themselves to cartographical delineation. Waste land often divided *tuath* from *tuath*, and the analogy of other tribal societies suggests that in some cases grazing, pannage, fishing and hunting rights may have overlapped topographically. However, in the eighth and ninth centuries territorialisation was definitely well under way and helped to shape the fortune of dynasties and develop new concepts of kingship.

It was Eoin MacNeill who first utilised the genealogies to complement the annals in making a coherent picture of early Irish history.[18] The nature of the annals does not afford an adequate framework for historical narrative. Early Irish history is a jigsaw that must be pieced together from a thousand fragments. No single source can supply enough of these, and we are in grave danger of obtaining a distorted picture from exclusive reliance on any one—annalistic, genealogical or legal.

Valuable work on the genealogies was also done by T. F. O'Rahilly, following closely on MacNeill's footsteps (in spite of his severe criticisms of the older scholar).[19] In my opinion, however, he made a fatal error in his use of these sources for the

[17] See for example my remarks on the tribes and kingdoms of Meath in Eogan, 'Excavations at Knowth,' *R.I.A. Proc.*, 66 C 4 (1968), pp. 392–5; for a fuller discussion see F. J. Byrne, 'Tribes and tribalism in early Ireland', *Ériu*, xxii. (1971), pp. 128–66.

[18] *Celtic Ireland* (Dublin, 1921), pp. 43–63; 'Early Irish population-groups,' *R.I.A. Proc.*, xxix. (1911).

[19] *Early Irish history and mythology* (Dublin, 1946).

reconstruction of the prehistoric Celtic invasions of Ireland—an error compounded by his almost total reliance on linguistic criteria. O'Rahilly castigated archaeologists for fitting their theories into the framework of the *Lebor Gabála*, but it is difficult to acquit him of the same charge.[20] (To be fair, here again he was progressing along a path first trodden by MacNeill.) Such is the fascination of the account given in *Lebor Gabála* of the successive invasions of Ireland in prehistoric times, that most modern scholars have sought to find in it memories of the Celtic conquest, and to assume that the *aithechthuatha* of historical times were aboriginal inhabitants enslaved by the newcomers. To O'Rahilly the Uí Néill, Connachta and Eóganachta were the 'Goidels' or Q-Celts, the last wave of Celtic invaders. They were preceded by several P-Celtic invasions. He says very little about the pre-Celtic population and tends to be rude about Pokorny's theories with regard to them.[21]

O'Rahilly, however, is forced to twist his own linguistic evidence. According to him the Dál Riata were P-Celts—and yet it was they who brought Q-Celtic to Scotland.[22] The Érainn were also P-Celts—and yet the ogam inscriptions, the earliest documents of the Gaelic language, are clustered thickest in their lands.[23] The geographical distribution of the Uí Néill and their historically documented expansion in the seventh and eighth centuries point conclusively to their origin in Connacht; this was seen by Mac-Neill, but O'Rahilly derided him and declared that they had landed on the Meath coast and pushed westwards.[24]

In fact it is more than doubtful if the *Lebor Gabála* preserves any genuine traditions of invasions, Celtic or otherwise. The story of Míl seems to have started in the eighth century with his two sons Éremón and Éber being invented as ancestors of the Connachta and Uí Néill and of the Munster Eóganachta respectively, in conformity with the political theory that Ireland was

[20] *Op. cit.*, esp. pp. 263–5, 419–43.

[21] *Op. cit.*, p. 439.

[22] This contradiction was pointed out by M. A. O'Brien, 'Irish origin legends,' in *Early Irish society*, ed. Dillon (Dublin, 1954), pp. 50f.

[23] O'Rahilly's attempt to extricate himself from this particular dilemma is worth quoting: 'The Goidelic invaders gradually won a dominating position in Ireland, not by force of numbers . . . but by their skill in war and politics. Doubtless they were also helped by the prestige of a superior civilization. It was they, for instance, who brought the Ogamic script to Ireland, though the later use of this script for epigraphic purposes acquired a greater vogue among the goidelicized tribes, especially those of the south of Ireland, than it did among the descendants of the original Goidels.' *Early Ir. hist.*, p. 495.

[24] *Ibid.*, pp. 161–83, 193–208, 478f., 489. Cf. MacNeill, 'Colonization under the early kings of Tara,' *Galway Arch. Soc. Jn.*, xvi. (1935), pp. 101–24; F. J. Byrne, *The rise of the Uí Néill and the high-kingship of Ireland*, O'Donnell lecture, 1969 (Dublin, 1970); id., *Irish kings and high-kings* (London, 1973), pp. 83f.

divided into two spheres of influence, Leth Cuinn and Leth Moga.[25] As the Ulaid in the north, however, did not belong genealogically to Leth Cuinn, and most inconveniently refused to succumb to the Uí Néill, they too were fitted into the scheme by the addition of Ír son of Míl as the remote ancestor.[26] Later again other dynasties and peoples who could not with propriety be regarded as 'non-Irish' were also traced back to Míl, whose progeny underwent an alarming if posthumous increase.

The Irish preserved no tradition of being Celts, and neither did the Welsh. The medieval pseudo-historical theories about their origin did not connect them either with one another or with the ancient Gauls. Their scholars relied on dubious etymological and antiquarian speculation derived largely from the works of Isidore of Seville.[27] Furthermore, it is improbable that the origin-legends of dynasties who came to power in the fifth century should tell us anything of the ethnic roots of the Irish people. Any such presumption would ignore a hiatus of several hundred, perhaps a thousand, years which yawns between the date of our earliest records and the hypothetical Celtic invasions. It should be remembered too that the names of the *aithech-thuatha* are by and large as Celtic as those of the dominant dynasties—indeed that the highly respectable Celtic root *rīgion* 'kingdom' (as found in Ciarraige, Calraige, Dubraige, Dartraige, Sordraige, Tradraige and countless other tribal names) is the exclusive property of these subject peoples.[28]

A new approach to the genealogical traditions is required.

[25] This theory is exemplified in several passages in the genealogical tracts and in the earliest stratum of the Irish World Chronicle. Cf. also Kelleher's remarks, *I.H.S.*, xvi. (1968), p. 143; the story of Míl may have been in existence as early as the seventh century, for Fiacc's hymn *Génair Patraic* refers to the Irish converted by Saint Patrick as *maicc Ébir maicc Érimón*—see Stokes and Strachen, *Thesaurus palaeo-hibernicus*, ii. (Cambridge, 1903), p. 316.

[26] However, it was not the true Ulaid, the Dál Fiatach, who were represented as descendants of Ír, since they were known to be Érainn; but the Cruthin dynasties of Dál nAraidi and Uí Echach Cobo, several of whose kings ruled the province from the fifth century to the tenth; see the notes to my edition of *Clann Ollaman uaisle Emna*, *Studia Hib.*, iv. (1964), pp. 61–94, and O'Rahilly, *Early Ir. hist.*, pp. 341–52. The Érainn were later fitted into the Milesian scheme—O'Rahilly, *op. cit.*, pp. 81f. The names Éremón and Éber apparently derive from the Irish and Latin names for Ireland, while the later Ír may have been suggested by the Old Norse *Íraland*, though O'Rahilly thinks otherwise, *ibid.*, pp. 195f.

[27] Thus the Welsh seem to have found the idea for their alleged descent from the Roman Brutus in Isidore's unflattering derivation of the name Brittones: *eo quod bruti sint* (*Etymol.*, IX. ii. 102), and MacNeill noted that the details of the story of the Milesian invasion involving the tower of Bregon and Inber Scéne resulted from a misunderstanding of a passage in Orosius—*Phases of Irish history* (Dublin, 1919) pp. 90–2. Meyer, however, notes that in some earlier versions a relationship with either the British Celts or the Gauls is recognised—*Ueber die älteste irische Dichtung*, i. (Berlin, 1913), p. 26.

[28] MacNeill, 'Population-groups,' p. 67.

Rather can we surmise that they reveal the political relations between the various tribes and dynasties that existed at the time of their compilation. We can even see at times the doctrine changing to adapt itself to new conditions. For instance, the north Sligo tribe of Calraige were no doubt connected with the others of that name scattered throughout Ireland, and the genealogists make all the Calraige descend from Lugaid Cál son of Dáire Sírchréchtach ancestor of the Corcu Loígde and other Érainn tribes. But they were soon absorbed into the Uí Néill overkingdom of Cairpre Dromma Cliab, and so we find a later tract claiming that they descend from a totally fictitious Cal son of Cairpre son of Niall Noígiallach.[29]

We may profitably compare the biblical genealogical scheme as set forth in Genesis x and the opening chapters of I Chronicles. Here the descendants of Ham, Shem and Japhet do not correspond very well with what modern scholars regard as the Hamitic, Semitic and Indo-European branches of mankind, but reflect instead the geographical and political relationships current at the time of writing.

The saga of the battle of Crinna tells how Cormac mac Airt defeated the Ulaid with the help of Tadg mac Céin and drove them from the Boyne, whereafter Tadg was rewarded with all the lands he could encompass in a chariot drive but cheated of Tara itself.[30] This tale has nothing to tell the historian of the third or fourth century, when Cormac is supposed to have lived, but is rather an origin-tale composed to explain in mythical terms the political situation which actually obtained in the eighth century. At this time the Uí Néill are dominant in the midlands, but the Ulaid are remembered to have once reached the Boyne and are still in their reduced state enemies of the Uí Néill. The lands north and south of the lower Boyne are occupied by the Ciannachta vassals of the Uí Néill, who are not eligible for the high-kingship. The situation is projected onto a mythological plane: it is the result of the exploits of the legendary ancestors of the Uí Néill and Ciannachta. At a second stage, perhaps, it was incorporated into the chronological scheme of the pseudo-historians and so 'dated' to the third century—in the teeth of

[29] See O'Brien, *Corpus geneal. Hib.*, i., pp. 155, 256, and compare O'Raithbheartaigh, *Genealogical tracts I* (Dublin, 1932), p. 153; D. ó Corráin, 'Lugaid Cál and the Callraige,' *Éigse*, xiii. (1970), pp. 225f.; id., *Ireland before the Normans* (Dublin, 1972), pp. 75–7 discusses the aetiological methods of the genealogists. Similarly the Fir Thulach of Mide, of Leinster origin but under the overlordship of the Southern Uí Néill, were later given pedigrees deriving them from a non-existent Fer Tulach son of Niall—Walsh, *The place-names of Westmeath* (Dublin, 1957), pp. 162–5.
[30] O'Brien, *op. cit.*, pp. 403–5; id., 'Irish origin-legends,' pp. 44f.; O'Grady, *Silva Gadelica*, i. (London, 1892), pp. 319–26.

evidence to the effect that the Ulaid were still powerful in Louth in the seventh.[31]

Similarly Carney has shown that the tale of the Birth of Cormac is neither pure literature nor historical saga in the usual sense but is political and didactic in purpose. The ancestor of the Uí Néill kings of Tara is made the subject of the universal Birth of the Hero Myth. Several versions have been combined, making for some confusion in the telling: the Romulus motif (hero suckled by wolf), the Cypselus motif (hero hidden in vessel), and a more obscure rescue by horses. Native Irish versions of these myths were in existence (and the circumstances of the hero's conception belong to the characteristically Irish form of the king-myth), but Carney believes that the author deliberately drew on Roman parallels to enhance the prestige of the Uí Néill. The story also serves to explain the special relations between the Uí Néill and Airgialla and the Corcorthrí and Luigne.[32] The same story tells how Eógan, ancestor of the Munster Eóganachta, was an ally of Cormac's father Art at the battle of Mag Muccrime and met a similar fate. Closely parallel to the conception of Cormac is that of the birth of Eógan's son Fiachu Mullethan: his maternal grandfather was the druid Treth moccu Creccai, 'hence it is a crime for any man of the Eóganacht to slay a man of the Crecraige'—the didactic purpose is here made explicit, and the parallelism reflects the eighth-century Leth Cuinn-Leth Moga division of hegemonies already referred to.

At this point it may be convenient to expatiate somewhat on the nature of Irish tradition. It is methodologically convenient to distinguish four categories: myth, legend, pseudo-history and fiction. Myth I use here in a strict sense: that which, irrespective of its objective historical truth, was at some period believed in and had a validity for and a function within the society that believed it. The importance of mythology for the historical understanding of an early society can hardly be overstressed. The Irish concept of kingship, for instance, is rooted in mythology. Myth in its turn counteracts upon history. If life may be said to imitate art, it is even more true that if in early Ireland we can isolate a characteristic myth of kingship we shall find historical kings attempting to live up to the demands of that myth. Unfortunately, it is not always easy to recognise the genuine myth from the accretions which have grown up around it. We have no purely pagan documents from Celtic Ireland. Contamination

[31] Byrne, 'The Ireland of St. Columba,' *Historical studies V*, ed. McCracken (London, 1965), pp. 49–52.
[32] 'Cath Maige Muccrime,' in *Irish sagas*, ed. Dillon (2nd edition, Cork, 1968), pp. 148–61; see further F. J. Byrne, *Irish Kings*, pp. 65–8.

from Christian monastic learning has set in before the date of our earliest written records. Euhemerisation was a favourite device with early Irish scholars and monks who wished to preserve ancient traditions without compromising their Christian beliefs. One reason for the apparent inconsequentialities and incoherences which prevent many of the Irish sagas from attaining the highest literary merit is that the events related have been historicised and the characters humanised, so that the author is often only dimly aware of the true nature of the motifs he uses. Paradoxically, it is only when the historian realises that these motifs are mythological that he can make full use of the stories. Once he has isolated the myth behind the pseudo-historical text he may be able to make valid deductions as to the nature of the society which produced it.

Legend, which in its most highly developed literary form is enshrined in saga or epic, relates historical memories. Where we can check later legends by contemporary records we can observe how the oral tradition tends to telescope historical perspective. Real persons may be confused with mythical figures and events which occurred in different generations be presented as contemporaneous. But normally, enough of the original milieu (which may of course differ considerably from that of the writer) is preserved so that we can speak with some confidence of the existence of a genuine tradition. It is however impossible for the actual historical course of events to be reconstructed from the saga accounts.[33] The *Táin Bó Cuailgne* reflects a Celtic heroic age of which we have independent evidence, but we can never know if Cú Chulainn, Conchobar or Fergus ever existed.[34] Less elaborate legends, often fragmentary or half-forgotten, are found in many other sources, notably the genealogies.

Pseudo-history is a deliberate attempt to construct a coherent chronological system from such myths and legends and even from wholly extraneous material. The introduction of Christianity, with its profound sense of history, resulted in such activity becoming the chief occupation of the Irish men of learning. One

[33] Cf. the remarks of Rhys Carpenter, *Folk Tale, fiction and saga in the Homeric epic* (Cambridge, Mass., 1946), p. 60: 'If there is one conclusion that stands firm in the study of mediaeval epic legend as it occurs in such poems as the Nibelungenlied, the Song of Roland, Beowulf and their kind, it is that one and all are dependent on actual incident and historic fact for some of their material, but that they present to the analyst an irreversible process. If he already knows the history from other sources (such as contemporary prose chronicles), he can discover how events have been distorted and transmuted to suit the irresponsible humors of the poets; but if, on the contrary, he knows only the epics, he can never hope to change them back into the history out of which they arose.'
[34] See Kenneth Jackson, *The oldest Irish tradition: a window on the Iron Age* (Cambridge, The Rede Lecture, 1964).

of the earliest such schemes for the prehistory of Ireland is found in the Irish World Chronicle, probably composed at Bangor in the eighth century by monks who had become accustomed to annalistic writing and who sought to fit ancient Irish traditions into the chronological framework of the Hieronymo-Eusebian chronicle.[35] It reached its culmination in the various recensions of the *Lebor Gabála*.[36] As we have seen, a favourite method among the Irish scholars was euhemerisation: the theory that ancient gods were in fact distorted memories of prehistoric kings and heroes.

Another type of pseudo-history is exemplified by the growth of the theory of the high-kingship: the use of genuine historical records to propagate a political programme. It is noticeable that kings who lived later than the early eighth century do not seem to have been considered suitable subjects for saga. However, annalistic records begin to become reasonably full from this period on, and in the later Middle Irish era a new type of pseudo-historical literature grew up, in which large elements of bardic panegyric were injected into the dry bones of the annals to give historical romances written in the newly fashionable bombastic and alliterative prose. Such works may keep reasonably close to the historical record, like the *Cogadh Gaedhel re Gallaibh*, or depart wildly from it, like the *Caithréim Cellacháin Chaisil*. Some such works even keep the annalistic framework around which they were woven, while a few are wholly in verse.[37]

Fiction on the other hand was composed primarily for entertainment. Pure fiction is relatively rare. Writers naturally used old motifs or played variations upon them, so that even a late work may preserve the remnant of a myth or legend whose earlier more authentic form has been lost. It is important to remember that although we have granted the Ulster saga-cycle an historical

[35] O'Rahilly, *Early Ir. hist.*, pp. 253f. In contradistinction to O'Rahilly, however, I believe that it can be shown that the World Chronicle was composed earlier than the ninth century: his statement (*ibid.*, p. 350) that its compiler 'evidently accepted the new doctrine which identified the ancient Ulaid with the early Dál nAraidi' can be shown to be mistaken.

[36] Edited by Macalister in five volumes, Ir. Texts Soc., vols. xxxiv, xxxv, xxxix, xli, xliv. (London, 1938, 1939, 1940, 1941, 1956).

[37] See Ryan, 'The battle of Clontarf,' *R.S.A.I.Jn.*, lxviii. (1938); 'The historical content of the *Caithréim Ceallacháin Chaisil*,' *ibid.*, lxxi. (1941). Pseudo-annalistic texts are best represented by Mac Firbhisigh's *Three fragments* ed. O'Donovan, The Irish Archaeological and Celtic Society, (Dublin, 1860), and by the Egerton *Mionannála*, ed. O'Grady, *Silva Gadelica*, i, pp. 390–413. The Northern Uí Néill counterblast to the *Cogadh* and *Caithréim* takes the form of a verse narrative on the circuit of Ireland by Muirchertach of the Leather Cloaks, allegedly composed by an eye-witness, the poet Cormacán Éices: *Mórthimchell Érenn uile*, ed. E. Hogan (Dublin, 1901); see B. ó Cuív, 'Literary creation and Irish historical tradition', *Brit. Acad. Proc.*, xlix. (1963), pp. 249f.

basis, when it gained literary popularity new stories were invented about the Ulster heroes which contain very little that may be termed genuine tradition. I would consider the tale *Mesca Ulad* such a work.[38] A late example of a medieval romantic tale using Ulidian characters is the *Caithréim Chonghail Chláiringnigh*.[39] This is in the main pure romance or fiction. It contains no genuine core of legend. But it is used for a pseudo-historical purpose. The hero Conghal is said to have been granted a third of Ulster— the region east of the Bann. This serves to create an 'ancient' name, *Trian Conghail*, for the territory conquered in the fourteenth century by a collateral branch of the O'Neills, the Clann Aodha Bhuidhe, and invests their lordship with an aura of spurious antiquity.[40]

It will be now be clear that, however we may try to keep these four strands of myth, legend, pseudo-history and fiction separate in our own minds, they tend to be inextricably ravelled in the texts as we have them. Monastic influence, with its bent for historicism, has been at work on most extant versions of our myths and legends. The authors of the sagas were Christian and composed consciously as literary artists.[41] We cannot therefore excise obviously Christian references as mere 'monkish interpolations' in the hope of recovering a genuine sample of Celtic paganism.

Furthermore, our texts, particularly when written in prose, rarely achieved canonical status. In the majority of cases we are dependent on late manuscripts, and the medieval Irish scribe frequently felt called upon to undertake the duties of editor or redactor. Apart from erratic modernisation of spelling or grammar, he would often introduce glosses, be stimulated into a digression, or interpolate new (or sometimes older) variants of a tale or genealogy. In the process anomalies might arise which his successors puzzled over and might attempt to harmonise. A medieval scribe with too lively an intelligence can be the modern editor's worst enemy. It is the discrepancies which most often afford us the clue to the original meaning, and we are fortunate that the mass of Irish tradition is so abundantly chaotic that no one man

[38] Ed. Watson, Mediaeval and Modern Irish Series, vol. xiii (Dublin, 1941); see Thurneysen, *Die irische Helden- und Königsage* (Halle, 1921), pp. 473–84.
[39] Ed. MacSweeney, Ir. Texts Soc., vol. v. (1904).
[40] A curious mixture of genealogical lore, sage and pseudo-historical propaganda in the interests of the Clandeboy O'Neills is presented by the *Leabhar Cloinne Aodha Buidhe*, ed. ó Donnchadha (Dublin, 1931). ó Ceallaigh, *Gleanings from Ulster history*, takes the antiquity of the term Trian Conghail too seriously.
[41] I believe that this principle emerges clearly from Carney's *Studies in Irish literature and history* (Dublin, 1955), even though one may disagree with details of his analysis.

or school could reduce it to a simple or coherent pattern.[42] A valiant attempt was made by Geoffrey Keating, and one must admire the skill with which he reconciles variant traditions to achieve a flowing and seemingly authoritative narrative of dignified prose. Only now, at the end of a thousand years of literary activity, did the art of history emerge in Gaelic Ireland. Too late. The foundations of scientific history in Ireland, based on the critical examination and edition of early documents, were already being laid by Ussher and Colgan, and the Gaelic world itself was about to collapse.

But if the Irish preferred to take their history in the form of fiction, this is a fact which the modern historian must face. We may deplore the dearth of orthodox documentation—what MacNeill dismissed in a splendidly partisan passage as 'the pomp and circumstance of Feudalism, with its archiepiscopal viceroys, its incastellations and its subinfeudations, its charters and its statutes, its registers and its inquisitions'[43]—but we have a mass of literature, interesting both in its own right and as a phenomenon of considerable historical significance. This literary bias extends right through the history of the Gaelic world down to the seventeenth century and surely has much to tell us of the nature of that world.

The literature extant from the Old and Middle Irish periods alone is so extensive as to afford us the luxury of selectivity. We are in a position to make aesthetic judgements based on familiarity with the cultural criteria of the time. We can understand the function of much that may seem valueless as literature and historically dubious; we can distinguish the tawdry from the genuine though uninspired; we can appreciate the craftsmanship of the more everyday products of the schools, and reserve our enthusiasm for the rarer jewels. Happier than students of many other early literatures, we are not obliged to treasure each fragment equally, simply because it is a fragment, nor to attribute to it qualities that it may never have been intended to possess.

In some ways such literature as takes a borrowed theme can give us a clearer insight into the preconceptions of its society than purely native writing, since we are then more acutely aware of the changes that the author has made in his material. Anglo-

[42] Kelleher, *I.H.S.*, xvi. (1968), p. 142: 'In these difficulties lies at least half the immense value the corpus has for the historian, for we may take it as an axiom of historiography that in source materials of this age and kind a good, glaring contradiction is worth a square yard of smooth, question-begging consistency. A permanently unresolved problem over which many men have laboured unsuccessfully at different times, for varying reasons, is generally replete with information or suggestion.' Cf. further, *ibid.*, p. 144.
[43] *Phases*, p. 240.

Saxon and Old Irish society were very similar in many respects, and their closeness is emphasised by the controversies between art historians as to the precise origins of the great illuminated books of Durrow, Lindisfarne and Kells. Yet we have two poems of roughly contemporary date which treat the identical theme of the Passion of Christ in radically different manners. The first is the justly famous Anglo-Saxon *Dream of the rood*; the other a poem by Blathmac mac Con Brettan, only recently discovered by James Carney.[44]

It has often been remarked how the anonymous Anglo-Saxon poet has fitted the Christian theme into the seemingly incongruous frame of Germanic heroic poetry. His success in achieving this remarkable feat is a measure of his greatness. The element of passive suffering has been banished, and the introduction of the Cross itself as narrator, constrained by obedience to its Lord's wishes to become the instrument of His death, enables the poet to play on the favourite heroic theme of the bond of loyalty between a man and his lord. (Although a similar bond existed in Irish society, it is notable how little impact it makes on the literary tradition).

> I saw the Lord of Mankind
> Courageously hasten to climb upon me.
> O then I dared not bend or break
> Against the wish of my Lord, though the surface
> Of the earth trembled with fear. I could have felled
> All my foes, yet I stood firm.
> Then the young warrior, God our Saviour,
> Valiantly stripped before the battle; with courage
> and resolve,
> Beheld by many, He climbed upon the Cross to redeem
> Mankind.

Ongyrede hine þā geong hæleð, þæt wæs God ælmihtig, strang and stīðmōd; gestāh hē on gealgan hēanne mōdig on manigra gesyhðe, þā hē wolde mancyn lȳsan.[45]

Blathmac's poem is much longer. It is more diffuse and elegiac. He has neither the intensity nor the blinding vision of the unknown author of the *Dream*. But he seems more civilised. We know in fact something of his background. He came from the Airgiallan family of Uí Ségáin, who were connected with the church of Lann Léire (Dunleer, county Louth). His father, Cú Brettan mac

---

[44] Carney, *The poems of Blathmac*, Ir. Texts Soc., vol. xlvii. (1964).
[45] *The Battle of Maldon and other Old English poems*, translated by Kevin Crossley-Holland and edited by Bruce Mitchell (London, 1965), p. 129.

L

Congusso, died in 740, and is in some sources described (perhaps anachronistically) as king of Fir Rois, a tribe whose territory extended from southern Monaghan into the centre of Louth. Blathmac's brother Donn Bó was slain in 759 by the king of Ulaid, Fiachnae mac Áedo Róin, at the battle of Emain Macha which was caused by rivalry between Airechtach priest of Armagh and the abbot Fer-dá-Crích.[46] He came therefore from petty royal stock and from a family closely connected with the church of Armagh and its dependencies. His poem is an address to the Virgin:

Come to me, loving Mary,
that I may keen with you your very dear one:
Alas! The going to the cross of your son,
that great jewel, that beautiful champion.

He describes Christ in the following terms:

Nícon fuair athair samlai,
a Maire, do macamrai;
ferr fáith, fisidiu cech druí,
rí ba hepscop, ba lánsuí.

Sainemlu cech dóen a chruth,
brestu cech sóer a balcbruth,
gaíthiu cech bruinniu fo nim,
fíriánu cech brithemain.

[46] Carney, *Blathmac*, p. xiv; Cú Brettan mac Congusso, king of Fir Rois, is as Carney notes, represented in the saga of the battle of Allen as one of the few in the high-king's army to escape alive (the correct date is 722 not 718), and the same saga seems to have preserved a garbled memory of Donn Bó, who is depicted as a poor widow's son whose severed head sang a lament after the battle—see Dillon, *The cycles of the kings* (London, 1946), pp. 99–102. Both the saga and the manuscript of the poem describe Cú Brettan as of the Fir Rois, but the genealogies show him to have been of the Uí Ségáin. Both Fir Rois and Uí Ségáin were related to the Airthir group of the Airgialla. *A.U.* 748 records slaying of Congal mac Éicnig, king of Airthir, at Ráith Esclai (probably Rathesker west of Dunleer, according to Hogan's *Onomasticon*), and *Ann. Tig.* say that Donn Bó mac Con Bretan was his killer. The Fir Rois do not appear to have been recognised as an independent kingdom until the ninth century; their emergence split the once important Mugdorna kingdom into two units, of which the Mugdorna Breg in northern Meath fell within the political overlordship of the Southern Uí Néill. The Uí Ségáin were the ruling family of the Airthir sept of Uí Chruinn, several of whom in the eleventh and twelfth centuries occupied the office of priest (*sacerdos*) of Armagh. It seems likely that after failing to secure the kingship of Airthir the Uí Ségáin turned their talents to the advancement of the neighbouring and related Fir Rois. See ó Fiaich, 'Uí Cruinn: a lost Louth sept,' *Louth Arch. Soc. Jn.*, xii. (1951), pp. 105–12; id., 'Armagh under lay control,' *Seanchas Ard Mhacha* (1969), pp. 103f.; Mac Iomhair, 'The boundaries of Fir Rois,' *Louth Arch. Soc. Jn.*, xv. (1962), pp. 144–79; and for the events of 759 see Kathleen Hughes, *The church in early Irish society* (London, 1966), p. 170. See further F. J. Byrne, *Irish kings*, pp. 29, 44f., 117f.

No father has found, Mary,
the like of your renowned son;
better he than prophet, wiser than druid,
a king who was bishop and full sage.

His form was finer than that of other beings,
his stout vigour greater than any craftsman's,
wiser he than any breast under heaven,
juster than any judge.[47]

The catalogue reveals the classes most honoured in Irish society. Notable is the mention of the craftsman, for the laws allow free status to any of unfree birth who practise a recognised craft. In curious contrast to the popular view of the early Irish as peculiarly wild and warlike, the poet only briefly uses a military metaphor before changing immediately to an ecclesiastical one:

'He called to him a stout band of people whose warrior qualities were renowned: twelve apostles to whom he was abbot, seventy-two disciples'.[48]

Christ is compared favourably to professional physicians:

'Every miserable condition that was brought to him which hand of leech could not cure—they would go home sound; they were not subject to nine-day periods.

'He would satisfy everyone in a gentle manner while he was curing their misery; he took no payment, demanded no fee'.[49]

He has the royal virtues:

'He used to go about for the good of all; he was affable,[50] gentle in manner; in the face of any affliction he did not inflict abusive rejection or repulse'.[51]

These last two terms (*etech n-aíre ná essáin*) were legal breaches of the Irish code of hospitality. It is remarkable how much legal phraseology is in fact employed by Blathmac. In a christianisation of the archaic 'virtues' of a tale or poem which are supposed to be procured by its correct recitation, and which derive ultimately

---

[47] Carney, *Medieval Irish lyrics* (Dublin, 1967), pp. 13–15.
[48] Id., *Blathmac*, p. 11.
[49] *Ibid.*, p. 15.
[50] *soācaldaim* 'easy to talk to; approachable.'
[51] Carney, *Blathmac*, p. 11.

from the primitive idea of the 'power of the word',[52] the Virgin is asked to grant salvation to those who recite the poem under certain conditions (much as the patron to whom a poem is addressed is asked for a reward by the bard), and Blathmac says:

> For you, beautiful Mary,
> I shall go as guarantor:
> anyone who says the full keen,
> he shall have his reward'.[53]

He also displays extreme legalism in his condemnation of the Jews: not only have they committed the ultimate crime in Irish law of kin-slaying (*fingal*), but they have rejected their king after accepting his sovereignty in a solemn contract:

> 'Opposing Christ, the son of the living God, was for them the opposing of a spear-point to (justly imposed) subjection; in the sayings of this kingly island: it was "denial after recognition." . . .
> 'Of shameless countenance and wolf-like were the men who perpetrated that kin-slaying; since his mother was of them, it was treachery towards a true kinsman.
> 'Besides that the son of God the Father, Christ, our royal gracious king (*Críst ar ruiri rígrathach*), had granted to them often after that many wonderful requests . . . .
> 'Every advantage that the King had bestowed upon the Jews in return for their clientship was "wealth to slaves"; they violated their counter-obligations'.

> Cach feb tecomnacht in rí
> do Iudib ara célsini,
> batar moíni do mogaib;
> ro-coillset a cobfolaid.[54]

This illuminates the semantics of the phrase *rath Dé* still used in modern Irish for 'the grace of God.' *Rath* is the legal term for the fief of stock given by a lord (*flaith*) to his client (*céle*— literally 'companion') which established between them the contract of clientship or vassalage (*célsine*). It is also used in the oldest texts for the gifts which an over-king (*ruiri*) gives to his subor-

---

[52] Cf. Dillon, 'The archaism of Irish tradition,' The Sir John Rhŷs Memorial Lecture, *Brit. Acad. Proc.*, xxxiii. (1947), pp. 4f.
[53] Carney, *Medieval Irish lyrics*, p. 19. For the technical meaning of the term *aitire* 'guarantor; hostage' see Binchy, *Críth Gablach* (Dublin, 1941), pp. 74f.
[54] Carney, *Blathmac*, pp. 35–7.

dinates (in the later Middle Irish *Book of rights* these are called *tuarastal* 'stipend' or 'wages') and which are a more essential symbol of his suzerainty than the tribute which he may also receive from them.[55] The actual term *rath* appears here in Blathmac's adjective *rígrathach* 'royally gracious or bountiful' applied to the *ruiri* Christ. In the Irish view, when the Jews accepted God's graces they implicitly acknowledged his kingship. Thus the verses listing these benefits, though obviously connected with the *improperia* of the Good Friday liturgy, are lent a peculiarly Irish legal flavour.[56] The Jews are accused of not fulfilling their counter-obligations (*cobfolaid*): another compound of the same word—*frithfolaid* 'mutual obligations' is found in two early tracts dealing with the relations between the king of Cashel and the tribal kings of Munster.[57]

Blathmac uses the *improperia* just as the Anglo-Saxon poet uses the *Vexilla regis*. But they have not merely borrowed: they have integrated the foreign material into their own world, giving it concrete meaning for their contemporaries and enriching for us the depth of its symbolism. This is true creativity, and can constantly be observed in the history of art. Isolation of the borrowed motifs can only be the first stage of our analysis: the very act of borrowing must be seen to have altered the material.

On a lower literary level the curious document known as the *Timna Cathaír Máir* or 'Testament of Cathaír Már' is clearly modelled on Jacob's blessings to his sons. The legendary ancestor of the Leinster dynasties leaves his bequests to his sons:

> Fergus is an untrustworthy man
> wayward like a child . . .
> thou shalt not be the venerable head of the province,
> thou shalt not be honoured like thy father.
> Strong kingship will not be transmitted
> from thy spiritless descendants . . .
>
> My stalwart Eochu Timíne,
> he shall not hoard property in land,
> he shall not raise strong men from the land . . .

[55] Cf. Binchy, *Críth Gablach*, p. 107, s.v. *sóer-rath*; Dillon, 'On the date and authorship of the *Book of Rights*,' *Celtica*, iv. (1958), p. 246.
[56] Carney, *Blathmac*, pp. 27–33.
[57] *Bk Lec.*, 192 b 36: '*Fritholad ríg Caisil fri thuathaib*'; *Y.B.L.*, col. 339: 'Dál Caladbuig and reciprocal services between the kings of Cashel and various Munster states,' ed. Grosjean and O'Keeffe, *Ir. texts*, i, pp. 19–21, of which §8 begins with the words '*Frithfolaith Caisil frt uatha Muman*'. See ó Buachalla, *Cork Hist. Soc. Jn.*, lvii. (1952) pp. 80–6; Dillon, *Lebor na Cert: the Book of Rights*, Ir. Texts Soc., vol. xlvi. (1962), pp. xvf.; Byrne, *Irish kings*, pp. 196–9.

My imprecation and my curse
be upon him for ever
apart from his handsome brothers!
Harsh is the deed in which he takes part,
to outrage the dignity of a noble father,
frolicking in an exalted bed,
grievous partnership in a mate.
Impure and ignoble
is the marriage-bed,
father and unruly son
tumbling and wantoning
with a fickle shameless woman,
with keen and noisy ardour . . .

My sea with its full harvest
to my sweet-voiced Bresal.
May each fierce warrior of thy numerous line
be the steersman of a well-laden fleet! . . .
On account of thy father's love for thee,
he has sent thee from him to the sea.[58]

Reuben, you are my first-born,
my might, and the first fruits of my strength,
pre-eminent in pride and pre-eminent in power.
Unstable as water, you shall not have pre-eminence
because you went up to your father's bed;
then you defiled it—you went up to my couch! . . .

Zebulun shall dwell at the shore of the sea;
he shall become a haven for ships,
and his border shall be at Sidon.[59]

The *Timna Cathaír Máir* was probably written in the eighth century, though its form—alliterative heptasyllabic verse—is archaic. But to show that it has a biblical model is to have explained little. The significance of the borrowing is that the model was suitable. The form is no mere literary flight of fancy or learned allusion but results from a very real similarity of tribal polity between the Old Testament and Irish cultures.

[58] Dillon, *Bk rights*, pp. 157, 161, 155; Byrne, *Irish kings*, pp. 138–42.
[59] *Genesis*, xlix. 3–4, 15 (R.S.V.) Note that it is the younger sons, Joseph and Benjamin in Genesis and Fiachu ba hAiccid in the *Timna*, who receive the final and culminating blessing. Compare the incident of the blessing by Jacob of Joseph's sons Manasseh and Ephraim in Gen. xlviii, 13–20; the etymology of Benjamin's name 'son of the right hand' makes one suspect that this story originally referred to him, not to Ephraim; the poem in Gen. xlix knows only of a single tribe descended from Joseph.

A healthy culture borrows only what is congenial to it and is thereby enriched. A weak culture is forced to borrow indiscriminately and becomes a mere province or colony. The impact of Christianity on early Ireland should, I suggest, be studied as an example of the former process.

Our use of literature as a valid historical source is to some extent imposed upon us by the literary bias of the Irish historical tradition.[60] By acknowledging this fact, however, we are not simply making a virtue of necessity. The ethos of any culture is most surely revealed in its literature. Historians have long since, one hopes, ceased to be satisfied with merely political data. And no-one who has learned to appreciate the delicate poetry and (what is more remarkable as an index of civilisation) the mannered yet elegant prose of *Acallam na Senórach*, that great repertoire of Fenian legend and topographical lore which was composed at the height of the Norman invasion, can be content to repeat the Ovidian rhetoric of Giraldus as a fair assessment of twelfth-century Ireland. Of equal significance is the fact that at this very time the bardic schools were elaborating rules of metre and were, quite deliberately and with considerable linguistic sophistication, establishing a literary language which was to remain standard for more than four hundred years.[61]

Sophistication is perhaps the key word in any estimate of classical bardic poetry. While such studies of individual poets and their patrons as Áine O'Sullivan's essay on Giolla Brighde Mac Con Midhe[62] or James Carney's work on Eochaidh ó hEodhusa[63] can afford the historian valuable new perspectives on persons and affairs with which he was perhaps only familiar from the State Papers, it seems unlikely that a perusal of the official bardic panegyrics from the thirteenth century to the sixteenth will yield any startlingly new fact for the writer of textbooks. A mere reading of the poems with such a purpose in mind can only too readily induce fatigue and disgust. They cannot be appreciated in translation, not because they are great poetry—they are not—but because their perfection resides in their use of the Irish language and their intricate deployment of metre. Even the most pedestrian poem in *dán díreach* has a certain

---

[60] Cf. B. ó Cuív, 'Literary creation and Irish historical tradition,' Rhŷs Lecture, *Brit. Acad. Proc.*, xlix. (1963), pp. 233–62.
[61] Bergin, 'The native Irish grammarian,' Rhŷs Lecture, *Brit. Acad. Proc.*, xxiv. (1938); Cuív, 'Linguistic terminology in the mediaeval Irish bardic tracts,' *Transactions of the Philological Society* (1965); id., 'The phonetic basis of Classical Modern Irish rhyme,' *Ériu*, xx. (1966), pp. 94–103; 'Some developments in Irish metrics' *Eigse*, xii. (1968), pp. 273–90.
[62] In *Early Irish poetry*, ed. Carney (Cork, 1965), pp. 85–99.
[63] *The Irish bardic poet*. (Dublin, 1967).

obligatory elegance of diction which speaks well for the society which appreciated such verse.

A feature of the Irish literary tradition which deserves some notice is its extraordinary continuity. There is no such break between the literature of Old and Middle Irish and Classical Modern Irish as exists between Anglo-Saxon and Middle English. This continuity no doubt explains its confidence and self-assurance. The political revolution which followed the Anglo-Norman invasion had of course its effects on Irish literature, though these may have been less than those produced by the ecclesiastical revolution which preceded it. But it was not until the seventeenth century that the Irish felt the need to defend themselves or their culture. They accepted it as self-evident that they were superior. They remained open to foreign influences, taking over the conventions of courtly love to render them in the traditional Irish metres. There was a lively trade in the translation of English and European best-sellers into Irish—an aspect of cultural history which has been hitherto rather neglected. There was similarly a more utilitarian traffic in translations of medical and philosophical texts.[64] After an apparent break in the thirteenth century,[65] Gaelic culture was once more in the ascendant. One has only to compare the sheer bulk of original writing and translation in Irish from the later middle ages with the Anglo-Irish and Norman-Irish literary remains to realise the unchivalrous enormity of this ascendancy.

In pre-Norman Ireland the learned caste had achieved a cultural unity which was independent of the political fragmentation of the country. It was the men of learning who largely created the idea of a high-kingship of Ireland which the kings were never quite able to put into practice. It is understandable that they should not have been unduly shaken by the further fragmentation introduced by the Anglo-Normans. Their doom, and the doom of Gaelic civilisation, came in the seventeenth century with the abolition of brehon law and its system of land-tenure, reinforced

[64] See e.g., O'Grady, *Catalogue of Irish manuscripts in the British Museum*, i. (1926), pp. 171–327; Shaw, 'Medieval medico-philosophical treatises in the Irish language,' *Féilsgríbhinn Eóin Mhic Néill*, pp. 144–57.

[65] Few Irish manuscripts have been dated to the thirteenth century, and while this may simply be due to the timidity of palaeographers it is notable that the thirteenth-century hands in *Ann. Innisf.* and the Cottonian Annals ('Annals of Boyle') write Irish in Anglo-Norman script and in a semi-phonetic orthography. The fourteenth-century Gaelic revival evidently modelled itself consciously on twelfth-century exemplars, both literary and scribal: see Carney, 'The ó Cianáin miscellany,' *Ériu*, xxi. (1969), pp. 122–47; B. W. O'Dwyer, 'The annals of Connacht and Loch Cé and the monasteries of Boyle and Holy Trinity,' *R.I.A. Proc.*, lxxii. (1972), pp. 86f. (based on information provided by the present writer, the folios from *Ann. Inisf.*, reproduced in plates II and III do not in fact illustrate the point).

by subsequent expropriation and confiscation—the destruction of a class rather than the defeat of a king or the overthrow of a political system.

For these reasons I believe that for future progress in the largely unexplored history of Gaelic Ireland in the later middle ages we shall be to a very great extent dependent on the literary historian and his like-minded colleagues. What type of economy, for instance, was it that produced the Books of Lecan, Uí Maine and Ballymote, and that was wealthy enough to erect those surprisingly functional Gothic structures to house the reformed mendicant orders in the fifteenth century?[66] Because its centres were in the west, in lands which had almost become *terra incognita* to the Dublin government, is it legitimate to assume that they were remote from the mainstream of European civilisation? The evidence of architecture and literary translation should cause us to think again.

I am not arguing for a return to the uncritical nationalist historiography of Alice Stopford Green, nor do I wish to idealise Gaelic Ireland at this period. As I said earlier, Gaelic culture is in many ways regressive during these centuries, and certainly its intelligentsia was backward-looking. But it is interesting and important enough to demand the serious attention of a sympathetic historian. Whoever he may be, he must at least pay the subjects of his study the elementary courtesy of learning their language.

[66] For the building activity of the friars see Leask, *Irish churches and monastic buildings*, vol. iii. (Medieval Gothic, the last phases), (Dundalk, 1960), Martin, 'The Irish friars and the observant movement in the fifteenth century,' *Ir. Cath. Hist. Comm. Proc.* (1960), pp. 10–16; id., 'The Irish Augustinian reform movement in the fifteenth century,' in *Medieval studies presented to Aubrey Gwynn, S.J.*, ed. Watt, Morrall and Martin (Dublin, 1961), pp. 230–64.

LIST OF ARTICLES IN *HISTORICAL STUDIES*,
VOLUMES I TO IX, INCLUSIVE

The articles in this and previous volumes of *Historical Studies* are listed here under the following headings:
  (i)   Irish History—Early and Medieval; Modern
  (ii) British History—Early and Medieval; Modern
  (iii) European and World History—Early and Medieval; Modern
  (iv) Historiographical and Other Articles.
Some articles are listed under more than one heading.

(i) IRISH HISTORY
Early and Medieval
Liam de Paor: 'The Aggrandisement of Armagh', VIII, 95,
Francis J. Byrne: 'The Ireland of St Columba', V, 37.
Marjorie O. Anderson: 'Columba and other Irish Saints in Scotland', V, 26.
Denis Bethell: 'English Monks and Irish Reform in the Eleventh and Twelfth Centuries', VIII, 111.
W. L. Warren: 'The Interpretation of Twelfth-Century Irish History', VII, 1.
Jocelyn Otway-Ruthven: 'The Character of Norman Settlement in Ireland', V, 75.
E. St John Brooks: 'The Sources for Medieval Anglo-Irish History', I, 86.
Aubrey Gwynn, 'Bibliographical Note on Medieval Anglo-Irish History', I, 93.
R. H. M. Dolley: 'Anglo-Irish Monetary Policies, 1172–1637', VII, 45.
Urban Flanagan, O. P.: 'Papal Provisions in Ireland, 1305–78', III, 92.
J. F. Lydon: 'The Bruce Invasion of Ireland', IV, 111.
'Senchas': the Nature of Gaelic Historical Tradition by F. J. Byrne.

Modern
R. H. M. Dolley: 'Anglo-Irish Monetary Policies, 1172–1637', VII, 45.
R. Dudley Edwards: 'The Irish Reformation Parliament of Henry VIII, 1556–7', VI, 59.
D. B. Quinn: 'Ireland and Sixteenth-Century European Expansion', I, 20.
Helga Hammerstein: 'Aspects of the Continental Education of Irish Students in the Reign of Elizabeth I', VIII, 137.
G. A. Hayes-McCoy: 'Gaelic Society in Ireland in the Late Sixteenth Century', IV, 45.
John Bossy: 'The Counter-Reformation and the People of Catholic Ireland, 1596–1641', VIII, 155.

List of Articles

H. F. Kearney: 'Mercantalism and Ireland, 1620–40', I, 59.

Aidan Clarke: 'The Policies of the "Old English" in Parliament, 1640–41', V, 85.

J. C. Beckett: 'The Confederation of Kilkenny Reviewed', II, 29.

J. G. Simms: 'The Irish Parliament of 1713', IV, 82.

Michael Drake: 'The Irish Demographic Crisis of 1740–41', V, 101.

J. A. Murphy: 'The Support of the Catholic Clergy in Ireland, 1750–1850', V, 103.

Maureen Wall: 'The United Irish Movement', V, 122.

Kennedy F. Roche: 'The Relations of the Catholic Church and the State in England and Ireland, 1800–52', III, 9.

J. J. Lee: 'The Dual Economy in Ireland, 1800–50', VIII, 191.

K. H. Connell: 'Illicit Distillation: an Irish Peasant Industry', III, 58.

P. J. Jupp: 'Irish M.P.s at Westminster in the Early Nineteenth Century', VII, 65.

Kevin B. Nowlan: 'The Meaning of Repeal in Irish History', IV, 1.

O. O. MacDonagh: 'The Irish in Victoria, 1851–91: a Demographic Essay', VIII, 67.

Donal McCartney: 'James Anthony Froude and Ireland: a Historiographical Controversy of the Nineteenth Century', VIII, 171.

F. S. L. Lyons: 'The Economic Ideas of Parnell', II, 60.

T. W. Moody: '*The Times* versus Parnell and Co., 1887–90', VI, 147.

The Government of Ireland Act, 1920: its Origins and Purposes. The Working of the 'Official' Mind by N. Mansergh.

The Catholic Clergy and Irish Politics in the Eighteen Thirties and Forties by K. B. Nowlan.

(ii) BRITISH HISTORY
Early and Medieval

Marjorie O. Anderson: 'Columba and other Irish Saints in Scotland', V, 26.

Denis Bethell: 'English Monks and Irish Reform in the Eleventh and Twelfth Centuries', VIII, 111.

G. W. S. Barrow: 'The Reign of William the Lion, King of Scotland', VII, 21.

J. W. Gray: 'The Church and Magna Charta in the Century after Runnymede', VI, 23.

Modern

B. H. G. Wormald: 'The Historiography of the English Reformation', I, 50.

Charles Wilson: 'Government Policy and Private Interest in Modern English History', VI, 85.

Kennedy F. Roche: 'The Relations of the Catholic Church and the State in England and Ireland, 1800–52', III, 9.

P. J. Jupp: 'Irish M.P.s at Westminster in the Early Nineteenth Century', VII, 65.

Brian Inglis: 'The Influence of *The Times*', III, 32.

Maurice Cowling: 'The Use of Political Philosophy in Mill, Green and Bentham', V, 141.
Asa Briggs, 'Chartism Reconsidered', II, 42.
T. W. Moody: *The Times* versus Parnell and Co., 1887–90', VI, 147.
C. L. Mowat: 'Social legislation in Britain and the U.S. in the Early Twentieth Century: a Problem in the History of Ideas', VII, 81.
Herbert Butterfield: 'Sir Edward Grey in July 1914', V, 1.
Ireland and the Eighteenth Century British Empire by R. B. McDowell.

(iii) EUROPEAN AND WORLD HISTORY
Early and Medieval
Herbert Ludat: 'The Medieval Empire and the Early Piast State', VI, 1.
D. M. Nicol: 'The Millenary of Mount Athos—963–1963', V, 59.
John Watt: 'The Development of the Theory of the Temporal Authority of the Papacy by the Thirteenth-Century Canonists', II, 17.
Christine Meek: 'The Trade and Industry of Lucca in the Fourteenth Century', VI, 39.
C. M. D. Crowder: 'Henry V, Sigismund and the Council of Constance: a Re-examination', IV, 93.
John B. Morrall: 'Pius II and his *Commentaries*', III, 25.
The Church in Italy in the Fifteenth Century by Denys Hay.

Modern
D. B. Quinn: 'Ireland and Sixteenth-Century European Expansion', I, 20.
H. R. Trevor-Roper: 'Religion, the Reformation and Social Change', IV, 18.
Helga Hammerstein: 'Aspects of the Continental Education of Irish Students in the Reign of Elizabeth I', VIII, 137.
Michael Roberts: 'Gustavus Adolphus and the Art of War', I, 69.
Richard Cobb: 'The French Revolution and Private Life', VIII, 3.
Albert Goodwin: 'The Recent Historiography of the French Revolution', VI, 125.
O. O. MacDonagh: 'The Irish in Victoria, 1851–91: a Demographic Essay', VIII, 67.
J. L. McCracken: 'The Members of the Cape Parliament, 1854–1910', II, 79.
Geoffrey Barraclough: 'German Unification: An Essay in Revision', IV, 62.
Theodor Schieder: 'The German Kaiserreich from 1871 as a Nation-State', VIII, 31.
C. L. Mowat: 'Social legislation in Britain and the U.S. in the Early Twentieth Century: a Problem in the History of Ideas', VII, 81.
V. Conzemius: 'Pius XII and Nazi Germany in Historical Perspective', VII, 97.
W. V. Wallace: 'An Appraisal of Edvard Beneš as a Statesman', VIII, 47.

T. D. Williams: 'The Historiography of World War II', I, 33.
Some Stoic Inspiration in the Thought of J. J. Rousseau by K. F. Roche.

(iv) HISTORIOGRAPHICAL AND OTHER ARTICLES

B. H. G. Wormald: 'The Historiography of the English Reformation', I, 50.

Charles Wilson: 'Government Policy and Private Interest in Modern English History', VI, 85.

Albert Goodwin: 'The Recent Historiography of the French Revolution', VI, 125.

Maurice Cowling: 'The Use of Political Philosophy in Mill, Green and Bentham', V, 141.

Donal McCartney: 'James Anthony Froude and Ireland: a Historiographical Controversy of the Nineteenth Century', VIII, 171.

Geoffrey Barraclough: 'German Unification: An Essay in Revision', IV, 73.

Theodor Schieder, 'The German Kaiserreich from 1871 as a Nation-State', VIII, 31.

C. L. Mowat: 'Social Legislation in Britain and the U.S. in the Early Twentieth Century: a Problem in the History of Ideas', VII, 81.

Jaroslav Kudrna, 'The Methodological and Political Foundations of Czech Historiogrpahy in the Twentieth Century', VIII, 61.

T. D. Williams: 'The Historiography of World War II', I, 33.

Michael Oakeshott: 'The Activity of Being a Historian', I, 1.

Denys Hay: 'Geographical Abstractions and the Historian', II, 1.

Alfred Cobban: 'History and Sociology', III, 1.

W. H. Walsh: 'The Limits of Scientific History', III, 45.

The Historian as 'Private Eye' by W. L. Warren.

Encore une Question. Lucien Febvre, the Reformation and the School of 'Annales' by Dermot Fenlon.